Social Change in a Peripheral Society

The Creation of a Balkan Colony

Neagoe Basarab, Prince of Wallachia 1512–1521, and his family, holding the church he renovated in the old capital, Curtea de Argeş. From a sixteenth-century church mural now in the Museum of Art, Bucharest.

Social Change in a Peripheral Society

The Creation of a Balkan Colony

Daniel Chirot

Department of Sociology
University of Washington
Seattle, Washington

ACADEMIC PRESS New York San Francisco London

A Subsidiary of Harcourt Brace Jovanovich, Publishers

ACADEMIC PRESS, INC.
111 Fifth Avenue, New York, New York 10003

United Kingdom Edition published by
ACADEMIC PRESS, INC. (LONDON) LTD.
24/28 Oval Road, London NW1

Library of Congress Cataloging in Publication Data

Chirot, Daniel.
Social change in a peripheral society.

(Studies in social discontinuity)
Bibliography: p.
1. Wallachia–Social conditions. 2. Wallachia–Politics and government. 3. Wallachia–Economic conditions. 4. Social change. I. Title. II. Series.
HN658.W35C54 1976 309.1′498′2 75-36645
ISBN 0–12–173150–2

PRINTED IN THE UNITED STATES OF AMERICA

To Henri H. Stahl—
A great social historian and teacher

Contents

Preface

My study has three purposes. First, I am interested in contributing to the long debate between those who seek universal laws and stages in history, and those who see only a lot of interesting, but always unique stories. I find merit in neither extreme, but propose a middle position. Second, I am particularly interested in extending the Marxist notion of "modes of production," to see if it is possible to rework the Marxist stages into flexible ideal-types that might be applied to societies outside Western Europe. It is now clear that as a set of universal evolutionary stages, the "slave," "feudal," "capitalist," and "socialist" modes of production have little if any bearing on change in most of the world over most of time. Similarly, it is certain that it is not possible to impose a single evolutionary schema, Marxist or not, on the succeeding modes of production that followed one another in various places. On the other hand, the notion of "modes of production" (more conveniently termed "political economies") is useful. If applied with caution, and filled with enough specific historical detail, the study of political economies can suggest some stages through which some, if not all, societies have passed in response to changing internal and external political and economic pressures. Third, I am interested in the nature of social change in peripheral societies, societies on the margins of the capitalist European world that have been absorbed by the dynamic industrial economies, and have, as a result, turned into "colonial" or "neocolonial" societies. This third interest is what led me to study the social history of Southern Romania, Wallachia, and therefore deserves more comment.

The theory of an interdependent world-system dominated by core (rich, highly diversified, and ultimately industrial) societies who subject, by direct or indirect means, peripheral (poor, overly specialized, and primarily agrarian) societies has been worked out in considerable detail, most recently by Immanuel Wallerstein. A good many peripheral societies have been studied, primarily those in the contemporary "third world," that is, in the former colonies of Europe in Latin America, Asia, and Africa. But much of Eastern Europe was colonized, at least economically, from the fifteenth to the early twentieth century. Poland and Hungary have been studied as peripheral societies, but Balkan societies have not, until now, been treated in the same theoretical framework, at least by Western scholars.

The notion of interdependent world-systems, however, can be extended beyond the study of the capitalist system, since there were smaller international systems before the Europeans spread their system throughout the globe. The Ottoman Empire was such a "world" system in that it included large number of diverse races, religious groups, and different types of social and economic structures. But whereas the capitalist world-system became so successful that it transformed the entire world, older putative world-systems did not have the same transforming power. They did not exploit their "colonies" in the same way as did the later capitalist system, and thus turned out to have much more limited capacities for growth. By studying the difference between Ottoman and capitalist exploitation of Romania, I hope to be able to add to the literature which seeks to explain the tremendous vitality of European capitalism. While this book is not about the Ottoman Empire as a whole, it does treat one important province of that empire, a province that might have been exploited to bring much greater rewards to Constantinople than the tribute that it actually collected.

The study of the international context in which societies exist explains much that happens within them. That is why social change in Wallachia cannot be explained in terms of universal laws acting on internal social structures. On the other hand, the international setting of a society does not explain all change either. It is a combination of the "world setting" and the state of internal development of social structures that I use to establish models of ideal--typical political economies.

Aside from the theoretical interest of this book, I hope that it also has some practical interest. Romania, after all, was an early example of a Western "neocolony." The consequences of this can now be studied with a good bit of historical perspective, and therefore, with somewhat deeper understanding than the more recent developments in contemporary "third world" societies. Many of the profound troubles which now beset the world capitalist system can be foreseen in the developments that occurred in Romania at the very start of the twentieth century. I hope, therefore, that this book contributes something to the study of all peripheral societies, not merely those in the Balkans, or even merely those in Eastern Europe.

Acknowledgments

Henri H. Stahl, Romania's greatest social historian, gave me the basic information and inspiration for this book as well as a great deal of his time. Were it not for the accidents of Romanian history, he would be well known in the West. Because his work is not now well known in English-speaking countries, I can say only that it should be.

Immanuel Wallerstein gave me the essential comparative perspective without which I could not have proceeded to make this research comprehensible to Western readers.

Sigmund Diamond and Terry Hopkins, whose patience and careful critiques helped me rewrite an earlier draft, also made this work possible.

Istvan Deak, Alexander Erlich, Michael Hechter, and Guenther Roth gave me valuable advice and much time.

In Romania, Ovidiu Bădina, Traian Herseni, Petre Datculescu, and Catalin Mamali helped me find my way around libraries and research institutes. They should not be blamed for any objectionable statements or errors, but only thanked a great deal. Their cordial hospitality saved me from sinking into bureaucratic imponderables.

Jim Bethel's fine maps will, I am certain, help make the book clearer, and I thank him for them. I thank Doris Saunders, who typed the manuscript, and Judy Sacks, who had to read it.

List of Tables

Notes on the Use of Romanian Terms and Letters

In order to avoid confusion, I have tried to use English instead of Romanian when possible. There are several important exceptions. Where changes in terminology over the years reflected social change, Romanian terms were used. These have been explained in the text. Three Romanian words, however, have been used throughout the text. These are:

boier (plural, *boieri*): nobles
moşneni: Wallachian free peasants
clăcaşi: peasants subjected to the corvée

I hope the frequent use of these terms will not cause any problems.

The following letters have distinct sounds:

ş: "sh" as in s*h*ot
ţ: "ts" as in sho*ts*
ă: "ẹa" as in l*ea*rn
î which used to be â in many words is the same as the Russian "yerry" which sounds somewhat like the "i" in t*i*ll. In post-World War II Romanian, the â version is used only in the words that stem from România.

STUDIES IN SOCIAL DISCONTINUITY

Under the Consulting Editorship of:

CHARLES TILLY *University of Michigan*	EDWARD SHORTER *University of Toronto*

William A. Christian, Jr. Person and God in a Spanish Valley

Joel Samaha. Law and Order in Historical Perspective: The Case of Elizabethan Essex

John W. Cole and Eric R. Wolf. The Hidden Frontier: Ecology and Ethnicity in an Alpine Valley

Immanuel Wallerstein. The Modern World-System: Capitalist Agriculture and the Origins of the European World-Economy in the Sixteenth Century

John R. Gillis. Youth and History: Tradition and Change in European Age Relations 1770 – Present

D. E. H. Russell. Rebellion, Revolution, and Armed Force: A Comparative Study of Fifteen Countries with Special Emphasis on Cuba and South Africa

Kristian Hvidt. Flight to America: The Social Background of 300,000 Danish Emigrants

James Lang. Conquest and Commerce: Spain and England in the Americas

Stanley H. Brandes. Migration, Kinship, and Community: Tradition and Transition in a Spanish Village

Daniel Chirot. Social Change in a Peripheral Society: The Creation of a Balkan Colony

In preparation

Jane Schneider and Peter Schneider. Culture and Political Economy in Western Sicily

Michael Schwartz. Radical Protest and Social Structure: The Southern Farmers' Alliance and Cotton Tenancy, 1880-1890

Dirk Hoerder. Crowd Action in Revolutionary Massachusetts, 1765-1780

1

Introduction: A Method for Studying Social Change

Every study of social history begins with a dilemma. Should the detail of particular situations dominate the work? Is social history best told as a set of interesting, but essentially unique, tales? Or should generalities be emphasized? Should there be a search for "laws" of social change? To pick the first course is to leave oneself open to the charge of being trivial. To pick the second is to invite the attacks of those who, like Karl Popper, believe that "laws" of social change are either self-evident or false. It was Popper, in fact, who wrote that, "history [should be] characterized by its interest in actual, singular, or specific events, rather than in laws or generalizations."[1]

Any detailed, empirical study of social change in a single society over a long period of time seems to confirm Nisbet's attitude that explanations of change, based on "stages of development" that inevitably lead to some logical, "ultimate end," tend toward futility. More and more events and changes intrude into the theoretical model until, finally, it becomes necessary to distort the record, or imagine events in order to save the theory.[2] This is particularly true in the study of non-Western European societies that have obviously failed to follow the

[1]Karl Popper, *The Poverty of Historicism* (New York: Harper Torchbooks, 1964), p. 143.
[2]Robert A. Nisbet, *Social Change and History* (New York: Oxford University Press, 1970), pp. 251–252.

supposed "progression of stages" from feudal to industrial society; for as Nisbet shows, all evolutionary theorizing rests on strong ethnocentric bias.[3]

Still, some level of generalization is necessary. There are recognizable similarities in the nature of social change across different societies and across different time periods. I take the position that the most interesting way of studying social change for a whole society within a comparative and theoretical framework—without slipping into the reification inherent in the various evolutionary theories attacked by both Nisbet and Popper—is by studying particular types of political economies. The reasons for this position should become clear in this study of social change in Southern Romania, Wallachia, over a period of some 650 years. I believe that the position I have stated allows for a clear identification of the major sources of change, and that this identification permits a coherent explanation of how and why Romanian society changed as it did. Therefore, while sidestepping any dogma about inevitable stages and the direction of change, I hope to present conclusions that are valid not only for Romania, but also for some other parts of the world at certain times.

The term "political economy" is an old one that has recently come back into vogue. Among current social historians, this term seems to have been used most brilliantly by Eugene Genovese in *The Political Economy of Slavery*. Political economy also has been a key concept among those who gathered around Karl Polanyi and collectively produced *Trade and Market in the Early Empires*. But to make use of this concept it is necessary to cite neither all those who now use that term nor its antecedents among eighteenth- and nineteenth-century political economists.

A political economy is characterized by a particular class structure—that is, the way in which a surplus is extracted from the economy, how and by whom it is distributed, and for what purposes. The concept of a surplus is central. Harry Pearson has shown that a surplus is not simply an excess resulting from improved technology; nor is a surplus necessarily the "cause" of further progress in cultural and political sophistication. Rather, the surplus is socially and politically defined from the very start. Though the extent of the surplus is limited by technology within broad bounds, it comes into being by a political act, by conquest, by the imposition of tribute, of a corveé, or of some other kind of tax.[4] As the nature of the surplus changes, as the way in which it is produced and collected changes, and as the uses to which it is put change, so do the political economy and the class structure of a society.

There have been cases in which the surplus was defined and enforced so stringently that the bulk of the population was forced down to, or even slightly

[3] *Ibid.*, pp. 189–192.

[4] Harry W. Pearson, "The Economy Has No Surplus: Critique of a Theory of Development," *Trade and Market in the Early Empires*, ed. Karl Polanyi, Conrad M. Arensberg, and Harry W. Pearson (New York: Free Press, 1957), pp. 320–341.

below, the level of bare subsistence. The surplus may also be defined so as to leave the producing population a rather large margin of comfort. Shifts from one situation to the other are possible without any significant technological change. However, a shift in the political economy may produce a technological change, or a technological change may facilitate a change in the political economy. The position that types of political economies must be studied in order to understand social change leaves open such questions as the relation of technology to culture and politics; the concept of a political economy is neither a form of technological determinism nor of cultural determinism.

A political economy comprises more than a particular class structure. It imposes certain forms of behavior on a people. Thus, the creation of a new surplus by a political act is likely to change property relations, which in turn may change family structure and the ways in which people behave in their daily lives. But again, as with technology, there is not necessarily a one-to-one relationship between people's daily lives and the nature of the surplus extracted from them. A set of limits is imposed on a social structure and on social attitudes by the political economy. Daily social forms may vary greatly within a particular type of political economy.

Family forms are a good example. It has been shown that there is a good deal of variation in family forms within and between industrial societies. But the variation has limits. For example, there are no advanced industrial societies in which property remains the exclusive possession of the large, extended family and in which the main unit of production is the family. Insofar as a society industrializes, such extended family forms decay, if they had existed at all. Industrial societies tend toward the conjugal family structure, although the extent to which this change takes place varies enormously, both within particular societies and between industrial societies. This does not preclude the fact that many nonindustrial societies also have been characterized by conjugal or some other restricted family form, rather than by extended families.[5]

Similarly, religion varies within and between industrial societies. No one would claim that all capitalist societies are Protestant. Yet, some movement toward rational religious belief, away from mysticism and the more sense-oriented religions, is apparent in the industrialization process. Of course, this trend does not influence all groups within the society equally; the fact that a long-term trend has existed in the past does not militate against at least a partial reversal of that trend within any particular industrial society.

So it goes with many other aspects of the social system. In other words, I believe that describing a particular political economy demonstrates only the limits within which a society is forced; it hardly explains the great variety of social forms and habits that exists within societies characterized by a certain

[5]See the various essays in Peter Laslett, ed., *Household and Family in Past Time* (London: Cambridge University Press, 1972).

type of political economy. A fuller explanation of any society must include a description of its past, with special attention to its unique or idiosyncratic aspects.

A final point in describing a political economy is that it exists only within a particular international system. At any given time, there may be several international systems, constituting an international division of labor and an international trade network. Such a network may be very large and powerful, like the contemporary world capitalist market,[6] or it may be very weak and of marginal importance for a particular society. Thus, in a world of purely primitive communal societies, there is no real international system. Should one society become more powerful, and force or somehow induce neighbors to trade with it, an international network is created.

For the present study of Romania, several international systems have been important. There was the European–Middle Eastern–Oriental network of organized trade routes in the Middle Ages. Later, there was the Ottoman Empire, which formed a distinctive international system of its own; however, this system was partially within the greater Mediterranean system of the sixteenth and seventeenth centuries. (I believe that Braudel's reputation as the best French historian since World War II rests in part on his proof of the existence of that particular international system.)[7] Finally, there was the Western capitalist system, dominated by the industrialized powers of Western Europe in the nineteenth century.

An international system influences a society within it because it sets a value on certain products that can be exported or imported. The system may define the nature of the surplus for a society within the system's range, especially if it has the economic or political power to extract that surplus for its own uses. International systems are the "rings" Nisbet discusses in his prescription for studying social change. Any system larger than a single society influences those societies within it, even if it does this differentially. That is not to say that all social change results from the intrusion of particular international systems, but much does. International systems vary, as do political economies; there are many types and they are characterized by different divisions of labor, by different "class structures" on the international level. Some systems are weaker than others, and these may be absorbed by their more powerful competitors; this is what happened to the Ottoman system in the eighteenth and nineteenth centuries.

International systems are not important simply because they are sources of technological and cultural diffusion. Primarily, they are important because they

[6] On the concept of "world systems" see Immanuel Wallerstein, *The Modern World-System: Capitalist Agriculture and the Origins of the World-Economy in the Sixteenth Century* (New York: Academic Press, 1974).

[7] Fernand Braudel, *La Méditerranée et le monde méditerranéen à l'époque de Philippe II* (Paris: Armand Colin, 1966).

impose certain economic and political patterns on their participants. As in the case of political economies, within the imposed limits considerable variation is possible.

It is the existence of international systems that makes much neoevolutionary theory invalid. A particular nonindustrial society, with its own technology and culture, will develop quite differently depending on whether it is absorbed by a modern industrial economy or taken into the network of a set of other nonindustrial societies. An understanding of evolutionary patterns is impossible without reference to the international context and, because this changes continually, evolutionary theory is constantly forced to appeal to a mysterious "diffusion" process. This is a failure of the theory because new ideas are not necessarily adopted at equal rates. Of importance is how and why certain economies become dependent on each other and how this causes change. It is now abundantly clear, for example, that participation in the capitalist colonial international system of the nineteenth century did not lead to industrialization for the colonies, but only for the colonizers. Only a theory of the effect of subordination or superordination within an industrial network, not a theory of diffusion, could explain this.[8]

Having spelled out a definition of "political economy" and of "international system," I have no intention of creating a new theory or a typology applicable to the whole world. I intend merely to point out why and how these definitions are useful for this particular study of social change in Wallachia from about 1250 until 1917. I further hope to suggest some modest generalities about other societies that also have been characterized by those political economies that existed in Wallachia during that period.

[8] This argument has been very popular recently. The best short statement about it is Andre Gunder Frank's "The Development of Underdevelopment," reprinted in *Imperialism and Underdevelopment*, ed. Robert I. Rhodes (New York: Monthly Review Press, 1970), pp. 4–17. An extremely persuasive and detailed version of the argument can be found in George L. Beckford, *Persistent Poverty: Underdevelopment in Plantation Economies of the Third World* (New York: Oxford University Press, 1972).

2

Wallachia

Eastern Europe is of particular interest to social historians for a number of reasons. The most important is the long-standing economic backwardness of most of Europe east of Germany, Bohemia, Austria, and Italy. From about 1500 to 1950, Western Europe north of Iberia and southern Italy forged far ahead of Eastern Europe in wealth as well as in the crystallization of nation–states. The lag behind the industrializing and modernizing countries was particularly evident in southeastern Europe, an area usually called the Balkans. What were the roots of this lag? To what extent were the causes of the lag exogenous or endogenous? How far back in history did the differences between Eastern and Western Europe arise?

A vital component of this problem is the distinctive nature of agrarian societies and economies in Eastern Europe. After 1500, Western Europe moved away from the feudal system that had evolved during the Middle Ages; the opposite seems to have happened in the East, where free men were turned into serfs and big landowning aristocracies began to dominate society after 1500. All subsequent agrarian history shows Eastern Europe falling behind in agricultural productivity, eventually entering the twentieth century with major agrarian crises.[1] Powerful landowning classes emerged which owned much, if not most, of the good land; below this elite there emerged a class of poor peasants—overcrowded on the land, hopelessly dependent on the landowners, and very backward with respect to literacy, national consciousness and, worst of all, technological competence in agriculture.

It is very difficult to generalize about all of Eastern Europe, and I do not propose to try. Between Polish social history and Russian social history, for example, there is a world of difference: Indeed, as the Polish state declined and vanished from the sixteenth to the eighteenth centuries, the Russian state grew from a weak political unit to a great world power. There are other significant differences in development throughout Eastern Europe. Those areas that the Ottomans ruled for long periods of time remain more backward than areas that escaped Turkish conquest; this difference can be seen within modern national units such as Yugoslavia, a part of which was long under Ottoman rule, while another part was only lightly touched by it. Even among areas within Ottoman rule, there are major differences. Bulgaria emerged as an independent nation without a landowning aristocracy; Romania became independent at about the same time, but was ruled by a powerful landed aristocracy.

This study is concerned with one part of Eastern Europe, southern Romania—that part of Romania called Wallachia by foreigners, and called *Țara Românească,* the Romanian land, by the Romanians. There are several compelling reasons for treating Wallachia as a distinctive unit. One is that the other provinces of Romania—Transylvania, the Banat, Moldavia, and Soviet Moldavia (Bessarabia)—had different histories. This is particularly true of Transylvania and the Banat, which were ruled by Hungarians from about the twelfth century until 1918. Moldavia and Wallachia, however, had more comparable histories. Both provinces were more or less independent, from their creation in the thirteenth and fourteenth centuries until they were conquered by the Turks in the fifteenth and sixteenth centuries. After that time, they had similar political histories and they were finally united into a single Romanian Kingdom in 1859. But from its creation until 1859, Wallachia was a separate political unit, and during the period I am studying—from about 1250 until 1917—Wallachia was a separate country for almost all of that time. Though there were important similarities between Moldavia and Wallachia, there were also some differences, and to discuss the two simultaneously would necessitate a considerable amount of explanation about these differences. These differences were more a matter of detail than of drastically different evolutions, however, and therefore I believe that relatively little is to be gained by studying the two

[1]Jerome Blum, "The Rise of Serfdom in Eastern Europe," *The American Historical Review* **LXII**, no. 4 (July, 1957): 807–836; Doreen Warriner, "Some Controversial Issues in the History of Agrarian Europe," *The Slavonic and East European Review* **XXXII**, no. 78 (December, 1953): 168–186; Doreen Warriner, *Economics of Peasant Farming,* 2nd ed. (New York: Barnes & Noble, 1965).

together. The same is not true of Transylvania and the Banat, which followed such different evolutions from Wallachia and Moldavia that for the period 1250–1918 they are best studied as parts of Hungary and, later, Austria-Hungary.

The issues involved in Wallachian social history are generally the same as those in Eastern European social history; they center on the transformations of agrarian society that led to the nineteenth and twentieth centuries' agrarian crisis. The key question may be posed simply: How did Wallachia come to be a backward economic area with a peasant problem? This question can be divided into several parts. Who were the peasants, and how did a class of peasants come into being? Who were the landowning nobles, and how did this class come into being? How did the lords come to have such power over the peasants? To what extent did external forces shape agrarian class relations, and to what extent did the evolution of Wallachian rural society stem from purely internal factors? What were the effects of Ottoman rule? What were the effects of Western capitalist development? Finally, why did the agrarian problem come to dominate Wallachia so totally, and how did the problem become so intractable that even today, after 30 years of Communist rule and intensive industrial development, it remains a virtually unsolved issue?

All these questions might be dealt with individually, but to do this would be extremely confusing and, in fact, misleading, because a common thread runs through all of them. This thread is suggested by the Marxist analysis of Eastern European agrarian history. Very briefly, Marx and Engels suggested that the reason for the difference in evolution between Eastern and Western Europe was that Eastern Europe became a grain exporting area after 1500,[2] while Western Europe began to industrialize. In return for grain exports, Eastern Europe received manufactured imports from the West. At the same time, the peasants in Eastern Europe were turned into serfs by the lords because there was a labor shortage and this was the only way to get the labor for growing grain surpluses to be exported. Thus, in the East, the coming of capitalism meant (1) a "second serfdom" (as distinct from the "first" or classical European serfdom in the feudal period), (2) a decline in artisans and urban life, and (3) a gradual regression to an atomized rural society similar to the one that had prevailed in the West during the Middle Ages. In a sense, then, Eastern Europe became the colony of Western Europe.

This analysis seems to fit fairly well for Poland.[3] It does not fit nearly so well for Wallachia. But the analysis can explain a great deal if it is modified to take into account the fact that Wallachia was first ruled by the Ottomans when it was

[2]Eric. J. Hobsbawm, Introduction to *Karl Marx: Pre-Capitalist Economic Formations* (New York: International Publishers, 1965), pp. 55–56.

[3]Wittold Kula, *Théorie économique du système féodal: pour un modèle de l'économie polonaise, 16e–18e siècles* (Paris and The Hague: Mouton, 1970).

primarily a pastoral country, and only later came into the Western market sphere as a grain exporter.

At the time of its political birth, Wallachia had a communal-trade political economy. The state's main source of revenue was its control of international trade routes, not the surplus taken from the free and communal rural villages. As the result of a shift in trade routes and of the Ottoman conquest in the fifteenth and sixteenth centuries, Wallachia eventually turned into a weakly developed colonial society. The protocolonial political economy was characterized by a modified form of "second serfdom." By this is meant a move toward the creation of a society in which the main surplus is produced by a servile (unfree) rural labor force, and in which a significant part of the surplus is designed for sale abroad to an economically and politically dominant society. The servile labor force was controlled by an aristocracy whose main power base was its control of the land. The free communal villages were destroyed.

In the nineteenth century, Wallachia was opened to Western commerce and freed from the Ottomans. It then became a strongly developed colonial society, characterized by a rigorous form of serfdom in which the serfs cultivated wheat for export to the West. The nobles became a true landowning class. Ultimately, as population density rose, the need for forced rural labor ended and the serfs were freed. But the landlords retained control of the land and of the peasants, and the colonial political economy remained intact until World War I.

This—the origins and growth of a colonial political economy—is the central theme of the present study. As such, I believe that it can shed some light on a great many colonial societies, particularly those that developed market-oriented, servile labor systems in agriculture.[4]

The Geography of Wallachia

Wallachia is the southern third of modern Romania. It covers about 76,160 square kilometers.[5] That is an area somewhat larger than the Republic of Ireland, and a bit smaller than Austria. From its eastern to its western end it measures some 400 kilometers; from north to south, about 150. The climate is temperate, having fairly cold winters and hot summers. It has the best soils in the Balkans on the extensive Danube plain, which occupies over half the total area. The southern and eastern boundary is the Danube River. The northern boundary, except at the eastern end, is the crest of the Carpathian

[4]Daniel Chirot, "The Growth of the Market and Servile Labor Systems in Agriculture," *The Journal of Social History* **VIII** (Winter, 1975): 67–80. This contains a review of some of the literature that pushes the argument linking the growth of the market to the spread of serfdom and slavery.

[5]For the physical characteristics of Wallachia see *Anuarul statistic al Republicii Socialiste România, 1970* (Bucharest: Direcția centrală de statistică, 1970), pp. 21–60.

Mountains. The northeastern boundary is not distinctive. A small tributary of the Danube, the Milcov, separates the Wallachian from the Moldavian plain, but the Milcov is hardly more than a large creek. In the west, Wallachia's boundary is formed by the Carpathians and the Danube, which runs through the mountains between Serbia and Romania. (See Map 1.)

In the Middle Ages, Wallachia was surrounded by Hungarian Banat and Hungarian Transylvania to the west and north, respectively, Moldavia to the northeast, Bulgaria (under Ottoman control from the thirteenth to the late nineteenth centuries) to the east and south, and Serbia (also in Ottoman hands from the fourteenth to the early nineteenth centuries) to the southwest.

For most of Wallachia's history, the only internal administrative boundary of concern was the dividing line between Oltenia and Muntenia. Oltenia was the western third of Wallachia, separated from Muntenia by the Olt River, which divides the country from north to south. In the nineteenth century, the country was divided into 17 counties. In Oltenia the plains counties were, from west to east, Dolj and Romanaţi. The hill and mountain counties, from west to east, were Mehedinţi, Gorj, and Vâlcea. In Muntenia, the plains counties were Olt, Teleorman, Vlaşca, Ilfov (which has Bucharest), and the steppe counties of Ialomiţa and Brăila. The hill and mountain counties were, from west to east, Argeş, Muscel, Dâmboviţa and Prahova. Two counties in the northeast, Buzău and Râmnicu-Sărat, were in both hill and plain country, but Buzău was chiefly in the hills and Râmnicu-Sărat chiefly in the plains. (For the purposes of this study, these distinctions become important only in the late nineteenth century, when statistical data were collected by county.)

In the nineteenth century, the foreign areas surrounding Wallachia had the same names; the major differences were that the Hungarian area was ruled by Austria, and that Serbia, and later Bulgaria, gained independence from the Turks. Wallachia was joined with Moldavia in 1859 to form the New Romanian state. In 1878, Romania received the land between the Danube and the Black Sea, the Dobrogea. These boundaries remained fixed until 1918.

Wallachia's geography has conditioned the direction of population movement and the types of agriculture that have been practiced there. It has four zones. There are the Carpathian Mountains in the north; farther south there are the sub-Carpathian depressions and hills, which were the most populated areas of Wallachia until the late nineteenth century; and beyond the hills are the flat plains, which run to the Danube in the east and south. The mountains, hills, and western plains are fairly wet; the southeastern plains are much drier, and suffer periodically from drought. The southeastern part of Wallachia is the Bărăgan steppe, which once was the home of Asiatic nomads, and which formed a virtually empty agricultural frontier area in the nineteenth century.

The Danube banks, the fourth geographical area of Wallachia, has long been more populated than the drier plains immediately to the north and west of the

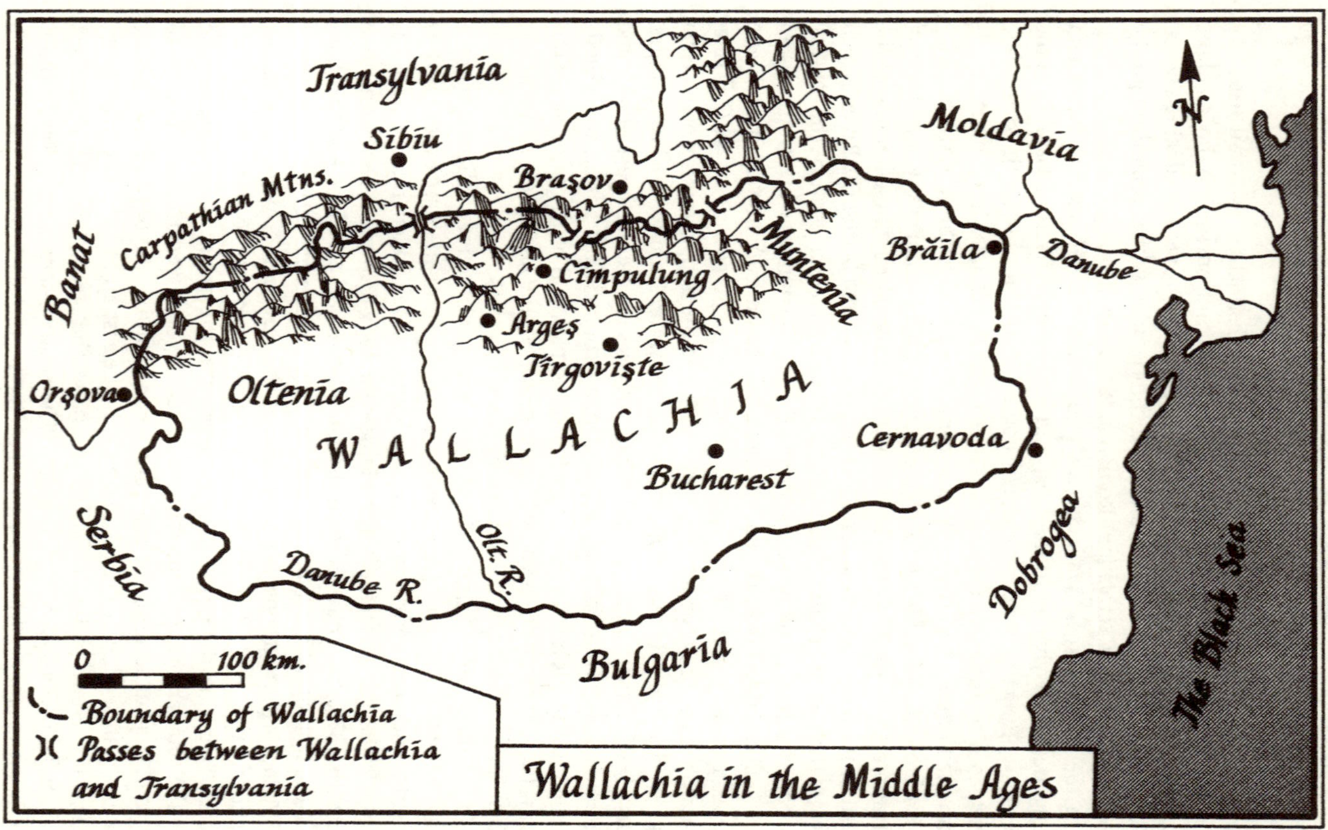
Transylvania
Sibiu
Carpathian Mtns.
Banat
Orşova
Oltenia
Braşov
Cîmpulung
Argeş
Tîrgovişte
Muntenia
Moldavia
N
Brăila
Danube
WALLACHIA
Cernavoda
Bucharest
Serbia
Olt. R.
Danube R.
Dobrogea
The Black Sea
Bulgaria
0
100 km.
Boundary of Wallachia
Passes between Wallachia and Transylvania
Wallachia in the Middle Ages

Map 1

river. Its fish and good grazing traditionally have provided a means of livelihood for a sedentary population, even when the steppes were dominated by nomads.[6] The mountain soils are poor, though well watered; the plains and steppe soils are good, though not well watered. The two best agricultural zones are along the banks of the Danube, and an east–west strip running just north of the steppes and south of the hill zone. This zone is particularly wide in Oltenia and in Western Muntenia.[7]

In the millenium between the withdrawal of Rome's legions and the establishment of an independent political entity, the plains were repeatedly overrun by invaders. This obliged the native population to remain in the safer hills and mountains. These people primarily were pastoralists, and were only secondarily engaged in agriculture.[8] When they began the long process of migration south and east into the plains, certain habits and types of social organization originating in the largely pastoral economy changed, adapting to the new conditions. Even today, the differences among the various geographical zones remain important. It is on the Bărăgan steppe that the collective farms are largest and most successful, just as the steppe had the largest estates earlier in history; in the mountains, the land is not collectivized and continues to house independent peasants who preserve their traditions more faithfully than do the plains people.

[6] C. Rusenescu and D. Bugă, "Territorial distribution and growth of the population between the Carpathians and the Danube, in the 19th and 20th centuries," *Revue roumaine de géologie, géophysique et géographie*, série de géographie **X**, no. 1 (1966): 76–77; D. Bugă, "Repartiția geografică a așezărilor omenești dintre Carpați și Dunăre la jumătatea secolului al XIX-lea," *Comunicări de geografie* **VII** (1969): 183–196; E. de Martonne, *La Valachie, essai de monographie géographique* (Paris: Armand Colin, 1902), pp. 42–44.

[7] G. Ionescu-Șișești, "Agricultura României," in *Enciclopedia Românieri*, **III** (Bucharest: Imprimeria națională, 1939), pp. 296–297.

[8] Some theories hold that the early Vlachs were entirely pastoral, but recent linguistic and archeological evidence now contradicts this. See N. Dunăre, "Interdependența ocupațiilor tradiționale la Români," *Apulum* **VII** (1968): 529–550.

3

The Dual Nature of the Communal-Trading Political Economy (1250–1500)

There has been a good bit of discussion about the nature of the "Asiatic mode of production."[1] But since Marx, a certain ambiguity has made the concept hazy. On the one hand, "Asiatic production" was characterized by self-sustaining, independent communal villages in which there was no private property in land, and in which conditions approximating primitive communalism prevailed. Thus, the state, located primarily in the princely cities, was superimposed on the real (rural) economy. It was superficial and likely to collapse rather easily, while underneath there remained the unchanging, self-sufficient village. (Marx was thinking mainly of Moghul India.[2]) On the other hand, most historians have stressed the all-powerful nature of the state and its role in maintaining irrigation works, and have noted that property was communal only because it belonged in its entirety to the state rather than to the local communities, and

[1]In particular see Karl A. Wittfogel, *Oriental Despotism: A Comparative Study of Total Power* (New Haven: Yale University Press, 1957); many articles in the journal *La Pensée*, particularly nos. 114 (1964), 117 (1964), 122 (1965), 127 (1966), 138 (1968), and 144 (1969); Eric J. Hobsbawm, *Karl Marx: Pre-Capitalist Economic Formations* (New York: International Publishers, 1965); and George Lichtheim, "Marx and the 'Asiatic Mode of Production,'" in *Karl Marx*, ed. Tom Bottomore (Englewood Cliffs, N.J.: Prentice-Hall, 1973), pp. 151–171.

[2]Hobsbawm, *Karl Marx: Formations*, pp. 33–36.

they have noted that the whole structure was highly despotic and centralized (ancient Egypt fits this description).[3]

The contradiction between these two aspects of the "Asiatic mode" of production has been serious enough that C. Coquery-Vidrovitch has attempted to resolve the question by inventing a new "mode" of production, the "African." In the large, precolonial African states there were no centralized irrigation networks; the states did not seem to control villages in a particularly strong way, but there were rich and powerful states nevertheless. Villages were more or less self-sufficient and communal, and were not strongly linked to each other or to the states. The states, it turns out, sustained themselves primarily by their control of international trade routes.[4] By leaving aside the nomenclature of "modes of production," and by dropping the reference to "Asiatic" or "African" types of production, this idea can be reworked to describe a type of political economy that was rather widespread throughout the world at various times. The early Wallachian state was one of the places characterized by what might be called the "communal-trading" political economy.

The communal-trading political economy can be characterized as follows:

1. There is a state that imposes a tribute on the rural population.
2. The tribute, however, is light, and the state "floats" above the rural population, interfering only slightly with village life.
3. The principal source of revenue for the state is the taxation of trade. This trade is based largely either on luxury items that are in transit through the state's area of control, or on relatively rare and expensive commodities mined or extracted from within the state's area of control. If the latter is the case, the extraction or production of the vital commodities requires relatively little labor and effort by the bulk of the population. Were this not the case, a different mode of production would exist—one that demanded far greater mobilization of mass labor by the state.
4. Villages continue to exist in a condition akin to "primitive communalism." The foundation of property is tribal or communal, and the small community is largely self-sufficient and closed off from the outside world.
5. Social differentiation is pronounced at the higher levels of the state apparatus, which enforces its monopoly over tribute collection and the collection of taxes on trade. The ruling elite, the head of state and his court of nobles, are thus primarily tax and tribute collectors and not landowners or managers of large numbers of slaves. They may own some land, and some slaves or serfs to produce their immediate food needs or even

[3]This is the aspect emphasized by Wittfogel and by most other interpretations, in particular Plekhanov's. See Samuel H. Baron, *Plekhanov, the Father of Russian Marxism* (Stanford: Standford University Press, 1963).

[4]C. Coquery-Vidrovitch, "Recherches sur un mode de production africain," *La Pensée* 144 (1969): 61–78.

to extract some trade goods; however, in general the amount of land and slaves or serfs owned is only a small proportion of the total land or population. Naturally, the elite tends to be strong militarily in order to protect its trade and tribute monopoly—its very existence depends on this key resource.

6. In the villages, however, the society is relatively undifferentiated and quite removed from the political life of the state as well as from direct involvement in the economic life of the state.
7. This situation should not be confused with the "hydraulic state," described by Wittfogel, in which the state rules the rural population quite directly and contributes important managerial inputs to the rural economy.[5] Nor should it be confused with a slave economy, in which the elite has enslaved a large part of the population in order to produce a substantial surplus.[6] Finally, this situation bears only the slightest resemblance to feudalism, in which the state is decentralized and the nobility directly controls local villages and the rural population.[7] The pure trading state is thus both much more centralized and much more superficial than the feudal state.

Actually, the rural hinterland controlled by such states may or may not consist entirely of communal villages. Some villages, near the main cities, may be directly owned by the state or its agents. Some of the hinterland may not be agricultural at all, but rather nomadic, or it may consist of hunter–gatherers. A wide variety of economic and cultural types may exist within a single trading state. The key is that the rural hinterland is not deeply involved in the economic life of the state, and that there exists a dual society consisting of the cities and main state structure on one side and whatever hinterland there may be on the other. Though Wallachian villages in the Middle Ages were communal, it would be misleading to insist on this as a characteristic of the type of political economy that prevailed—unless, of course, the notion of "primitive communalism" is defined broadly enough. It would then include all types of rural societies that were relatively uninvolved in outside trade, relatively free of outside control, and relatively classless. (Classlessness refers to an absence of social strata with differing amounts of economic power, not to an absolute lack of division of labor.) Even in cases where the tribute raised was important for the state, it was a relatively small burden for the villages, and did not alter their basic independence from state control.

Some examples of this kind of dual state are the Western Sudanic Empires of

[5] Wittfogel, *Oriental Despotism.*

[6] For example, in Greece. See M. I. Finley, "Was Greek Civilization Based on Slave Labor?" in *The Slave Economies: Historical and Theoretical Perspectives*, ed. Eugene D. Genovese (New York: Wiley, 1973), I, pp. 19–45.

[7] See March Bloch, *Feudal Society* (Chicago: University of Chicago Press, 1961), pp. 441–447.

Ghana, Mali, Songhay, and Kanem-Bornu,[8] the Khazar Empire based on the Caspian Sea and the Volga,[9] the Laotian state of the fourteenth to the seventeenth centuries,[10] and probably the Yucatan Maya city–states.[11] Carthage, for most of its history, was probably another example of this type of political economy.[12] There are other examples that seem to fit this description, but for which data are scarce. It seems that the early Varangian state in Russia was of this type,[13] as well as the pre-Khmer Funan state in lower Cambodia and Vietnam,[14] a great many pre-Islamic Arabian states such as Palmyra and later Mecca,[15] and many others. The societies mentioned were very different from one another, but all had two key points in common: The state depended on its control and taxation of long-distance trade for its survival; and the state loosely ruled populations that were peripheral to the trade and were not important providers of sustenance for the state. These populations were more or less left alone as long as they provided a small tribute and did not harm the trade routes. Some of these societies exported slaves, but even in this case, as in the Sudan, the majority of the population was not enslaved. Rather, the state either raided for slaves outside its boundaries, or collected some slaves from within its boundaries in periodic raids and tribute-raising operations. Within the state itself, it was not the productive power of the slaves that was important but rather their value as a trade good, similar to a valued mineral or vegetable product.

Some of these states, called "ports of trade" by Polanyi, did not even control a hinterland. They were purely trading cities, sufficiently important to adjoining states that they were left independent and free to carry out their vital function. Pre-Columbian Mesoamerica, the coast of West Africa in the sixteenth to nineteenth centuries, the ancient eastern Mediterranean coast, the Persian Gulf, the Sahara oases in the Middle Ages, and no doubt many other areas had such

[8]Daniel Chirot, "Urban and Rural Economies in the Western Sudan: Birni N'Konni and its Hinterland," *Cahiers d'études africaines* 4 (1968): 547–550; C. Coquery-Vidrovitch, "Recherches sur un mode," *La Pensée* 144: 64.

[9]René Grousset, *L'Empire des steppes* (Paris: Payot, 1960), pp. 236–238.

[10]Kéo Manivanna, "Aspects socio-économiques du Laos médiéval," *La Pensée* 138 (1968): 56–70.

[11]Anne C. Chapman, "Port of Trade Enclaves in Aztec and Maya Civilizations," in *Trade and Market in the Early Empires*, ed. Karl Polanyi, Conrad M. Arensberg, and Harry W. Pearson (New York: Free Press, 1957), pp. 131–133.

[12]Raymond Bloch, "Rome et l'Italie des originies aux guerres puniques," in *Histoire Universelle*, ed. R. Grousset and E. G. Léonard (Paris: Gallimard, 1956), I, pp. 890–892. This is generally used to explain Carthage's weakness in the First Punic War. Carthage fought to maintain trade routes, not for territory, and it was incapable of fighting a sustained imperial war.

[13]Jerome Blum, *Lord and Peasant in Russia from the Ninth to the Nineteenth Century* (New York: Atheneum, 1964), pp. 20–21.

[14]Christopher Pym, *The Ancient Civilization of Angkor* (New York: Mentor, 1968), p. 28. The Soviet historian L. Sédov feels that the successor of Funan, the Khmer Angkor state, became a "hydraulic society" in the ninth century when it seized free villages and inaugurated an economy based on large scale irrigation of rice. L. Sédov, "La société angkorienne et le problème du mode de production asiatique," *La Pensée* 138 (1968): 71–84.

[15]Bernard Lewis, *The Arabs in History* (New York: Harper Torchbooks, 1966), pp. 27–28 and 34–35.

"ports of trade."[16] Like the other trading states mentioned earlier, these were most prevalent and successful wherever they served to link two or more rich societies that traded with each other, acting as intermediaries in this trade. As such, the amount of territory they controlled and the size of the population they ruled did not matter greatly. Slaves, spices, cacao, gold, leather, cloth, salt, or any number of other products were the trade items.

The great Portuguese Sea Empire in Asia was merely an expansion, on a gigantic scale, of this kind of political economy. Portugal's success was due to its usurpation of trade routes previously controlled by numerous Indian Ocean "ports of trade."[17] Venice and Genoa also had a similar kind of political economy, as is shown by their tendency to grab trading rights and entrepot enclaves rather than territory for its own sake.[18]

The Early Communal-Trade Wallachian Political Economy

Keeping some of these examples in mind can help us understand some of the more peculiar aspects of medieval Wallachian social history, particularly in light of the common assumption made by many Romanian historians that medieval Wallachia and Moldavia were, in some real sense, "feudal."

The nature of the villages, the origins of the Wallachian nobility, the state, and the role of trade all must be examined in order to present a complete picture of this particular political economy. Keeping the model in mind, it then becomes possible to pinpoint which forces destroyed the communal-trading state and created a different type of society in the sixteenth century.

The origins of Wallachia are lost in such a heavy overlay of pseudohistorical myth, supported by the most fragmentary documentation (i.e., chance phrases in Byzantine documents here and there), that little can be said about it. All that is known is that somehow a population of Latin-speaking shepherds survived in the Carpathian mountains through some 10 centuries of successive foreign rule: German, Hun, Avar, Bulgarian, Magyar, Pecheneg, Cuman, and Mongol.[19] This group surived, with some mixture of Slavic populations that is reflected in the Romanian language, because the land was controlled by tributary states that skimmed off certain taxes from the Romanian villages and profited from the taxation of trade routes, fishing, and salt mines, but did not interfere in local village life, or even profoundly change it at all. Tribute collection was the

[16] See the various essays in Polanyi *et al., Trade and Market.*

[17] C. R. Boxer, *Four Centuries of Portugese Expansion, 1415–1815* (Berkeley and Los Angeles: University of California Press, 1972).

[18] Fernand Braudel, *La Méditerranée et le monde méditerranéen à l'époque de Philippe II,* 2nd (Paris: Armand Colin, 1966), I, pp. 312–315.

[19] A history of all these people after the Germans can be found in Grousset, *L'Empire*, pp. 226–242 and 468–486.

highest goal of the state, not direct ownership or control of local lands or people. Rulers could come and go, as they did, but underneath the political life of the large yet superficial imperial structures there lived the same shepherd village society.[20] Only Slavs moved into the area in sufficient numbers to influence the language and institutions of the local villages,[21] and these Slavs themselves were not, for the most part, organized into anything greater than village-sized communities.[22]

The villages were communal; that is, land was not private except for house and garden plots. Land was available to all the members of the community according to need. There was some agriculture, but only enough to satisfy a few needs. Animals were the main resource, along with the products of the forest (honey, wax, and lumber), and the pasture and forest land were collectively owned. Villages were organized into confederations whose primary task was to regulate land disputes between communities.

Evidence about the Early Communal Villages

By the greatest of chance, something is known about the social organization of these communal villages, because a few of these ancient communities survived into the nineteenth and even into the twentieth century to be studied by contemporary sociologists. In these villages in the Vrancea (in southwestern Moldavia bordering on Wallachia), the principal law was that all village lands except for gardens, vineyards, and house plots, were available for use by villagers, but not by outsiders. A family could use any clearing it made for as long as it wanted, but once the plot was abandoned, it reverted to the community. Forests and pastures were open to general use.

By the time the Vrancea was studied, communal institutions were in an advanced stage of decay, but there is ample documentation from the nineteenth century to show that they were still quite lively then.[23] The communal insti-

[20] Henri H. Stahl, *Studii de sociologie istorică* (Bucharest: Editura ştiinţifică, 1972), pp. 5–62.

[21] On the early Vlachs, their economy, and Latin and Slavic influences on their economic vocabulary see the unusually clear article by Nicolae Dunăre, "Interdependenţa ocupaţiilor tradiţionale la români," *Apulum* **VII** (1968): 529–550.

[22] The date of conversion to Christianity is unknown. It is assumed to have been sometime during the period of Bulgarian rule. All that is clearly known is that in 1234 the Vlachs were Orthodox Christians. A papal bull of that year states that in the land of the Cumans there were men called "Walati" who received sacraments from "pseudo-bishops who belong to the Greek rite." Cited in Andrei Oţetea, "La formation des états féodaux roumains," *Nouvelles études d'histoire* (Bucharest: Académie roumaine, 1965), **III**, pp. 95. See also B. Câmpina, "Le problème de l'apparition des états féodaux roumains," *Nouvelles études* (1955), **I**, pp. 147. On the history of the first Bulgarian Empire see Stephen Runciman, *A History of the First Bulgarian Empire* (London: G. Bell and Son, 1930).

[23] The term "communal" is used for the Romanian word *devălmăşie* which means joint property, or held in common. The word for communes themselves is *obşte*. The best, though highly controversial, work on Romanian communal villages is Henri H. Stahl's *Contribuţii la studiul satelor devălmaşe româneşti*, 3 vols. (Bucharest: Editura academiei, 1958–1965). A synthesis of this work appeared in French: Henri H. Stahl, *Les anciennes communautés villageoises roumaines* (Bucharest and Paris: Académie roumaine and C.N.R.S., 1969).

tutions declined because of population growth and economic changes. A high population density and a change from a primarily pastoral to an agricultural economy caused disputes over land usage as the shifting cultivation practiced in the past was replaced by the establishment of more permanent fields. Another reason for the decay of communal institutions was the intrusion of the outside world. Originally, all of Vrancea had paid a tax to the Moldavian princes. In the nineteenth century, several Moldavian nobles and monasteries tried to claim the region as theirs and collect dues for the use of the land. To protect themselves, the Vranceans raised money for a long series of law suits which they eventually won. But in the process, some individuals contributed more money than others and so claimed a larger share of the land. Then, in the late nineteenth and early twentieth centuries, lumbering became important and some Vranceans abused their communal rights to the forests and seriously deforested the area.[24]

The form of organization that existed in the Vrancea in the nineteenth century apparently was not new, for in 1716, Dimitrie Cantemir, a one-time Moldavian prince then living in Russia, wrote about it, assuming that the form dated back to the earliest times of the principality. He described the Vrancea and two other similar areas in Moldavia in his *Description of Moldavia.*

> The second lesser republic in Moldavia is Vrancea in the country of Putna near the boundary of Wallachia, surrounded on all sides by very wild mountains. It numbers twelve villages and two thousand farms, and is ignorant of cultivation, being content like Câmpulung with the grazing of sheep. Similarly the inhabitants pay a definite fixed tribute yearly to the prince, are ruled by their own laws, and utterly reject the prince's orders and his judges alike.[25]

Cantemir seems to have exaggerated his description of the Vrancea's independence, because there was a Moldavian court official called the "Vornic of the Vrancea" who was the prince's tax collector in that region. This office once may have been held by a local chief, but the position had certainly turned into a state office by Cantemir's time. Furthermore, the state was recognized as the highest judicial authority.[26]

Might that form of society, which still survived in isolated places during the nineteenth century, have been the general form in early Wallachia from the thirteenth to the sixteenth centuries? Several facts suggest this.

During its early history, Wallachia was chiefly a mountain and hill state. The very name Muntenia (used for the eastern two-thirds of the principality) means "Mountain Land." The early capitals of the Wallachian state were Curtea

[24] Henri H. Stahl, *Nerej, un village d'une région archaïque* (Bucharest: Institut de sciences sociales de Roumanie, 1940), I, pp. 225–378.

[25] Section reproduced in *Contrasts in Emerging Societies*, ed. Doreen Warriner (Bloomington, Ind.: Indiana University Press, 1965), p. 129.

[26] Stahl, *Nerej*, p. 227.

de Argeş, and Câmpulung—not the same Câmpulung mentioned by Cantemir, which is in northern Moldavia, but Câmpulung in the Wallachian Carpathians. Only in the fifteenth century was the capital moved, first to Târgovişte on the edge of the mountains, and finally, in the middle of the fifteenth century, to Bucharest in the plains.[27] As mentioned earlier, it is known that the Vlachs of this period were primarily pastoralists. And, while they undoubtedly used the plains in their annual migration toward winter pastures along the Danube, their villages were situated in the safer hills and mountains where they could hide or defend themselves against the numerous invaders who troubled Wallachia.[28]

Old boundary markings delineate village areas. The earliest documents that make mention of the division of land into villages date from the fourteenth century, and these documents state that such divisions existed "from time immemorial." Because the establishment and maintenance of such boundaries between villages was one of the principal functions of the assembly of Vrancean villages, and because the establishment of such boundaries throughout much of Wallachia antedated the creation of an independent state, it can be inferred that federations of communal villages, interested in defining and protecting their grazing rights, existed from at least the thirteenth century, and probably before.[29]

Division of lands within villages into private plots is much more recent. Most recorded divisions occurred in the sixteenth, seventeenth, and eighteenth centuries,[30] and in some areas they were still occurring in the nineteenth century.[31] That the division into private plots is relatively recent supports the notion that the villages were communal before the division.

There are thus four major pieces of evidence that suggest the early Wallachian villages were communal:

1. the remnants of communal institutions found in the Vrancea and the Vrancea's traditional distance from the Moldavian state;
2. the fact that, during the thirteenth to the sixteenth centuries, Wallachia had mostly a mountain or hill population and was primarily pastoral, just as the Vrancean population remained until the nineteenth century;
3. signs of the existence of village federations even before the creation of the state in the thirteenth century which suggest that there existed institutions,

[27] P. P. Panaitescu, *Interpretări româneşti* (Bucharest: Editura universul, 1947), pp. 222–223.

[28] In the sixth and seventh centuries there were the Avars, in the eighth and ninth the Bulgars, in the tenth the Magyars, in the eleventh the Patzinaks, in the twelfth the Cumans, in the thirteenth the Mongols (Tartars), and from the fourteenth to the nineteenth centuries the periodic Ottoman raids.

[29] Stahl, *Les anciennes communautés*, pp. 32–35.

[30] Constantin Giurescu, *Studii de istorie socială* (Bucharest: Editura universul, 1943), p. 253.

[31] Stahl, *Contribuţii la studiul*, **II**, pp. 321–341.

similar to those found in the Vrancea, that regulated the use of land between communal villages; and

4. the division of village lands into private family plots took place only in the sixteenth to nineteenth centuries, not before.

Having shown that most Wallachian villages were probably communal during the first few centuries of the Wallachian state, it is easier to proceed to interpret the evidence about these villages' relations with the state, its prince, and its nobles.

According to the available documents from the second half of the fourteenth century, the state taxed villages by taking a part of their production. The village unit was collectively responsible for the tax. The tax included some cereals (a tithe), wine, vegetables, and fruit. But as might be expected from a mostly pastoral economy, the tax principally took the form of animals, most of all sheep (and wool), pigs, cows, oxen, and hides. The part paid in forest products was also important—mostly honey and beeswax, but also firewood and lumber for construction. There was also a tax in fish and hay.

Villages could be called upon for defense (proving that they had arms), for the construction of fortifications, and for the maintenance of roads. They provided the local police, which was supposed to keep local routes clear of brigands, and were obliged to furnish transportation and food for the state's agents whenever they were in their area on a mission. In some cases, villages had to maintain the prince's mills and ponds, to provide some game for the court, and to take care of the prince's animals (sheep, cows, horses) if the need arose. A few villages near salt mines had to provide them with labor.[32]

From the time of the origins of the state, the prince could cede some of his powers of taxation to nobles or monasteries; numerous acts describe such gifts," which in fact were often sales or leases. These "gifts" led many Romanian historians to believe that this was evidence of seignorial property of villages,[33] but actually the "gifts" were revokable and generally amounted to a part, not the whole, of the dues owed the state. Only later, beginning in the fifteenth century

[32] Stahl, *Les anciennes communautés*, pp. 167–169.

[33] The most noted proponents of this theory of seignorial property in Wallachia and Moldavia are Giurescu, *Studii*; Ioan C. Filitti, *Proprietatea solului în Principatele Române până la 1864* (Bucharest: Fundaţiunea Regele Ferdinand I, 193?); and the more recent historians Andrei Oţetea and Barbu Câmpina (see articles cited in note 22). The issue has revolved around whether the early Wallachian state was "feudal" and whether there were free village communities at this time rather than serfs bound to the land. The issue remains controversial in Romanian historiography. Aside from Stahl's work, on which I base myself, some other noted historians have agreed that the villagers were originally free and that the rights of nobles over them were weak. See Radu Roşetti, *Pământul, sătenii, şi stăpânii în Moldova* (Bucharest: Socec, 1907); Marcel Emerit, *Les paysans roumains depuis le traité d'Andrinople jusqu'à la libération des terres, 1829–1864* (Paris: Recueil Sirey, 1937); and the recent qualified acceptance of this thesis in Ştefan Ştefănescu, "Consideraţiuni asupra termenilor 'vlah' şi 'rumîn' pe baza documentelor interne ale Ţării Romîneşti din veacurile XIV–XVII," in *Studii şi materiale de istorie medie*, 5 vols. (Bucharest: Editura academiei, 1956–1962), **IV** (1960), p. 75 (hereafter cited as *S.M.I.M.*).

and increasingly in the sixteenth century, was the whole of the state's taxing powers in some villages ceded to nobles or monasteries.[34] The "gifts" were rights to dues, not to the land as such, and when the "gifts" were sales, the price was very low. In the fifteenth century, the rights to dues for a whole village cost hardly more than one or two Gypsy slaves. This was because the dues themselves were quite light.[35]

The Nobles

The origins of the nobility are not very clear, and are the subject of controversy. Nicolae Iorga, Romania's best-known historian, believed that the nobility originated as an administrative class created by the princes. Although this theory is consonant with the existence of a state that ruled generally free communal villages (in which Iorga also believed), some of the evidence indicates that matters were not so simple.[36] As might be expected, those who believe that the nobility started as an administrative body also believe that, in early times, they did not own land, and that early villages were free and communal.

Dimitrie Cantemir stated that the ranks of the Moldavian nobility included high court officials; "knights," who received land from the prince in return for military service; and various groups of less important officials, including the descendants of former officials who had received villages in return for their services. These descendants might not have been officials themselves, but they clearly came from officials' families. Given the changes that had occurred between the fifteenth and the early eighteenth centuries when Cantemir wrote, this description supports the theory that the nobility originated as a service aristocracy, but says little about whether or not villages were originally free.

But Cantemir further listed another class of noble, called *răzăşi*, comprising simply free peasants.[37] The same class of free peasants also existed in Wallachia, where it was called *moşneni*. According to Radu Rosetti, these free peasants descended from nobles who had become impoverished and reduced to the level of the peasantry, even though they retained their freedom and still considered themselves noble.[38] Furthermore, in the late sixteenth to the early eighteenth centuries, free peasants in Wallachia were called *cnez* or *judec*. But the word *cnez*

[34]Stahl, *Les anciennes communautés*, pp. 170–172 and 175–176. From the documents ceding "gifts" to Wallachian monasteries it is evident that they did not have even the means to collect dues, but had to get dues collected for them by the prince who remained responsible for the collection. Only in the fifteenth and sixteenth centuries, particularly in the latter, did monasteries evolve their own collecting apparatus. Stahl, *Contribuţii la studiul*, **III**, pp. 94–97.

[35]Marcel Emerit, "Reflexions sur le régime seigneural en Roumanie," *Revue historique du sud-est européen* 4–6 (1938): 10–17.

[36]Nicolae Iorga, *Geschichte des Rumänischen Volkes* (Gotha: F. A. Perthes, 1905), **I**, pp. 252–253.

[37]Dimitrie Cantemir, trans., *Descriera Moldovei* (Bucharest: Editura Cartea Românească, 1923), pp. 139–143.

[38]Rosetti, *Pământul*, pp. 38–40, 232–235, 299.

comes from the Old Slavonic КЪНѦЗЬ, meaning prince. *Judec* was the Latin version of the same word and is the origin of the modern Romanian word for county, *judeţ*; in thirteenth- and fourteenth-century documents, it referred to an important class of leaders of the Vlach population in both Wallachia and Transylvania.[39]

Unfortunately for Rosetti's argument, in an Austrian census of Oltenia taken in 1722, about 47% of all the peasant villages were listed as "free," and in the mountainous district of Gorj, the proportion of free villages was about 60% of the total.[40] As late as 1912, more than 60% of the inhabitants of the mountainous districts of Gorj, Vâlcea, and Argeş, in the Wallachian Carpathians and sub-Carpathians, considered themselves descendants of *moşneni* (the word replaced *cnez* and *judec* in the eighteenth century), and they tended to be clustered in certain areas. In the more recently settled plains of Eastern Wallachia, on the other hand, fewer than 10% of all peasants claimed to be descendants of *moşneni*. In the Vrancea, the last region of communal villages, all of the inhabitants claimed to be *răzăşi* (the Moldavian equivalent of *moşneni*).[41] It is obvious that such large, clustered portions of the population could not all be descendants of an impoverished aristocracy. Yet, the facts that they were recognized as having a connection to the old nobility, and that from the late sixteenth to early eighteenth centuries they were called by a name that signified a noble origin have to be explained.

It is likely that the early Wallachian villages had headmen who acted as intermediaries between their people and the authorities who collected taxes from them. Such headmen are called *kenezi* in early fourteenth-century Hungarian documents. They were Vlachs (Romanian-speaking) who apparently were village chiefs among the Vlach people of Transylvania. A document from the Banat, dating from the second half of the fourteenth century, emphasizes these headmen's "middleman" role between Hungarian nobles and Vlach commoners. Eventually, some members of this group receded into the mass of Romanian peasants while others were absorbed into the Magyar aristocracy, so that by the end of the sixteenth century the class had disappeared.[42]

But in Wallachia, the *cneji* (i.e., plural of *cnez*) evolved differently. In all probability, they performed a function similar to that of their Transylvanian

[39] Ioan Bogdan, "Despre cnejii români," in *Ioan Bogdan: Scrieri alese*, ed. G. Mihăilă (Bucharest: Editura academiei, 1968), pp. 180–183 and 201–203 (reprint of an essay written in 1903). The Bulgarian rulers of the first Bulgarian Empire called themselves *Cneaz* before being accorded the title of Czar by Constantinople but after they had become sufficiently slavicized to drop the Hun title of Khan (See Runciman, *First Bulgarian Empire*).

[40] Stahl, *Les anciennes communautés*, p. 23.

[41] Henri H. Stahl, "Organizarea socială a ţărănimii," in *Enciclopedia României* (Bucharest: Imprimeria naţională, 1938), I, p. 575.

[42] Ioan Bogdan, "Despre cnejii români," *Scrieri alese*, pp.182–185; and M. Hoblan, "Mărturii asupra rolului cnezilor de pe marile domenii din Banat în a doua jumătate a secolului al XIV-lea," in *S.M.I.M.* (1957), II, pp. 407–417.

counterparts while Wallachia was ruled by the Cumans and Mongols, but in the second half of the thirteenth century, Mongol rule was replaced by native rule.[43] A Hungarian document of 1247 mentions Vlach *voievods* (military chiefs), who ruled what must have been village federations that had united to fight against the nomads. Though the Hungarian King claimed that these *voievods* owed him allegiance, and he even used Western crusading knights to try to gain control over them, Wallachia remained independent except for a tribute it paid to Hungary.[44] The *cneji* thus formed the original base of the prince's (*Voievod*) administration. Later, there was a differentiation of the *cneji* into high and low nobles; the former became the court service and military aristocracy (*boieri*), and the latter remained village headmen.[45]

In later centuries, particularly in the sixteenth, most villages lost their freedom and were seized by *boieri* and monasteries. The institution of *cneji* vanished, based as it was on free villages dealing through their representatives with the state. The Wallachian *cneji* thus followed their Transylvanian counterparts' decline into obscurity, except in those villages that remained free after the sixteenth century. These were mostly in the hills and mountains, and they came to be called *cneji* villages. From this came the logical development of calling all free villagers *cneji*.[46] This change and the terminology associating "free" with "noble" both support the notion that all villages originally were free, and show the origins of the nobility.

The State

The explanation of the origins of the nobility does not, however, explain the origins of the Wallachian state itself, nor of the institution of *Voievod* (Prince). One interesting and frequent documentary clue to the origin of the *Voievodat* was the use of the prefix *Io* (Old Slavonic Iѿ) in front of the *Voievods*' names in acts from the fourteenth century on. The term first appeared in the mid-fourteenth century, probably at the same time that a permanent princely chancellory was established in Wallachia.

This prefix seems to have been employed by the Czars of the Second Bulgarian Empire (1187–1393). It is known that this Empire arose from a mixed Bulgar, Vlach, and Cuman population. Though the Vlachs mentioned in the sources were probably mostly southern Balkan Vlachs (the "Meglenoromanians" and the "Aromanians"), the Empire was certainly in contact with Cumans north

[43] Henri H. Stahl, *Controverse de istorie socială românească* (Bucharest: Editura ştiinţifică, 1969), pp. 261–271.

[44] Bogdan, "Originea voievodatului la români," in *Scrieri alese*, pp. 177–178; and A. Oţetea, "Etats féodaux roumains," in *Nouvelles etudes*, **III**, pp. 96–97.

[45] Stahl, *Controverse*, pp. 272–275.

[46] *Ibid.*, p. 266; and Bogdan, "Despre cnejii români," *Scrieri alese*, p. 204.

of the Danube.[47] It is impossible to tell whether the Bulgarian Czars of the Second Empire exercised any control in Wallachia, but given the connections between Bulgaria and Wallachia, it is likely that some of the forms of the Bulgarian court were imitated in Wallachia even though it was ruled by the Cumans. The word *voievod* meant "general" (or as Ioan Bogdan called them, "belli dux") in Bulgarian (as it originally did in Serbian, Polish, and Russian).[48]

As stated previously, the nomad rulers of Wallachia probably ruled it as a communal-trade state. They imposed taxes on the communal villages and probably used native village headmen as their intermediaries. Though virtually nothing is known about the period of Patzinak domination, and only little about the Cumans, it is known that this was the pattern adopted by Mongols, who ruled Wallachia for only a few years. The fact that such a system of organization emerged in the independent Wallachian state suggests it antedated the Mongols. (In Moldavia, which the Mongols ruled for over 100 years, they left deeper, traces.)

Thus, when the Wallachian state took possession of Wallachia, it inherited a system of administration shaped by several centuries of nomadic rule and Bulgarian influence. Of interest is the fact that the new Wallachian ruling class found itself in possession of a group of nomadic slaves who had been abandoned by their former rulers. These were the Gypsies (brought from central Asia by the Cumans? Mongols?), who were to remain slaves in Romania until the nineteenth century.[49]

The number of nobles, *boieri*, was too small to rule the state. There were also lesser functionaries, the *curteni* (courtiers) and *slugi* (servants). These minor

[47] Ioan Bogdan, "Iw̃ din titlul domnilor români," in *Scrieri alese*, pp. 146–158; George Ostrogorsky, *History of the Byzantine State* (New Brunswick, N.J.: Rutgers University Press, 1957), pp. 358–361, particularly note 4. p. 358. This question touches on the sensibilities of nationalist historians in the Balkans. The Bulgarians tend to believe that there were no Vlachs involved in the Second Bulgarian Empire. The Romanians go to the other extreme of suggesting that the Vlach element was dominant. (See P. P. Panaitescu, "Les relations bulgaro-roumaines au moyen âge," *Revista Aromânească* I (1929); and N. Bănescu, *Un problème d'histoire médiévale. Création et caractère du second empire bulgare* (Bucharest: Institut roumain d'études byzantines, 1942). This might be a good place to add that a similar controversy exists between the Hungarians and Romanians about the nature of the indigenous population of Transylvania. In that case, however, the evidence is much clearer. To claim that there were no Romanian speakers in Transylvania before the arrival of the Magyars is absurd in view of the evidence, some of which was used earlier to discuss the origins of the *cneji*. For a brief review of some of the nationalistic arguments about early Romanians see Robert L. Wolff, *The Balkans in Our Times* (New York: Norton, 1967), pp. 31–36.

[48] Bogdan, "Originea voievodatului" in *Scrieri alese*, pp. 175–176. In Slavic countries, *voievod* never signified prince or king, but remained a term for military leaders beneath the prince. This suggests that the term was adopted in Romania before independence. When the Wallachians reconquered their territory from the Mongols, their *voievod* was elevated to the rank of prince. The Romanian term for nobles, *boier* (plural, *boieri*) also has a Slavic origin, probably Bulgarian. (Runciman, in *The First Bulgarian Empire*, suggests that the Slavs took it from the Huns.)

[49] Nicolae Iorga, *Points de vue sur l'histoire du commerce de l'orient au moyen âge* (Paris: Librairie universitaire J. Gamber, 1924), pp. 75–76 and 83–85; and various parts of his *Histoire des roumains et de la romanité orientale* (Bucharest: Académie roumaine, 1937–1945). Also, Stahl, *Les anciennes communautés*, pp. 42–44.

officials constituted the bulk of the army, for there was no distinction between civil and military office. Many were directly attached to princes, but others were attached to particular *boieri*. Their military role was considerable, for they were the enforcement branch of the state as well as its administrators and tribute collectors.[50]

The Role of Commerce

Thus far in the discussion, the account of the probable origins of the Wallachian princes, court, and nobles and their relations with the free village communes has left aside a consideration of both the dynamic forces at work in the creation of the new state, and how that state became relatively wealthy in a short time. In 1330, the Hungarian King Carol Robert invaded Wallachia, and *Voievod* Basarab I tried to buy him off with a payment of 7000 silver marks—an enormous sum for the period, amounting to about 1200 kilograms of pure silver. Carol Robert refused the offer but was beaten off. It is difficult to imagine that a state subsisting entirely from lightly taxed, rather primitive semipastoral villages would be able to raise such a large quantity of precious metal. Though there were some gold mines in Hungarian Transylvania, Wallachia did not have its own source of precious metals.[51] There must have been a fairly active commerce with other areas, and the nature of this commerce proves to be the element that has been missing in the account thus far.

The Mongol conquest, far from being a simple, destructive raid, opened up or at least greatly expanded a major commercial route between the West and Asia. The Mongols left a network of roads and customs posts which was taken over by the new rulers.[52] The Khans granted Caffa (in the Crimea) to the

[50] N. Stoicescu, "Contribution à l'histoire de l'armée roumaine au moyen âge," *Revue roumaine d'histoire* **VI**, no. 5 (1967): 731–738. Stoicescu claims that the existence of these officials shows the feudal nature of the Wallachian and Moldavian states, but given the absence of feudal domains, this is hard to accept. He throws doubt on his own theory by showing that these officials in the seventeenth century were divided into princely officials and those controlled by independent high nobles. He concludes that if this was the case in the seventeenth century, it must have been even more so in the fifteenth when the state was weaker. But as will be shown later, the seventeenth-century state was much weaker than the earlier state, and by the seventeenth century a real "feudalization" had occurred. No such decentralization can be demonstrated in the early state.

[51] O. Iliescu, "Despre natura juridică și importanța despăgubirilor oferite de Basarab voievod regelui Carol Robert, 1330," in *S.M.I.M.*, **V**, pp. 145–147.

[52] This is one of the basic themes in Iorga, *Points de vue*. See also P. P. Panaitescu in *Interpretări românești*, pp. 136–137. Panaitescu believes that the reason two separate Romanian states developed was that they were based on two different trade routes, one going north from the Black Sea to Lvov and on to the Baltic (the Moldavian route), and the other more directly west from the Black Sea through Wallachia. The fact that each of these states produced similar goods and had a similar commerce running through it, but in different directions, would explain why they were politically distinct, and even rivals.

The prevailing view in Romanian historiography is that Iorga was wrong, and that the Mongols were a purely destructive force. (See A. Oțetea, "Etats féodaux roumains" in *Nouvelles études*, **III**, p. 93.) Unfortunately, this

Genoese for the purpose of promoting trade.[53] From there the Genoese established coastal trading enclaves around the whole northern coast of the Black Sea. Some of their most important ones were on the Bessarabian coast and the Danube Delta (which were then Mongol territory and later by the mid-fourteenth century, Moldavian territory). It is not known precisely how far up the Danube the Genoese reached, but it is certain that they traded at least as far as Cernavoda, on the opposite side of the Danube from Wallachia. A Hungarian document of 1349 mentions Genoese traders as far West as Orşova, a Danube port on the boundary between Wallachia and the Banat. It is quite conceivable that the Genoese transshipped goods by land from the Adriatic port of Ragusa to the Danube, and then down to the Black Sea by boat.[54]

Another source of trade was the German Transylvanian cities established just north of Wallachia on the other side of the Carpathians. These cities probably originated in the early thirteenth century, when the Hungarian kings invited Germans to populate their eastern marches with reliable elements as part of an attempt to extend their influence into "Cumania" (Wallachia). But the formation of semi-independent, Royal German trading cities did not occur until the second half of the thirteenth century after the passage of the Mongols.[55]

There were two types of trade in early Wallachia. There was the long-distance trade that passed through Wallachia from the Black Sea toward the Adriatic, or northward into Transylvania, from which it moved into Central Europe, to Buda, and to Germany. Second, there was a trade in Wallachian products that were exported toward Constantinople by the Genoese, and north to the German cities of Transylvania (which possibly re-exported a part of these goods farther

Ftn. 52 (continued)

position can not be taken at face value since it is taken from a similarly biased and ideologically based position adopted by Soviet historians. Officially, the period of the early Wallachian state was characterized by the "feudal" mode of production, and facts that might indicate the contrary are not viewed with favor. In the last several years, the rehabilitation of Iorga and the renewed independence of Romanian historians have indicated that the official position may swing back to Iorga.

This point of view is strengthened by the more recent research of Sigismund Pach carried out from the Hungarian point of view. He shows the importance of the "Wallachian" connection via the Transylvanian Saxon cities in the Hungarian spice trade. See, "La route du poivre vers la Hongrie médiévale," in *Histoire économique du monde méditerranéen 1450–1650. Mélanges en l'honneur de Fernand Braudel* (Toulouse: Privat, 1973), pp. 449–458.

[53] Iorga, *Points de vue*, p. 92. It is conceivable that the Genoese enclaves on the sea borders of the Golden Horde's territory were "ports of trade" such as those described by Polanyi *et al., Trade and Market.* As far as these enclaves and their relations with Moldavia and Wallachia are concerned, too little is known about their nature to be very specific. But Polanyi's theory of neutral enclaves where trade was regulated by administrative arrangements between the rulers of the hinterland and the port merchants offers an interesting hypothesis about the relations between the Wallachian voievods and the Genoese.

[54] Constantin C. Giurescu, "Le commerce sur le territoire de la Moldavie pendant la domination tartare (1241–1352)," in *Nouvelles études*, **III**, p. 56, particularly note 6. Also G.I. Brătianu, "Vicina I. Contributions à l'histoire de la domination byzantine et du commerce génois en Dobrodgea," in Académie Roumaine, *Bulletin de la section historique* (Bucharest, 1923), **X**, pp. 113–189.

[55] Nicolae Iorga, *Istoria comerțului românesc* (Bucharest: Tiparul românesc, 1925), **I**, pp. 32–34.

north and west). The main items that passed through Wallachia toward the East were artisan items from Germany, Bohemia, and the Transylvanian cities—cloth, tools, and arms. Goods passing from the East toward the West and North were mainly spices, silks, and jewelry.[56] (The Adriatic–Black Sea trade in the east–west direction was probably similar.) Wallachia itself imported Western artisan goods and Oriental luxuries and exported fish, animal and forest products, and salt. Cereals were too bulky to be transported over the mountains to Transylvania, but some were exported to Constantinople by sea. In the fourteenth century, the Genoese became a key food supplier to Constantinople, and there are records of major wheat shipments from Kilia on the Danube Delta toward Pera, the Genoese enclave in Constantinople.[57]

There is little doubt that the long-distance trade passing through Wallachia was more valuable to the state than was the trade that originated from within the state. The long-distance trade going to and from the Black Sea did not decline until the general decline of Levantine trade during the sixteenth century. This was probably due more to the Portuguese circumnavigation of Africa than to the Ottoman seizure of Constantinople in 1453.[58] In 1503, records from Braşov, the major Transylvanian trading city, showed that the value of Oriental goods entering the city after passage through Wallachia and Moldavia (about 90% of the goods through Wallachia) was four times as great as the value of imports from the Romanian principalities. It was only by the middle of the sixteenth century, when total trade to and through Braşov had fallen to half of what it was at the start of the century, that the value of Wallachian and Moldavian imports into Braşov became greater than the value of Oriental goods passing through to Braşov.[59]

From the little that can be deduced about the organization of the transit trade through early Wallachia, it is possible to see the great importance it had for the state. There is, first of all, the documentary proof mentioned earlier that large sums of precious metal were apparently in the hands of the princes. Second, there was the customs organization that had been taken over from the Mongols and earlier nomad empires and maintained by the state, with fixed points on trade routes where customs agents collected a tax.[60] Third, from the mid-

[56] Radu Manolescu, *Comerţul Ţarii Romîneşti şi Moldovei cu Braşovul* (*Secolele XIV–XVI*) (Bucharest: Editura ştiinţifică, 1965), pp. 16–17.

[57] *Ibid.* Also, Constantin C. Giurescu, *Istoria pescuitului şi a pisciculturii în România* (Bucharest: Editura academiei, 1964), I, pp. 58–59, 65–66, and 73–76—on fish; A. Ilieş, "Ştire în legătură cu exploatarea sării în Ţara Românească pînă în veacul al XVIII-lea," in *S.M.I.M.*, I, pp. 156–158—on salt; O. Iliescu, "Notes sur l'apport roumain au ravitaillement de Byzance d'après une source inédite du XIVe siècle," in *Nouvelles études*, III, pp. 105–116. This last article refers more to Moldavia than to Wallachia, but it can be supposed that it also holds for the latter. Along with wheat, the Genoese document discussed in this article mentions transactions with Pera in salt, wine (presumably from Dobrodgea), beeswax, and honey.

[58] Manolescu, *Comerţul Ţării*, p. 174. A. H. Lybyer, "The Ottoman Turks and the Routes of Oriental Trade," *English Historical Review* XXX (October, 1915): 588.

[59] Manolescu, *Comerţul Ţării*, pp. 177 and 180.

[60] Iliescu, "Regelui Carol Robert" in *S.M.I.M.*, V, pp. 144–145.

fourteenth century on (possibly earlier as well, but there are no known records), the Wallachian princes issued "authorizations" to foreign merchants to pass through Wallachia. They even made efforts to increase the importance of their main Danube port, Brăila, by exempting foreign merchants entering Wallachia there from paying a tax on their goods. But on their way back through Wallachia, they were obliged to pay the normal tolls (thus indicating that the main purpose was to stimulate the transit trade).[61] Finally, the early Wallachian capitals of Câmpulung and Târgovişte were situated on the main trade route going from the Danube to Braşov.[62]

In the early fifteenth century, the Wallachians seized the Moldavian outlets to the sea on the Danube Delta. This was at a time when Bulgaria had lost its independence to the Turks (thus cutting off a rival trade route from the Black Sea to the Adriatic), and when the Ottoman Empire itself was in temporary eclipse because of Tamerlane's victory at Ankara. It was also during this period, under the rule of Prince Mircea the Elder, that the Wallachian trading state reached its apogee.[63] This occurred at a time when it had the greatest control over the Black Sea and Danube Delta ports in its history, illustrating the importance of the long-distance trade that crossed its territory. (In the second half of the fifteenth century, as the Turks re-entered Wallachia and as Moldavia regained command of its entire coastline, the main trade route shifted northward, and Moldavia reached its apogee under *Voievod* Stephen the Great.)[64]

A detailed knowledge of both the types of men who composed the body of merchants active in Wallachia from the thirteenth to the fifteenth century, and the extent to which they acted as agents of the Wallachian state would be very useful for fully understanding the nature and organization of commerce. Little is recorded about these matters before the sixteenth century, but from the evidence that is available, some important inferences can be drawn.

As might be expected, foreigners played an important role in commerce. There were "Latins" (Italians) from Ragusa and Genoa—not only those living in the port cities, or those merely passing through Wallachia, but others permanently established in the interior cities on the main trade routes such as Câmpulung and Târgovişte. There were also Greeks, and there were a few Armenians (though fewer than in Moldavia). Some of the permanent foreign residents were agents of the princes, as well as important international figures with personal connections with neighboring kings and princes.[65]

Wallachians participated in commercial relations with other states, and by the second half of the fifteenth century, their importance seemed to be increas-

[61] Iorga, *Istoria comerţului*, I, pp. 46–47.

[62] Panaitescu, *Interpretări*, p. 222.

[63] Iorga, *Istoria comerţului*, pp. 57–59; Andrei Oţetea *et al.*, *Istoria Romîniei* (Bucharest: Editura academiei, 1962), II, pp. 362–384, section by B. Câmpina and D. Mioc.

[64] Oţetea *et al.*, *Istoria Romîniei*, II, pp. 488–550, section by B. Câmpina and M. Berza.

[65] Iorga, *Istoria comerţului*, I, pp. 77, 118–119, 129–133, 144. Some Turkish merchants began appearing in the late fifteenth century.

ing while that of foreigners was decreasing. The princes themselves were among the biggest merchants in Wallachia, though of course they acted through their foreign and domestic merchant agents. *Boieri*, both high court officials and lesser ones, also were active either independently or as agents of the state. But most of the Wallachian merchants apparently were commoners from the towns, and by the late fifteenth century, men from small towns (and even villages) played an increasingly significant role in commerce.[66]

The major piece of evidence about the various types of merchants from Wallachia and the types of goods they handled is from Braşov, the main German Transylvanian trading town. Fairly complete customs records exist which list all merchants and goods involved in trade between Wallachia and Braşov for the year 1503, half of 1530, and the years 1542–1550. Although by 1503 commercial relations between Braşov and Wallachia were already changing from what they previously had been, it is possible to draw a great many conclusions about the trade situation in the fifteenth century.[67]

As in earlier times, the trade between Braşov and Wallachia in 1503 had two basic components: the local production moving between the towns, some for their own consumption, and goods in transit between the Orient and the West which passed through each town but did not originate in either. The same Wallachian products were being exported to Braşov as in previous centuries. (Of course, a significant proportion of these exports were re-exported to the rest of Transylvania and beyond into Hungary.) These products were salted fish, honey, wax, animals, hides, and smaller amounts of wool, bacon, and other animal fats, cheese, and wine. Cereals are mentioned only in the records of 1530, and then only a very small quantity was involved.[68] The Western artisans' goods imported into Wallachia (both those made in Braşov and those originating in points farther north and west) were cloth, knives, and a category labelled as "small items"—that is, tools, rope, some clothing, footwear, and other items that were exported from Braşov in small quantities.[69] Because the items re-exported by Wallachia were the same as those consumed there, these items were thus also the main ones involved in the long-distance trade from West to East. The items originating east and south of Wallachia, and entering Braşov after passage through Wallachia, were cotton, spices, lemons, raisins, figs, incense, rice, fine woven products of cotton, silk, and gold thread, carpets, and a host of similar products.[70]

By 1503, the number of foreigners (Italians, Greeks, and others) participating

[66] *Ibid.*, pp. 137–142. Also R. Manolescu, "Schimbul de mărfuri dintre Ţara Românească şi Braşov în prima jumătate a secolului al XVI-lea," in *S.M.I.M.*, **II**, pp. 169–170.

[67] Manolescu, "Schimbul," in *S.M.I.M.*, **II**, p. 117.

[68] *Ibid.*, pp. 126, 133, 136, 139, 145–148.

[69] *Ibid.*, pp. 147–149.

[70] *Ibid.*, pp. 172–173.

in the commerce between Braşov and Wallachia had fallen to almost none.[71] This was, however, a temporary stage, for later in the sixteenth century a large number of "Levantine" merchants from the Ottoman Empire came into Wallachia. Almost all of the merchants mentioned in the 1503 records were Wallachians and Transylvanians.[72]

There were two categories of Wallachian merchants: the "big" merchants, agents of the princes, important *boieri,* and men from the larger cities whose degree of independence is unknown, but who dealt mainly with the court and high nobles; and "little" merchants, many of whom were from smaller towns and villages and who dealt with the less important elements of the society. In 1503, the Braşov records listed 204 "little" merchants who made 323 trips to Braşov, and 59 "big" merchants who made 126 trips. The average "little" man's trip involved a load worth 2835 aspers (an Ottoman unit of money), while the average "big" merchant's trip involved a load worth 25,267 aspers (about 10 times as much). But, of all the Wallachian products imported into Braşov and carried by Wallachians, 97% were carried by "little" merchants. On the other hand, 46.5% of the imports of Western artisans' goods were carried by "big" merchants, and they carried 89% of all cloth imports and all of the knives (96% of which were expensive luxury knives); the big merchants carried only 5% of the miscellaneous small items listed in the records. (All these percentages refer to the value of the goods, not to weight or number, except for the breakdown of types of knives, in which the percentage refers to numbers of knives.)[73]

In the transit trade of Oriental goods through Wallachia toward Braşov, the disproportion was even greater. Of all the Wallachian merchants involved in this trade (70% of the Oriental goods brought into Braşov through Wallachia were handled by Wallachians rather than Transylvanians), more than 99% were brought by "big" merchants. As for the proportionate values of the various types of commerce, only 5% consisted of Wallachian exports to Braşov, 29% consisted of imports (a significant portion of which were re-exported east and south, as mentioned previously), 64% of Oriental goods passed through Wallachia toward Braşov (of which most were re-exported north and west).[74]

Several conclusions can be drawn from these statistics. In the second half of the fifteenth century, after the Ottoman seizure of Constantinople, the number of Italians involved in the Black Sea trade fell sharply, but at least some of the Black Sea commerce remained (though Iorga feels it fell sharply).[75] The princes, important *boieri,* and their agents, who formed the class of "big" merchants, controlled the transit of Oriental goods toward the West. It may be

[71] Iorga, *Istoria comerţului,* I, p. 144.
[72] Manolescu, *Comerţul Ţării,* p. 144.
[73] Manolescu, "Schimbul," in *S.M.I.M.,* II, pp. 154–155, 158–160, 173.
[74] *Ibid.,* pp. 196–197.
[75] Iorga, *Istoria comerţului,* I, p. 67.

that, in the decline of this commerce during the sixteenth century, they kept only that part of the commerce that they had previously run themselves, and the Genoese and Ragusan shares simply vanished. It is more likely, however, that at an earlier stage, when the Wallachian state was less developed and the Italians were more active, the state only taxed the trade without directly involving itself in it, and that by the sixteenth century the state and its direct agents found it necessary to take over what was left of the trade in order to secure a vital element in state revenues. The same situation prevailed for the passage of Western goods toward the East. The "big" merchants handled virtually all of the cloth and knives destined for re-export, and the trade in the small items destined for the general Wallachian population was left to the "little" merchants.

The export of Wallachian products does not conform to the above pattern. Though left mostly to "little" merchants, this trade was but a very small part of the total trade between Braşov and Wallachia. There is no way of ascertaining the volume of that trade with the Black Sea ports and with Constantinople from the thirteenth to the fifteenth centuries. It is quite likely that the state and "big" merchants took a more active part in it than they did in the same type of trade with Braşov, if only because Braşov was much closer to Wallachian centers of population than were the old Genoese ports and, of course, Constantinople. But given the seeming lack of interest of "big" merchants in this trade with Braşov, it is probable that even in earlier centuries the export of Wallachian products in any direction was not too important. In any case, taxation of the transit trade was always more important.

By 1503, Wallachian villages obviously were involved at least partially in a money economy, because they provided small goods for Braşov and the "little" merchants purchased the various small items imported from Braşov. The role of commerce must not have been very important, but it did have a steady (and, by the sixteenth century, growing) place in the village economy, so that some sort of rudimentary differentiation between richer and poorer villages was possible. This differentiation was to have major consequences in the later sixteenth century, when a great crisis overtook Wallachian villages.[76]

The following conclusions about rural life in Wallachia during the time of the communal-trade state can be made from the evidence on trade presented so far.

(1) The nature, organization, and extent of the trade, especially the long-distance trade, explain both the relative wealth of the Wallachian state and the high level of exchange that existed, even though most of the population lived in primitive communal villages that were neither heavily taxed nor greatly

[76] G. Zane, "Originea şi desvoltarea economiei de schimb," in *Enciclopedia României* (Bucharest, 1939), III, p. 248. Documents show that by the fifteenth century money had penetrated into village life, and that its use spread during that century.

involved in the main economic concerns of the court and nobility. Of course, evidence about trade does not establish the existence of communal villages. That is done by the more direct historical evidence presented earlier. But it does counter the arguments of those historians (such as Câmpina and Oţetea) who claim that this trade and the wealth of the state resulted from the princes' and *boieri's* selling a substantial and increasing quantity of products appropriated from their hypothetical "feudal" estates.

(2) The evidence on trade in Wallachia explains why the new state expanded so rapidly in the late thirteenth and early fourteenth centuries, despite a seemingly flimsy social base after a period of 1000 years, during which the Latin-speaking Vlachs had lived in obscurity in the mountains while Wallachia was politically dominated by a long series of passing nomads.

(3) Finally, the role of trade in Wallachia until the end of the fifteenth century sets the stage for the transformation of rural society in the sixteenth century, when the long-standing patterns of trade and tribute were altered by the Ottomans.

4

The Collapse of the Communal-Trading Political Economy and the Rise of the Seignorial State (1500–1600)

The Ottoman conquest of Wallachia was a gradual and confused affair that lasted from the late fourteenth to the early sixteenth centuries. Even after this there were revolts, and the last major Wallachian military effort against the Turks finally ended in the first years of the seventeenth century. At first, the Turks demanded only a small tribute. Gradually, they raised their demands and interfered in Wallachia's internal affairs, mainly by taking part in the selection of princes. The first period of Ottoman domination ended in the early fifteenth century when, as we have seen, Mircea the Elder ceased paying tribute.[1] But Ottoman raids resumed in 1419, and by the mid-fifteenth century Wallachia was again paying a small tribute of 10,000 ducats.[2]

[1]Andrei Oţetea *et al.*, *Istoria Romîniei* (Bucharest: Editura academie, 1962), **II**, p. 382.

[2]*Ibid.*, p. 466. In order to give a rough idea of the weight of this tribute, it is possible to see to what proportion of Wallachia's Western-oriented foreign trade it added up. In 1503 the total value of Wallachia's trade with Braşov amounted to about seven million aspers (see R. Manolescu, "Schimbul de mărfuri dintre Ţara Românescă şi Braşov în prima jumătate a secolului al XVI-lea," in *S.M.I.M.* (Bucharest: Editura academiei, 1957), **II**, pp. 196–197. Of course this was not the whole of Wallachia's trade because Braşov was only one of several major Transylvanian trading cities, and some of the transit trade headed west toward the Adriatic instead of going north into Transylvania. A rough translation of ducats can be made into aspers (see D. Mioc, "Cuantumul birului în Ţara Românească în secolul al XVI-lea," in *S.M.I.M.*, **V**,

From 1456 to 1462, under the rule of Wallachia's most famous prince, Vlad the Impaler (popularly known as *Dracula,* a man fond of impaling his enemies and leaving their putrifying bodies on stakes in open fields), the Turks were held off. But the reign of Vlad also marked the opening of a serious struggle for control of the villages between the prince and the nobility, and in this struggle the nobles were helped by the Turks. (The nature of this internal struggle will be explained in greater detail below.) In 1462, a pro-Turkish *boieri* revolt overthrew Vlad, and Wallachia again became a subject state. In 1476, Vlad made a brief comeback with the aid of the Moldavian Prince Stephen the Great.[3] But after this, *boieri* collaboration with the Turks and the overwhelming power of the expanding Ottoman Empire put Wallachia under increasing subjugation. Between 1521 and 1527, the Wallachian tribute to the Empire was 24,000 ducats a year. From 1558 to 1566, it rose to 50,000 ducats a year; from 1567 to 1581, to 65,000 ducats a year; from 1582 to 1584, to 95,000; from 1585 to 1591, to 125,000; and finally from 1592 to 1594, it was 155,000 ducats a year. This represented the maximum tribute, and during the temporarily successful revolt of Michael the Brave from 1596 to 1600 the tribute declined to 8000 ducats.[4]

The relative burden of Wallachia's taxation may be inferred from a comparison with general Ottoman and Mediterranean revenues at that time. At the end of the sixteenth century, the Ottoman annual budget was on the order of 6 million ducats, the French budget about 5 million ducats, and Spain's 9 million. A tribute of 150,000 ducats in Wallachia therefore amounted to 2.5% of the Ottoman budget, 120,000 amounted to 2%, and 90,000 to 1.5%. But the Ottoman Empire as a whole had about 16 million people, and Wallachia had only about

Ftn. 2 (continued)

p. 160). The 10,000 ducats were then worth about one-half million aspers. If it is assumed that at most Braşov handled only one-third to one-half of Wallachia's western trade, then the tribute demanded by the Ottomans amounted to about 2% or 3% of the value of that trade. The proportion of that trade's value that wound up in the Wallachian state's coffers as profits and customs duties is not known, but clearly a major portion of the tribute, if not its entirety, could be paid from these earnings. As will be seen later, as trade declined and the tribute rose sharply in the sixteenth century it became impossible for the Wallachians to pay the tribute out of foreign trade earnings. This demonstrates the fiscal imperatives that generated social and political changes in the sixteenth century.

[3] Oţetea, *Istoria Romîniei*, **II**, pp. 465–477 and 523–524, section by B. Câmpina and Şt. Ştefănescu. As for the notorious Dracula, his fame spread through Transylvania (he impaled a number of Braşov merchants, among others, whom he accused of evading Wallachian customs duties) to Hungary, Germany, and Russia where he was a source of popular legends and stories from the fifteenth to the eighteenth centuries. Several manuscript and printed fifteenth- and sixteenth-century versions in German have been found. A sample version published in Bamberg in 1491 was called *Ein wunderliche und erschruckenliche hystoryi von einem grossen wuttrich genant Dracole wayda* [An astounding and terrifying story about a great tyrant named Dracula voda]. See Ioan Bogdan, "Vlad Ţepeş şi naraţiunile germane şi ruseşti asupra lui," in *Scrieri alese*, ed. G. Mihăilă (Bucharest: Editura academiei, 1968), pp. 468–481. Evidently Vlad made a great impression in a different context, as a fighter for national liberty and as a champion of the little people against the avaricious and treacherous *boieri*. This is the way he is viewed today in Romania.

[4] Mioc, "Cuantumul birului," in *S.M.I.M.*, **V**, p. 160.

150,000 people at the end of the century. Thus, Wallachia could not have had more than 1% of the Empire's population, yet it was paying from one and one-half to two and one-half times its share to the imperial budget. France at that time had some 16 million inhabitants, and because its state budget was 5 million ducats, Wallachia's population was providing three times as many ducats per capita in Ottoman tribute as the French were providing in taxes to their state in the early 1590s.[5]

The other effect of the rise to power of the Ottoman Empire was a major disruption of old trade routes. The Italians were driven out of the Black Sea trade, and the Genoese lost their major Black Sea port, Caffa, to the Turks in 1475. The value of Wallachia's trade with Braşov fell from about 7 million aspers in 1503 to a yearly average of about 3¼ million aspers between 1542 and 1554, and from the middle to the end of the sixteenth century it remained about steady (taking into account the decline in the value of the asper).[6] The shifting content of the trade with Braşov during the sixteenth century shows an even more dramatic change than the decline in total trade. Between 1503 and the 1550s, the value of Wallachian exports of local products increased by about 40 to 50%. The value of imports from Braşov (including Western goods passing through Braşov toward Wallachia, and Western goods re-exported from Wallachia) fell by about two-thirds from the early part of the century until mid-century. The value of Eastern goods passing through Wallachia toward Braşov also fell by about two-thirds from the early part of the century to the 1540s.[7] So while the value of trade passing through Wallachia between the West and the Orient fell very sharply, some of the difference was made up by an increase of Wallachian exports.

Braşov was not, of course, Wallachia's sole trading partner. In the mid-sixteenth century, Wallachia also traded with Germany, Poland, Venice (presumably mostly overland to the Adriatic), and increasingly with the Ottoman Empire.[8] The emergence of Bucharest as Wallachia's capital largely resulted from the increasing trade with the Ottomans, because it lies midway between the Carpathians and the Danube. During the second half of the sixteenth century, while the old trading cities experienced sharp population declines, Bucharest was the only Wallachian city to grow.[9] However, the commerce with the Otto-

[5]Fernand Braudel, *La Méditerranée et le monde méditerranéen à l'époque de Philippe II*, 2nd ed. (Paris: Armand Colin, 1966), I, pp. 361–362 and 411. For Wallachian population estimates see Şt. Ştefănescu, "La situation démographique de la Valachie aux XIVe, XVe, et XVIe siècles d'après les conjonctures socio-politiques," in *Nouvelles études d'histoires* (Bucharest: Editura academiei, 1970), IV, pp. 47–61.

[6]Oţetea, *Istoria Romîniei*, II, p. 517; and R. Manolescu, *Comerţul Ţării Romîneşti şi Moldovei cu Braşovul (Secolele XIV–XVI)* (Bucharest: Editura ştiinţifică, 1965), pp. 180–181.

[7]Manolescu, "Schimbul," in *S.M.I.M.*, II, pp. 153, 164, and 176.

[8]L. Lehr, "Comerţul Ţării Romîneşti şi Moldovei în a doua jumătate a secolului XVII," in *S.M.I.M.*, IV, p. 243.

[9]Nicolae Iorga, *Istoria comerţului românesc* (Bucharest: Tiparul românesc, 1925), I, pp. 239–257.

man Empire was conducted on terms that were highly unfavorable to Wallachia. The animals, animal products, grain, salt, and copper that Wallachia exported at this time to the Empire were sold at special low prices, which were enforced by law, to Turkish merchants and to an increasing number of Levantine merchants (Greeks, Armenians, and Turkish Jews) who became an important segment of Wallachia's urban population during the sixteenth century.[10] The Sultan protected these merchants—many of whom apparently acted as Ottoman agents—because Wallachia, like Moldavia, had become a vital source of food for Constantinople. Romanian sheep seem to have been a major source of Constantinople's meat supply, as is shown by Suleiman the Magnificent's special order in 1560 to make every effort to keep open the overland flow of sheep from Wallachia and Moldavia to Constantinople.[11] To some extent, an East–West trade continued to pass through Wallachia, but it was carried by caravans from Constantinople rather than depending mainly on the Black Sea.[12] As shown by the Braşov data, this trade was certainly less active in the second half of the sixteenth century than it had been in the fifteenth and early sixteenth centuries.

The change in trade patterns, the losses involved in the redirection of trade into Turkish and Levantine hands at special low prices, and the accompanying growth of the Ottoman tribute presented serious problems for the Wallachian princes. Though the total value of trade and the taxes it provided in the fifteenth and sixteenth centuries is not known, and though the precise source of the state's income is not known, it is certain that during the sixteenth century taxes on commerce were an important source of revenue, as they had been earlier.[13] The partial figures provided by the Braşov register reveal the scope of the problem the Wallachian state faced in the second half of the sixteenth century. In the late fifteenth century, the Ottoman tribute amounted to between 5% and 10% of the total value of the Wallachia–Braşov trade (and, of course, a considerably smaller portion of total foreign trade). By the mid-sixteenth century, the tribute equaled the value of the Wallachia–Braşov trade. During the next half-century, the tribute tripled while the value of the Wallachia–Braşov trade remained roughly stable.[14] Thus, while Wallachia might easily have raised much of the tribute from taxes on commerce in the early sixteenth century, this was obviously no longer possible by the end of the century, and a new source of revenue had to be found to pay the tribute. It was this need that radically transformed rural Wallachian society during the sixteenth century.

An important consequence of the spread of Ottoman rule, which aggravated

[10] *Ibid.*, pp. 181–184, 208; and Lehr, "Comerţul Ţării," in *S.M.I.M.*, **IV**, pp. 231, 243–244.

[11] Lehr, "Comerţul Ţării," in *S.M.I.M.*, **IV**, p. 245.

[12] *Ibid.*, pp. 285–288.

[13] *Ibid.*, pp. 294–296.

[14] Manolescu, *Comerţul Ţării*, p. 180.

its other effects, was a sharp population decline. Each of the Ottoman invasions, the civil wars, the raids, and the passage of foreign armies through Wallachia because of the Turks' wars with the rest of Central and Eastern Europe provoked population losses. Men were killed, enslaved, and starved by the requisitions of food and animals. At the start of the fifteenth century, during the reign of Mircea the Elder, Wallachia probably had about 500,000 people. In 1460, at the time of Vlad the Impaler, it had about 400,000 people. One hundred years later, Wallachia had between 300,000 and 350,000 people. The worsening economic and political conditions of the late sixteenth century caused a further sharp drop as emigration compounded the problem. A Turkish account of 1591–1592 cites a population of only from 150,000 to 180,000 people, and though this may have been too low an estimate, other accounts by Western European travelers agree that large parts of Wallachia were deserted in the 1590s. It has been estimated that by the early 1600s the population was down to about 150,000—that is, 30% of what it had been at the height of the "communal-trade" state 200 years before.[15] Naturally, this posed a grave problem: The need for taxes was greatly increasing, while the taxable population was greatly decreasing.

The New System of Taxation

As might be expected, the system of taxation changed considerably during the latter part of the fifteenth century and especially during the sixteenth century. In the late fifteenth century, the state's fiscal apparatus began to grow, so that by the middle of the sixteenth century Wallachia was divided into "tax counties" (*judeţi de bir*). By the second half of the sixteenth century, the traditional custom of having each district and village pay a fixed tithe and tax had changed, and the state continually raised taxes and even levied extra taxes periodically to meet its needs. A fiscal census was taken every 3 years, and taxes were levied according to district and village wealth.

Within villages, the same system prevailed. Family heads were obliged to pay according to their wealth—not simply a fixed proportion of their produce as before but, increasingly, as much as could be taken from them. The partial introduction of an exchange economy in the villages (see the evidence given earlier about the role of villages in the trade with Braşov), the growing distinction between wealthier and poorer villages, and the increasingly heavy taxes eroded the principle of collective village responsibility for the tax. Some form of collective responsibility was maintained, but in a rather different way from before. When a family could not pay its share, then relatives, neighbors, or ultimately anyone the authorities regarded as capable of paying was obliged

[15] Şt. Ştefănescu, "La situation démographique," in *Nouvelles études*, **IV**, pp. 47–61.

to do so; in return, those who paid gained temporary rights to use the land worked by the defaulting party. If the defaulter proved incapable of paying his taxes over a longer period of time, he lost all his rights to use of land, and those who were obliged to assume the responsibility gained the defaulting villager's rights. This was instrumental in destroying the village communes and in inaugurating the divisions of common land into private family strips, because those who assumed heavier taxes insisted on receiving greater, permanent rights to the use of land. (There were other reasons for the decay of communal villages, but those will be dealt with later.)[16]

Another change in the structure of taxation was the spread of tax farming. During the fifteenth century, the princes attempted to keep the fiscal apparatus under their direct control, and this may well have been one of the chief sources of contention between the *boieri* and the state; as will be shown later, the late fifteenth and sixteenth centuries saw the *boieri* becoming an increasingly independent class separated from the direct state administration. After the mid-sixteenth century, however, the central power of the state was broken by the Ottomans in favor of the *boieri*, and taxes were then collected by a complex system of tax farming handled by important *boieri* at the county (*județ*) level, and by lesser *boieri* at the village level.[17]

In the sixteenth century, the tax on villagers ceased to be raised entirely in kind and, though it probably remained largely in kind, the tax began to be measured in money equivalents.[18] This development built upon earlier involvement of villagers in petty trade—small surpluses for coin, coin for small trade items. The setting of money values on the tax increased the tendency to measure animals, produce, and eventually land itself in money, just as the villagers' need to raise increasing amounts of tax money stimulated their tendency to buy and sell.

Considering changes in prices through the sixteenth century and the tax load on each village family, equivalents in produce can be worked out which show how much the weight of taxation increased. Between 1521 and 1557, the average village family had to sell the equivalent of 5 sheep a year in order to pay its tax. Between 1592 and 1594, it had to sell the equivalent of 21 sheep. During the same period, the quantity of wheat that had to be sold for taxes (assuming that only one product was sold to pay for the whole tax is, of course, a convenience for purposes of calculation only) more than doubled, the quantity of

[16] D. Mioc, "Despre modul de impunere și percepere a birului în Țara Românească pînă la 1632," in *S.M.I.M.*, **II**, pp. 102–112 and 114–116.

[17] *Ibid.*, pp. 82–96.

[18] Henri H. Stahl, *Les anciennes communautés villageoises roumaines* (Bucharest and Paris: Académie roumaine and C.N.R.S., 1969), p. 211. See also D. Mioc, H. Chirca, and Șt. Ștefănescu, "L'évolution de la rente féodale en Valachie et en Moldavie, du XIVe au XVIIe siècles," in *Nouvelles études*, **II**.

cattle increased more than 4½ times, the number of horses more than 5 times, and the amount of ordinary land (not in vines) increased 18 times.[19]

The Growth of the Nobles' Power

The changes in trade patterns, population density, tax structure, and the growth of Ottoman political power in Wallachia caused a major change in class structure. The nobles and monasteries became more powerful at the expense of both the princes above them and the villagers beneath them. The power they gained over the villagers in the sixteenth century was maintained, in one way or another, until 1864 in the case of the monasteries, and until the end of World War I in the case of the nobles. Even though the noble families of the late nineteenth century were not the hereditary descendants of the late sixteenth-century nobles, with very few exceptions, they were nevertheless very much their institutional descendants. The changes brought about by the great crisis of the sixteenth century thus stand out as among the most important in Wallachian history, and they form an essential background to nineteenth and even twentieth century Romanian social problems.

There are five sorts of documents from the late fourteenth to the early seventeenth centuries that reveal the growth of the nobility's power. These are: (1) documents issued by the princes releasing certain nobles, monasteries, and villages from taxes; (2) documents that mention gifts of horses and other goods and money to the princes by *boieri* and monasteries, in return for the princes' "gift" of villages to them; (3) documents that describe the rise of monastic fiscal

[19]D. Mioc, "Cuantumul birului," in *S.M.I.M.*, V, p. 165 and pp. 172–173. Mioc established a chart for the period that shows the variation in tax per free village family per year by taking the average of all tax amounts paid by village families recorded during each of the sets of years.

Years	Tax in aspers	Tax in ducats	Worth in sheep	Worth in oxen	Worth in horses	Worth in hectares of land
1521–1557	86	1.31	5.06	0.48	0.18	about 1.5
1558–1566	212	3.32	—	2.12	0.11	about 4.3
1567–1581	265	4.25	—	1.77	0.31	about 5.7
1582–1584	301	5.01	—	—	0.37	about 7.2
1585–1591	550	5.50	—	2.11	0.47	about 9.6
1592–1594	946	7.37	21.02	2.36	1.05	about 27.2
1595–1600	577	3.37	—	1.55	0.30	about 11.0

The last set of years, from 1595 to 1600, saw the sharp drop in Ottoman taxes caused by the temporarily successful revolt of Wallachia under Michael the Brave. It must be noted that this chart reflects a sharp fall in the value of land throughout the sixteenth century, particularly toward its end. This was caused by the depopulation which left a great deal of land empty.

organs for collecting dues from villages under their control; (4) princely acts allowing *boieri* to dispose of villages by sale or to members of their family, as they wished; and finally, (5) acts between villagers and *boieri* in which the latter were admitted as "brothers" of the former, thus giving rights to communal village lands. Other sorts of documents also reflect the transformation that took place during this time, particularly acts in which free villagers sold themselves to *boieri* in return for relief from taxes; these will be dealt with later in describing the fate of communal villages.

Beginning in the late fourteenth century, but most commonly in the fifteenth century, the state began to issue acts releasing from taxes certain villages belonging to monasteries and nobles. This indicates that during the fifteenth century, numerous villages passed out of state control and into the hands of the church and nobles. There had been "gifts" of villages before, but these had been temporary and partial sales or leases of rights to village dues. In the fifteenth century, these "gifts" began to be permanent. (The late fourteenth-century examples refer to monasteries, not to nobles.) In the mid-sixteenth century such "gifts" ceased, not because the state regained greater control, but because it lost control entirely over noble and monastery seizures of villages.[20]

Starting in the mid-fifteenth century, culminating between 1470 and 1540 and virtually ending after 1550, there exist references to "gifts" of horses by *boieri* and monasteries to the princes in return for rights to villages. Some Romanian historians have explained these "gifts" as normal "feudal dues" by nobles to their prince, but in fact, they were nothing of the sort. Rather, they were payments made to the princes by *boieri* and monasteries in return for which the princes surrendered taxing power over villages. This is proved by the fact that, though horses were an important part of the payments, other goods and money were frequently included as payment as well, and in many instances, the "gift" of the horse was excused in return for extra payment in some other kind. Furthermore, monasteries were more frequently exempted from the "gift" of a horse or horses because pious princes favored the growth of monastic lands. If the "gift" of a horse had simply been a token feudal due, as some have maintained, there would have been no reason to exempt monasteries. But given that horses were the most valuable animals in Wallachia, and that good horses had considerable value when compared to the rather feeble price paid for villages in the fifteenth century, it becomes clear that horses were real payment.[21]

It was only in the second half of the fifteenth century that the state began to give monasteries full rights of tax collection over villages from which they drew dues. Before then, the state had collected the dues and given them to

[20] Stahl, *Les anciennes communautés*, pp. 176–181, particularly the charts on pp. 178 and 181.

[21] *Ibid.*, pp. 185–188; and the much more complete discussion on the "gift" of horses in Henri H. Stahl, *Controverse de istorie socială românească* (Bucharest: Editura ştiinţifică, 1969), pp. 124–187.

monasteries. This reflects the declining power of the state and the rise of local power,[22] clarifying Damaschin Mioc's assertion that, in the sixteenth century, a system of tax farming was established that gave local *boieri* the rights to collect village taxes. Mioc explains this by saying that it was to "compensate" nobles for the loss of their immunity from taxes.[23] But this is not correct. The rise of a tax farming system does, indeed, coincide with the gradual disappearance of the granting of tax immunities to nobles who held villages, but the replacement of immunities by the development of *boieri*'s and monasteries' direct powers to collect taxes indicates that there was a transfer of power from the central government to local potentates. After 1550, it was pointless for the state to give nobles and monasteries exemptions from taxes because it was losing the power to collect its own taxes. Thus, the old system of granting immunities was replaced by a tax farming system in which the nobles became even more powerful than they had previously been.

The earliest "gifts" of villages to nobles were not permanent, as stated earlier. But gradually, rights to villages became hereditary. If, however, the noble had no sons, the villages reverted to the state. This began to change about 1450, when acts were issued decreeing that nobles holding villages could leave them to daughters if there were no sons. Then acts were issued allowing nobles to contract "brotherhood" with others so that they could pass their villages to them. One noble would declare another to be his "brother," generally in return for a payment. Acts allowing villages to be passed to such "brothers" were in fact legitimizing barely concealed sales. Gradually, then, nobles began selling villages, and this marked the defeat of the state's claim to possess all the villages, especially those that had been "granted" to nobles. Acts legitimizing this process were most common in the first half of the sixteenth century; by 1550 they had become rare, and by 1600 they had almost disappeared. This marked the complete abandonment of the old law prohibiting nobles from alienating villages "granted" them by the state.[24]

A final proof of the growth of the nobles' power over villages is the development of the institution of "brotherhood" between nobles and common villagers. Because the villages traditionally were communal, only members of the community had the right to use its lands. As nobles began to seize free villages, they needed a legitimization for interfering in village affairs. Presumably, had the old *cneji* been directly transformed into some sort of "feudal" aristocracy, such legitimization would have been unnecessary. But the *cneji* who formed the

[22] Henri H. Stahl, *Contribuţii la studiul satelor devălmaşe româneşti* (Bucharest: Editura academii, 1958–1965), **III**, pp. 77–97.

[23] Mioc, "Despre modul," in *S.M.I.M.*, **III**, p. 115.

[24] Stahl, *Les anciennes communautés*, pp. 182–185. The tendency to contract "brotherhoods" continued and even grew after 1550. But after 1550, decrees allowing property transfers by this means declined because the principle was accepted as legitimate. For the institution of "brotherhood" between unrelated nobles, see G. Cronţ, *Instituţii medievale româneşti* (Bucharest: Editura academiei, 1969), pp. 64–70.

boier class earlier had passed through a stage of being state functionaries, divorced from membership in the village communities, and thus they had to find a way to get back into these communities.

Beginning in the fifteenth century, but especially in the sixteenth, nobles paid certain villagers to adopt them as "brothers," giving the nobles rights to use communal lands. They thereby became the most powerful members of these communities because of their greater wealth and political weight, and accordingly tended to take over the whole community. This process not only reveals a way by which nobles inserted themselves into free communes, but also provides even further proof of the existence of such communes.[25]

The growth of local nobles' power is shown by the documentary evidence, but this evidence does not explain *why* the process took place. By collectively examining the evidence on (1) fifteenth- and sixteenth-century trade patterns, (2) the growing Ottoman tribute, and (3) the increasing interference of the Turks in internal Wallachian affairs, the dynamics of the change become evident.

There may well have been centrifugal tendencies in the early Wallachian state. But as long as the state and its officials drew their main income from taxation of the long-distance trade passing through Wallachia, there was also a strong force diverting the attention of the trading state's nobles away from the seizure of the free communal villages. Also, these villages were strong and viable institutions, as long as taxes remained low. But as the long-distance trade declined simultaneously with the introduction of the Ottoman tribute, and as the endless chain of wars between Wallachia and the Empire began to require higher state revenues, taxes rose. One solution was to increase direct exports from Wallachia. This involved obliging the villages to yield a greater surplus, as well as involving a change of emphasis in trade patterns from an intermediary role for the elite to an emphasis on production that could be profitably carried out by local controllers of the land.

Insofar as the importance of direct Wallachian exports increased during the fifteenth and sixteenth centuries, it is correct to say, as does Henri Stahl, that this was in part a function of the "capitalist" transformation of Western Europe that spread to the German Transylvanian cities.[26] There is some truth to the claim that the growth of the nobles' power and the decline of free villages were linked to the more widespread phenomenon of the "second feudalization" that took place in Europe east of the Elbe at this time.[27] For Wallachia, however, this

[25] Stahl, *Les anciennes communautés*, p. 184 (chart); and Cronţ, *Instituţii*, pp. 70–73 and 226–233.

[26] Stahl, *Les anciennes communautés*, pp. 13–18.

[27] Doreen Warriner, "Some Controversial Issues in the History of Agrarian Europe," *The Slavonic and East European Review* XXXII, no. 78 (December 1953): 176–177; Jerome Blum, "The Rise of Serfdom in Eastern Europe," *The American Historical Review* LXII, no. 4 (July 1957): 819–830; Maurice Dobb, *Studies in the Development of Capitalism*, 2nd ed., (New York: International Publishers, 1963), pp. 39–41. Stahl's thesis in this

explanation is quite insufficient, because the sixteenth century was not marked by a greater over-all integration with Western economies. Indeed, during the sixteenth century Wallachian artisanry developed and Wallachia became less rather than more dependent on Transylvanian imports.[28] Instead, the rising taxes imposed on villagers because of the Ottoman presence and the probable decline of state revenues from the transit trade (and thus the decline of state power) explain the change.

The entire shift of the Wallachian political and economic structure into the Ottoman sphere of power suggests that at this time Wallachia was becoming more detached from the Western economic sphere. Wallachia was becoming virtually an Ottoman colony, and it was Ottoman power—not Western—that was forcing changes strikingly analogous to those that were occurring in the more northerly parts of Eastern Europe at this time. This is not really as contradictory as it might seem, for the eventual degeneration of the Ottoman Empire in the centuries that followed should not imply that in its more dynamic period of existence it somehow had failed to transform its provinces, as had the contemporaneous Western European economic inroads into Eastern Europe north of Wallachia.

Apparently, the Wallachian state at first tried to maintain its old power by assuming more direct control over the villages. Official Romanian historiography labels the second half of the fifteenth century the "period of struggle for the centralization of the state."[29] Had it not been for Ottoman interference, this attempt at tighter centralization of the state might have succeeded. But, given the fact that the Turks played off *boieri* attempts at becoming more independent from princely power, the attempt failed and Wallachia was transformed from a trade state to a seignorial state.

In the fifteenth century, some time after the reign of Micea the Elder (who died in 1418), records appeared that mentioned an assembly of nobles who elected the princes. Throughout the fifteenth and sixteenth centuries, this assembly is mentioned, but it never took a definitively institutional form, as did

Ftn. 27 (continued)

matter, like Dobb's, is basically that first presented by Engels. But as Doreen Warriner shows, this argument may have a great deal of merit in so far as Poland and the Baltic countries were concerned, but it seems inadequate for the Balkans. And as Blum shows, it does not hold for Russia either even though during the sixteenth century Russian peasants became serfs. It seems that Romanian historians have found the argument appealing because it is an orthodox Marxist line of reasoning, and also because during the nineteenth century Romanian peasants were bound more tightly than ever before to the land during a period of rising grain exports to the West. But drawing an analogy between nineteenth and sixteenth century events on the basis of circumstantial evidence based largely on general European history is not necessarily sound procedure. Though Stahl irrefutably shows that nobles seized Wallachian and Moldavian free villages during the late fifteenth and sixteenth centuries, he fails to tie this into his more general thesis based on Engels' arguments.

[28] Lehr, "Comerțul Țării," in *S.M.I.M.*, **IV**, pp. 241–242 and 299–300.

[29] Oțetea, *Istoria Romîniei*, **II**, chaps. 6 and 7.

analogous institutions in Western Europe. The nobles' assembly did not disappear, however, until the eighteenth century.[30] There thus existed institutional means for the Turks to play on *boier*—prince hostilities and to influence the selection of princes favorable to the nobles and Turks.

The most notable fifteenth-century example of *boieri* treason to the state in favor of their own ambitions and Ottoman power was the overthrow of Vlad the Impaler in 1462, just after he had beaten back a Turkish invasion (see earlier discussion). Vlad had waged a bitter struggle against the nobles and Turks, and the failure of his attempt against the nobles also meant the failure of his fight against the Turks. In the sixteenth century, the struggle became more acute. One modern Romanian historian has written:

> Treason was an incurable boyard disease, particularly in the XVIth century, as has been pointed out by [contemporary] foreigners. In August, 1534, the Wallachian boyards asked the emissary of the sultan Suleiman the Magnificent for another prince . . . but the prince [Vlad Vintila] succeeded in arresting them, mutilating their noses and mouths and jailing them in the castle of Poienari. The boyards did not, however, give up their vendetta, and in the next year, they murdered him during a deer hunt. The chronicle of Wallachia is full of mentions of the permanent conflict between the lord of the land and the boyards who fought to enlarge their privileges and immunities. The expression "the lord slit the throats of boyards" appears frequently in the chronicle. Mention is also made of the episode in which the Wallachian Prince Radu of Afumaţi, hero of the fight against the Turkish invader, and his son Vlad, were murdered by the boyards who had secretly raised an army in 1529, at Rîmnicu Vîlcea. The boyards separated themselves from their lord in conditions that were tragic for the country in 1538, 1574, and 1594. The Prince John was accused by the chronicler-monk Azarie of being a "lion" who wanted to drink the blood of the boyards, who betrayed him.[31]

This completes the list of main causes for the rise of the nobles and the decline of the communal-trade state. The state lost revenues because of the change in trade patterns. It therefore lost the ability to reward the nobility, which then began to seize villages in order to extract taxes for itself, and probably to engage in small-scale commercial activities by exporting village products. Rising Ottoman taxes further weakened the state, as did Ottoman political interference and, as the population declined and taxes on free villages became ever more onerous, these villages were unable to maintain their freedom. The conjunction of circumstances played directly into the nobles' hands, and by 1550 they were a dominant seignorial class, in almost permanent revolt against the state and with local power bases in the villages they controlled.

[30] P. P. Panaitescu, "La grande assemblée du pays, institution du régime féodal en Moldavie et en Valachie," in *Nouvelles études*, **III**, pp. 117–139.

[31] D. Ciurea, "Quelques considérations sur la noblesse féodale chez les Roumains," in *Nouvelles études*, **IV**, pp. 87–88.

Serfdom

The last phase in this process, however, occurred between 1593 and 1601 under the rule of Michael the Brave. Michael was the last *Voievod* to try to resurrect the Wallachian state, but the economic basis of his attempt was quite original. As a young *boier*, he had made some money as a merchant, and had acquired four villages as a dowry from his wife. Between 1585 and 1592, he purchased 40 villages for 1,515,700 aspers, becoming the largest individual landowner in Wallachia. He owned 36 of these 40 villages entirely, and the others partially. Of the 36 he had purchased entirely, 27 previously had been free villages. It was his wealth in villages that probably was a decisive factor in his selection as *Voievod.* As prince, he used the state treasury to increase his holdings, and during his reign he purchased 129 whole villages as well as parts of 20 others. Of the wholly purchased villages, 103 previously had been free (and were thus purchased from the villagers themselves), as had been 10 of the partially purchased villages.[32] Given that there were at most 20,000 to 25,000 families in Wallachia, and probably about 20 families in a village, there must not have been more than about 1000 Wallachian villages in 1600. Michael owned about 20% of these.[33]

Using this base, Michael raised an army sufficiently large to defeat the Turks and conquer Moldavia (and for a brief while, even Transylvania), thus uniting all three Romanian principalities for the first and last time until 1918. This effort was unrealistically ambitious and aroused the opposition of the Transylvanian and Moldavian nobles, the Turks, and the Poles. In 1600 the short-lived unity collapsed, and in 1601 Michael was murdered.[34]

Michael's brief reign was marked by two important changes. The Wallachian state attempted to reconstitute itself on the basis of the prince's private ownership of villages, and some time during his reign, Michael passed a law binding the residents of purchased villages to the land, thus completing the process of transforming a possible majority of Wallachian villagers into serfs.[35] However, in order to understand the background and significance of this act, the fate of the villagers in the sixteenth century must be examined more closely.

[32] I. Donat, "Satele lui Mihai Viteazul," in *S.M.I.M.*, **IV**, pp. 466–477 and 505–506.

[33] Based on the various estimates in Şt. Ştefănescu, "La situation démographique," in *Nouvelles études*, **IV**, pp. 57–60.

[34] Oţetea, *Istoria Romîniei*, **II**, pp. 95–1016 (section by B. Stănescu); and Nicolae Iorga, *Istoria lui Mihai Viteazul* (Bucharest: Editura militară, 1968).

[35] Stahl, *Les anciennes communautés*, pp. 188–189; and Constantin Giurescu, "Legătura lui Mihai Viteazul," *Studii de istorie socială* (Bucharest: Editura universul, 1943), pp. 51–69. Stahl sees this act of binding villagers to the land as the culmination of the set of transformations that occurred in the late fifteenth and sixteenth centuries. Giurescu sees it as a sign of the beginning of the end of serfdom, and feels that the act was less important than was previously thought. Because of the evidence presented throughout this book, I consider Giurescu wrong.

The partial transformation of village economies into money economies, the rise in taxes, and the nobles' efforts at seizing villages for their own account combined to present serious dangers to the village communes. When certain villagers who had become more wealthy than their neighbors were obliged to pay a higher proportion of the tax, and even to take responsibility for poor villagers' taxes, they naturally demanded control over the use of communal lands. At the same time, there was the danger that a noble could buy his way into the village community by paying a poorer villager and by taking over his tax payments. If a village remained communal, it thus risked being taken over by nobles whose wealth and political power would allow them to dominate the previously egalitarian community.

As a result, large numbers of communal villages divided their lands into family strips. This process took several forms. The division could be egalitarian, each family receiving an equal amount, or it could be unequal, the rich receiving more. The division could be total or else it could proceed in stages, some lands being divided with others—particularly more distant pastures and forests—remaining common.[36] Once this procedure became fairly routine, as it did during the sixteenth century, it became possible for nobles to take over parts of villages by purchasing certain families' strips, or by seizing the strips of families unable to pay their taxes. Thus, villages could be partly owned by a *boier*, or owned by several *boieri*, each of whom owned a part; or, alternatively, a village could be partly owned and partly free. In fact, because all that was required for a purchase was money and not necessarily a title, free peasants could purchase whole other villages or parts of villages.[37] This was certainly one of the factors contributing to the relatively great social fluidity in sixteenth-century Wallachia; a commoner who accumulated enough land could enter the ranks of the nobility, while nobles who lost their land and could not find service with the state administration fell to the rank of simple villagers.[38]

On the other hand, a village might be seized before it was divided. Or else, particularly in those parts of the plain that were repeatedly devastated by war, a village might be abandoned by its inhabitants and then taken by a noble who would try to resettle it. Such villages were in effect undivided, because they belonged entirely to the nobles. The owner would then replace the village council and have greater control than in divided villages where clear ownership rights had been established. As a result, many purchased villages looked like old communal villages, lacking distinct strips of land belonging to particular families, and having many of the old traditions of land usage that had predominated in the free communal villages.

Because the nobles did not directly cultivate much land for their own account,

[36] Stahl, *Les anciennes communautés*, pp. 77–95.

[37] *Ibid.*, pp. 200–202 and 213–222.

[38] Ciurea, "Quelques considérations," in *Nouvelles études*, **IV**, pp. 84–87.

but instead seized villages in order to collect their taxes in kind and in money, communal forms could persist for a long time after the loss of village freedom. Such villages were still very common in the eighteenth and nineteenth centuries, and when viewed from the air in the twentieth century they have the characteristic layout (not uniform strips that came from a rational division, but irregularly shaped plots that grew into each other) of villages, as in the Vrancea, that were still living according to free communal laws.[39]

There were thus four possible types of villages: undivided free communal, undivided but not free, divided free, and divided but not free. This mixture of types is one of the factors that makes the interpreting of history from the observation of twentieth century village fields so complex.[40] A further complication is the fact that as of the late sixteenth century, but especially in the seventeenth century, some purchased villages repurchased their freedom and promptly divided their lands. The process could be repeated several times, if villages were seized, then repurchased their freedom, then were seized again, and so on.[41]

During most of the sixteenth century, villagers in nobles' or monasteries' villages were free to leave if they paid their back taxes.[42] During the crisis of the latter part of the sixteenth century, however, the depopulation of these villages became a serious problem for the owners because empty villages obviously could not be taxed. This explains Michael the Brave's act binding villagers of owned villages to the land.[43] It also accounts for the important terminology changes in Wallachian documents at the end of the sixteenth century. Previously, there had been a differentiation in the words for commoner and noble (*Vlah* and *boier* in the Slavonic documents, but in Romanian the commoners were simply called Romanians, or *Rumîn*). As of the late sixteenth century, however, the term *Rumîn* came to mean a serf legally bound to his lord's land.[44] As has been ex-

[39]Stahl, *Les anciennes communautés,* pp. 153–156. See also Daniel Chirot, "The Romanian Communal Village: An alternative to the Zadruga," in Robert F. Byrnes, ed., *The Zadruga: The Extended Family of the Balkans. Essays by Philip E. Mosely and Essays in His Honor* (South Bend, Ind.: Notre Dame University Press, 1976), pp. 139–159.

[40]Henri H. Stahl, "Paysages et peuplement rural en Roumanie," in *Nouvelles études,* **III**, pp. 72–73.

[41]Such, for example, was the case of Runcu in Gorj. Personal communication by Henri H. Stahl to the author, 1970, and again, 1975.

[42]Even proponents of the theory that there were "feudal" lords from the earliest days of the Wallachian state admit this important fact. See P. P. Panaitescu, "Dreptul de strămutare al ţăranilor în Ţările Romîne (pîna la mijlocul secolului al XVII-lea)," in *S.M.I.M.*, **I**, pp. 74–76 and 121–122.

[43]Stahl, *Les anciennes communautés,* p. 205.

[44]Şt. Ştefănescu, "Consideraţiuni asupra termenilor 'Vlah' şi 'Rumîn' pe baza documentelor interne ale Ţării Romîneşti din veacurile XIV–XVII," in *S.M.I.M.*, **IV**, pp. 66–70, 75. In fact, the changes were more complicated. As of the late fifteenth century there appears the term *vecin*, neighbor, which referred to bound villagers. As might be expected, the change from freedom to serfdom was gradual, and did not come about with a single act. It would certainly have been in the interests of village owners to bind their villagers to the land, and the attempt to do so began at the time when nobles were beginning to seize villages. But as the sixteenth-century change of word for serfs, from *vecini* to *rumîni* (or *rumâni*) indicates, Michael's act coincides with the full legitimization of this tendency, and with its culmination. A large enough proportion of the population then became serf to warrant the adoption of the term "Romanian" for serf.

plained previously, it was at this time that the term *cnez* came to mean a free villager. This new terminology remained current until the early eighteenth century, when it changed again because of shifts in the relationship between nobles and their serfs.

It would be wrong to assume that all villagers became serfs at this time; in fact, documents after 1600 showed that some free villages survived until the nineteenth century. Even in the census of 1912 it was possible to reconstruct a map of the location of free villagers by asking peasants whether they had come from free or serf families.[45] Even in the period after the Second World War, the distinction between formerly free and serf peasants (legally abolished in 1864) was still very much alive in certain parts of Romania, and collectivized peasants of one village would sneeringly refer to the equally collectivized peasants of another village as "serfs."

The distribution of free and serf villages in the nineteenth century reveals a great deal about the process of seizure that had taken place centuries before. It was in hills and mountains that there continued to exist free villages, while the plains villages tended to be overwhelmingly serf.[46] A map showing Michael the Brave's purchases of villages shows that this generalization holds for the late sixteenth century as well. Only 11 of the 193 villages he purchased and seized were in the hill and mountain zone (and his accounted for a majority of purchases carried out in his time),[47] despite the fact that the hills and moun-

[45] Stahl, *Les anciennes communautés*, map between pp. 24 and 25.

[46] *Ibid.*, map, pp. 24–25.

[47] Though most Romanian historians believe that a large majority of villagers had become serfs by 1600, I think this may not actually have been the case. The fact that the free villages were in a zone that probably had a majority of Wallachia's population indicates that though an overwhelming majority of the plains people became serfs, they may not have constituted an absolute majority of the whole population. Another doubt is raised by the statistics of Michael's acquisitions. Of the 40 recorded sales of entire villages that took place between 1585 and 1592, Michael purchased 36, or 90%. While he was prince, Michael purchased almost twice as many villages as had all of his sixteenth-century predecessors together. (See Donat, "Satele lui Mihai Viteazul," in *S.M.I.M.*, **IV**, pp. 70–74.) Michael seems to have been responsible for almost two-thirds of all recorded village purchases between 1512 and 1627. (Compare Stahl, *Les anciennes communautés*, chart on p. 220, to Donat's charts.) Yet, Michael's some 200 villages could hardly have been more than 20% of all existing Wallachian villages, so that as few as 30% of all villages might have been serf in the first years of the seventeenth century. The proportion was almost certainly larger because acts pertaining to purchases by a prince were more likely to be preserved than acts pertaining to purchases that might never have been officially recorded at all. Even among partial purchases that have been recorded, the figures are revealing. Though only 40 villages were wholly purchased between 1582 and 1592, there were 551 partial purchases. Michael's innovation was to concentrate almost entirely on outright whole purchases, and only 10% of his purchases were for parts of villages. On the other hand, the other nobles who purchased villages purchased four whole ones and 227 parts of villages. Of the 316 purchases by men who were not identified by rank (presumably commoners), all were for parts of villages, and none for entire villages. Of the four purchases made during this time by monasteries, all were partial. Therefore, though less than one-third of all villages in the early seventeenth century may have been wholly serf, a large enough number of parts of other villages *may* have been purchased to make a majority of the entire population serf. But this is not certain. In any case, it is safe to say that by 1600 close to half of all villagers were serfs, but it is unlikely that the proportion was much more than 50%.

tains were considerably more densely populated that the plains.[48] The reason for this is that it was easier to take over partially or wholly abandoned villages than stronger hill and mountain villages that had been less ravaged by war.

That it was mostly plains villages, and often partially or wholly abandoned villages, that fell into noble hands in the late sixteenth century had two important effects. The first was that almost as soon as the law creating serfs was passed, serfdom began to decay. In order to attract villagers, nobles had to offer favorable conditions—that is, they had to promise to lighten the tax load. Because some nobles offered better conditions than others, and because they were obliged to attract a labor force, the movement of villagers from one area to another continued, even though it was technically illegal.[49] Given the inevitability of flight when conditions became too harsh, nobles could not exploit villagers as much as they might have wished, and many chose to sell their villages back to their inhabitants in order to avoid the problem of extracting an income from them.[50] In the seventeenth century, this practice became common. Most of Michael's villages, for example, were gradually sold by his successors, and 85% of the sales were to villagers rather than to nobles or monasteries.[51] This does not mean that purchases of new villages ceased, but only that the process of village seizures was hardly irreversible.[52]

The second effect of the pattern of village seizures was more nefarious for the villagers. Originally, when a village was purchased or taken by a noble, this gave him only rights to collect village dues. It did not give him the right to dispossess villagers who had an inalienable right to their lands. The same was true for partial purchases, and when a strip of land was purchased, it was understood that the family that had previously owned it continued to have rights of usage.[53] Land by itself had relatively little value, and in the late sixteenth and early seventeenth centuries a distinction was made between villages purchased with serfs and villages purchased without them. Nobles then began to purchase serfs to populate their villages, and though this was in violation of the traditional custom, the nobles had become sufficiently powerful to do it anyway. This, of course, increased the temptation to flee, because a villager with inalienable rights to the use of some land was less likely to flee than one who had been reduced to virtual slavery and had no inalienable rights.[54] But under different circumstances, the precise opposite could take place. Once the inalienability of

[48]This, at least, was the pattern throughout most of Wallachia's history.

[49]Stahl, *Les anciennes communautés*, pp. 233–235.

[50]*Ibid.*, pp. 222–238; and Giurescu, *Studii de istoria socială*, pp. 68–69.

[51]Donat, "Satele lui Mihai Viteazul," in *S.M.I.M.*, **IV**, p. 478.

[52]From 1601 to 1627, 64 recorded villages sold themselves but 84 repurchased themselves. Stahl, *Les anciennes communautés*, p. 220.

[53]*Ibid.*, pp. 201–202.

[54]*Ibid.*, pp. 203–205.

the serfs' rights to their land was dissolved, certain nobles might choose to sell a serf his freedom while keeping his land. This was particularly common in the case of a troublemaker, or of an especially insubordinate villager. There even were cases in which a noble chased out a village population when he felt he could purchase or attract a more amicable set of villagers.[55]

By the early seventeenth century, there had thus appeared several new social categories whose existence would have been impossible in the traditional society: free rural people without land, villagers who were bought and sold like Gypsy slaves, nobles who did not hold court office but whose position rested on their ownership of villages, serfs tied to villages that were still communally organized, free villagers who owned their own private land and, paradoxically, even serfs who had purchased other serfs. At the same time, there were still older types of villages that remained both free and communal, and of course their remained a powerful segment of the nobility that held state offices.

This list of social categories clearly shows that the imposition of "serfdom" did not totally destroy the old social order, although it greatly modified it. Some remnants of the village communities survived. Nor was the new system stable. Underneath the complex legal and political changes, Wallachian villagers remained predominantly pastoral. This precluded the development of a primarily agricultural feudal order, such as had existed earlier in Western Europe. It also prevented the "hardening" of serfdom into an inflexible order, thus precluding the development of a peasant society analogous to that in seventeenth-century Russia, to which Romania has too often been compared.[56]

[55] *Ibid.*, pp. 228–229.

[56] For the changes that transformed Russian peasants into serfs in the sixteenth and seventeenth centuries, see Jerome Blum, *Lord and Peasant in Russia from the Ninth to the Nineteenth Century* (New York: Atheneum, 1964), pp. 247–269. Certain Romanian historians, most notably P. P. Panaitescu, have drawn a great many conclusions about Romanian social history in the Middle Ages by drawing analogies with Russia. The parallel is tempting because there seem to have been many similar elements: communal villages, Mongol rule, early states based on trade with the Black and Baltic Seas, tardy feudalization and, in the nineteenth century, the emergence of a similar peasant problem that eventually destroyed the monarchy. But easy analogies are misleading. In the first place, though village communes were indeed ancient Russian institutions, they were destroyed in the fifteenth and sixteenth centuries, and the redistributive *mir* which were common in the nineteenth century were rather new institutions to which there are no Romanian analogies. (*Ibid.*, pp. 504–534.) The remnants of communal villages found in Wallachia and Moldavia in the late nineteenth and early twentieth centuries were not newly created institutions, but old ones. Second, the Russian heartland does not seem to have ever been primarily pastoral, though large parts of later conquests were. Third, even in Kievan Russia there were large noble and monastery estates, long before any sign of such estates ever appeared in Romania (*Ibid.*, pp. 33–43). Fourth, a three-field system appeared in Russia, at the latest in the fifteenth century (*Ibid.*, p. 23). The three-field system, common in large parts of feudal Europe, never appeared in Moldavia or Wallachia (though it did in Hungarian Transylvania). Many other distinctions could be drawn, but even with these few facts it is evident that rural Wallachian society in the sixteenth and seventeenth centuries was very different from rural Russian society at the time, and that many of the historical parallels are more apparent than real.

The Fall of Communal-Trading Political Economies

Communal-trading political economies are both extremely durable and extremely vulnerable. As long as the key trade route remains uninterrupted, they survive. Conquest by outsiders who do not place heavy new demands on the rural inhabitants changes little; in fact, there may be a string of political entities that succeed each other, as in Wallachia through much of the Middle Ages, without changing the type of prevailing political economy. But if the trade route is broken, or if new economic demands are placed on the rural population, the system must collapse. Inevitably, then, there must be a struggle between the state, its former administrative nobility, and the rural population. Deprived of old revenues, the state must seek new ones. It must fight its nobles in order to retain control of the surplus, and at the same time, the rural inhabitants will fight both nobles and the state in order to escape the new demands for a surplus. Depending on who wins this three-sided struggle, a new political economy will emerge.

The rural population may win the struggle. This, essentially, is what happened to the Songhay Empire after its Saharan trade route was destroyed and the value of western Sudanic gold on the Mediterranean market fell because of the importation of precious metal from America. The conquering Moroccans failed to subdue most of the population. This spelled the end of the state and the return to a local subsistence agriculture after the disappearance of the trading and political urban centers. In Songhay after the end of the sixteenth century, the imperial structure was destroyed, taking with it the high culture and the importance of the main cities.[57]

The state may win the struggle. It can then establish itself on a new basis and begin to extract a significant and large surplus from the rural population. The state's strict control of the villages must also be accompanied by strict control over the nobility. This sort of development occurred in Russia during the long series of wars against the Mongols. The peasantry was ultimately reduced to subservience, and so were the nobles. The surplus extracted from the peasantry was used to maintain the military power of the state, and this formed the basis for Russian expansion. At the same time, Ivan the Terrible's purge of the nobility prevented any move toward political and economic feudalization that would have resulted had control of the rural surplus fallen into the hands of the nobles.[58]

The formation of the Aztec and Inca empires in the period preceding the Spanish conquest is another example of this kind of development. Certainly,

[57] Daniel Chirot, "Urban and Rural Economies in the Western Sudan: Birni N'Konni and its Hinterland," *Cahiers d'études africaines* 4 (1968): 547–565; E. W. Bovill, *Caravans of the Old Sahara* (London: Oxford University Press, 1933).

[58] Blum, *Lord and Peasant*, pp. 135–151.

traces of communal village institutions existed, but there is no question that these two new empires ended local freedoms in order to extract a considerable surplus from agriculture in the villages they controlled. In both empires, the main danger was a possible revolt of the nobles on the one hand, or of whole rural areas on the other.[59] A successful revolt by either nobles or peasants would have resulted in their gaining supremacy over the state.

The third possible outcome is that the nobles may win. The rural population then becomes subject to the local controllers of the land, and is forced to yield a surplus to the aristocracy. But the state is greatly weakened, and may virtually disappear (as it did in large parts of feudal Europe). This is also what happened, more or less, in Wallachia—but with a twist. The process took place along with, and in large part because of, the Ottoman conquest. The Ottoman demand for tribute prevented the final collapse of the state, and a feudal political economy did not develop. The empire retained central power, and it obliged the rural nobles to export much of the surplus extracted from the villagers. Thus, while Wallachia came to acquire some characteristics of a feudal political economy, it actually became something quite different.

The workings of Wallachian society in the seventeenth and eighteenth centuries can best be understood in terms of a modified model of colonial societies, for in many ways, Wallachia became a colony surprisingly similar to European colonies of the sixteenth to the twentieth centuries. The Wallachian society that emerged after 1600 was characterized by strong nobles, weak and bound villagers, and a weak state structure. The society itself was bound to the requirements of a foreign imperial power, and this maintained the state and took much of the rurally produced surplus out of the hands of the Wallachians. Had the Turks simply been one more warrior aristocracy conquering a communal-trading society, and had the old trade routes been maintained, there would have been no substantial change in Wallachian society. But the Ottoman Empire was not a simple new version of the Cuman or Mongol state, and its effects were much more profound.

[59] Sergio de Santis, "Les communautés de village chez les Incas, les Aztèques et les Mayas; contribution à l'étude du mode de production asiatique," *La Pensée* 122 (1965): 79–95; and John H. Rowe, "Aspects of Inca Socio-Political Organization and Religion at the Spanish Conquest," *The Indian Background of Latin American History*, Robert Wauchope, ed. (New York: Knopf, 1970), pp. 147–177.

5

The Protocolonial Political Economy (1600–1821)

The changes that took place in the sixteenth century and were consolidated in the seventeenth amounted to nothing less than the transformation of one mode of production into another. It is obvious that there was no fundamental technological change. Indeed, as will be shown, Wallachia's agri-pastoralists continued to use the same general economic techniques practiced since prestate times. What changed was the political order and, more important, the nature and collection of the surplus extracted from the society in order to sustain the new system. The state became weaker, the nobles became more powerful, and the villagers lost their freedom as they became burdened with the heavier taxes imposed on them.

Much as the communal-trade state depended on a particular international setting (chiefly the existence of lucrative trade routes through Wallachia), so the transformation of the sixteenth century followed from a change in that setting. As such, it was part of a larger change that took place throughout the Mediterranean world—not only in the Ottoman sphere, but also in the Spanish sphere of influence. The new political economy may be characterized as a protocolonial system. In many ways, it was similar to the colonial system that was developed by the Northern European states and extended throughout the world in the eighteenth and nineteenth centuries. But unlike Northern Europe, the Mediterranean colonial systems did not lead to the creation of modern nation–states or to the industrialization of the dominant societies. Therefore, the effect of the Mediterranean type of system on the colonies was somewhat different from the effect of colonization on societies dominated by industrializing states. Still, the similarities between protocolonial societies and fully colonial societies is worth noting. These similarities explain how Wallachia emerged in the nineteenth century as a full colony of Western Europe, while retaining many of the characteristics it had developed earlier under Ottoman domination.

Imperial structures are characterized by the existence of core and peripheral areas. The core dominates and uses peripheral areas in order to sustain and expand its own economy. Peripheral areas become primary producers and sources of tribute; they also become enclave societies. An enclave develops—the chief port or trading city, and usually the chief administrative center as well—and this enclave becomes a direct extension of the core's economy, polity, and culture. Mines and plantations are limbs of this enclave, but the majority of the population is left out of the enclave. Natives may work for the enclave, but it remains culturally alien to them. Insofar as rural natives work for the enclave, they compose an exploited "under race" working for the ultimate benefit of the core society or metropole. The natives are left out of the political process, which is ruled by the interests of the core society. The surplus is therefore not channeled into domestic investment, but instead goes to the metropole.

There also exists an intermediate class which is tied to the enclave, and which benefits from its collaboration with the metropole. This class is composed of two groups that overlap: the landowners, who directly extract a surplus from the native rural laborers; and the town merchants and administrators, who serve the metropole's interests as well as their own. This intermediate class becomes acculturated to the dominant ways of the metropole, and it tends to adopt its speech patterns, ways of dress, and religious attitudes. (This class may also consist of people from the metropole, but it need not.) This acculturation process distinguishes the intermediate class from the run-of-the-mill natives who perpetuate the more traditional cultural patterns. Thus, a great gulf begins to separate the beneficiaries of the enclave society and the mass of rural folk. The local elite becomes a class of strangers in its own society, while the bulk of the population becomes a class of "inferior" natives.[1]

In such a system, the political development of the colonial area is stunted because a powerful, centralized state is prevented from emerging (unless there is

[1]Andre Gunder Frank, "The Development of Underdevelopment," *Imperialism and Underdevelopment*, ed. Robert I. Rhodes (New York: Monthly Review Press, 1970), pp. 4–17; Immanuel Wallerstein, *The Modern World-System* (New York: Academic Press, 1974), pp. 67–129; Barrington Moore Jr., *Social Origins of Dictatorship and Democracy: Lord and Peasant in the Making of the Modern World* (Boston: Beacon, 1967), section on China, pp. 162–227, particularly p. 176 on the role of the *compradors*.

a successful anticolonial revolt). Economic development is also stunted, in that the economy takes a path that benefits the metropolitan economy. Further, within the colonial society, the local elite resists change because its position is based on the exploitation of the existing system. It resists the emergence of a strong, native state, which would weaken links with the metropole and threaten the elite's control of rural areas (that is, the elite's source of revenues). A powerful, centralized state would appropriate the rurally produced surplus.[2]

Balandier has listed the key aspects of "enclave" economies in the nineteenth and twentieth centuries, and some of these are appropriate for sixteenth- and seventeenth-century Mediterranean empires:[3]

(1) The economy is characterized by a quest for raw materials or agricultural products to be used by the metropolitan economy.

(2) Import–export trade is either in the hands of foreigners from the metropolitan country, or in the hands of agents acting for that country. Native business is fragmented and replaced either by "metropolitans" or by "pariah capitalists," foreign merchants who stand between the natives and the metropolitans, but who can be trusted to act in the interests of the enclave economy because that is the main source of their support in an alien and hostile culture.

(3) There is a partial "property dispossession" of native peasants, either by local landowners or by foreign ones, as every effort is made to break village self-sufficiency in order to produce an exportable surplus.

(4) The purely indigenous economy stagnates as it becomes more subordinate to metropolitan interests and foreign domination.

(5) A great "distance" separates the metropolitan agents and the natives who are relegated to the roles of laborer, servant, and peasant.

(6) A native landowning elite develops, capable of exploiting the situation by growing exportable cash crops.

The sixteenth century saw the emergence of such imperial structures throughout much of the European world and areas that it controlled or bordered. The core areas were Spain and Portugal, northwestern Europe, Russia, and the Ottoman Empire. The peripheral areas were the Americas, Eastern Europe, and areas incorporated by the Russian and Ottoman states in Europe, Asia, and Africa. But, while a certain European "world system" was emerging, Russia and the Ottoman Empire were evolving their own somewhat distinct "world systems." These systems were *not* subordinate to the West, even though developments within these systems were similar to those occurring in the Western world and its colonies.[4]

Throughout the peripheral areas of these imperial structures, similar trans-

[2]Wallerstein, *Modern World-System*, pp. 310–321 argues this point for Eastern Europe.

[3]Georges Balandier, "The Colonial Situation: A Theoretical Approach," *Social Change: The Colonial Situation*, ed. Immanuel Wallerstein (New York: Wiley, 1966), pp. 41–42.

[4]Wallerstein, *Modern World-System*, pp. 321–326.

formations took place. This striking similarity has been noted by many, particularly by Genovese, who saw the extension of serfdom in Eastern Europe as a direct analog of the creation of slave plantation systems in the Americas, especially in Brazil and the Caribbean. In both cases, the source of change was the same: It was necessary to find a labor force for the production of agricultural export goods. The stratification in both areas was similar—landowners tied to the Western market at the top, and slaves or serfs at the bottom.[5] In both situations, the orientation to the Western European market was the same, the nature of the social struggle between landowners and rural producers was the same, and the cultural split between the two classes was similar.[6] Because both areas were too lightly populated to provide an adequate labor force, it was necessary to resort to bondage; this took the form of slavery in the Americas and serfdom in Eastern Europe.[7] In Russia, a similar process took place, but the surplus went to the maintenance of the Russian state rather to Western exports.[8]

In Poland and Hungary, the growing demand from the West for grain and animal products (1) strengthened the high nobility, (2) weakened the state, (3) weakened the indigenous bourgeoisie, and (4) reduced the peasantry to serfdom. Taking advantage of the higher prices for rural products, the high nobles used their political power both to extract more dues from the peasants and to reduce the power of the state.[9] Thus, the extension of the Western market in these areas had opposite effects in Eastern and Western Europe.[10]

Despite all the differences between Eastern Europe and America, an analogous transformation took place in sixteenth-century America, particularly in those areas that developed as primary agricultural exporters. Spain tended to use its colonies as metal producers, but Portugal began to develop the sugar economy in Brazil in the sixteenth century.[11] Again, to solve the labor problem, slaves were imported. Later, this pattern spread to the West Indies, and ultimately to parts of North America as well.[12]

[5]Eugene Genovese, *The World the Slaveholders Made* (New York: Vintage Books, 1971), pp. 22–23.

[6]Wallerstein, *Modern World-System*, p. 90.

[7]Daniel Chirot, "The Growth of the Market and Servile Labor Systems in Agriculture," *The Journal of Social History* **VIII** (Winter, 1975): 67–80; Evsey Domar, "The Causes of Slavery or Serfdom: A Hypothesis, *The Journal of Economic History*, 30 (1970): 18–32.

[8]Jerome Blum, *Lord and Peasant in Russia from the Ninth to the Nineteenth Century* (New York: Atheneum, 1964), pp. 135–151, 235.

[9]S. P. Pach, "Sixteenth-century Hungary: Commercial Activity and Market Production by the Nobles," *Economy and Society in Early Modern Europe. Essays from Annales*, ed. Peter Burke (New York: Harper Torchbooks, 1972), pp. 113–133.

[10]*Ibid.*, also, Witold Kula, *Théorie économique du système féodal: pour un modèle de l'économie polonaise, 16e–18e siècles* (Paris and The Hague: Mouton, 1970); Maurice Dobb, *Studies in the Development of Capitalism* (New York: International Publishers, 1963), pp. 39 and 51.

[11]Celso Furtado, *The Economic Growth of Brazil* (Berkeley and Los Angeles: University of California Press, 1963), pp. 1–23.

[12]C. L. R. James, "The West Indies in the History of European Capitalism," *The Slave Economies: Historical and Theoretical Perspectives*, ed. Eugene Genovese (New York: Wiley, 1973), **I**, pp. 195–209.

The same pattern occurred in the Mediterranean. As Braudel has shown, that area was characterized by one key, dramatic social change in the second half of the sixteenth century: A new class of nobles seemed to emerge, and this class became very rich while most of the population became poorer. Rural poverty led to a dramatic rise in brigandage in Spain, Italy, and throughout the Balkans. Whatever putative bourgeoisie existed in these areas was ruined.[13] In the Ottoman Empire there developed *Ciftliks*, which were large, efficient serf estates given to the production of cereals. Braudel likens them to the Polish and eastern German wheat-producing estates and to colonial plantations.[14] In Egypt, the Ottoman conquest did not disturb the Mamluke estates, and Egypt became a chief provider of food for Constantinople.[15]

Spain avoided a "second feudalization," but only because the crown and nobility were more interested in raising sheep than in cultivating grain. Consequently, the high dues imposed on the peasants there, as in other parts of the Mediterranean, led to flight to the towns and the gradual erosion of the rural labor force, as well as the rural tax base, of the state. This was particularly the case in the late sixteenth century, and the decline of Spanish agriculture in this period foreshadowed the economic collapse of Spain in the seventeenth century.[16] But the exception proves the rule. Spanish agriculture was characterized by an increasing effort to produce a marketable good. The fact that the peasantry escaped renewed bondage neither prevented Spain's ruin nor affected the basic transformation that occurred.

What is most noteworthy about the Mediterranean pattern is that the same process took place within the core areas of Spain and Turkey and in the peripheral areas of these empires. If Poland can be viewed as a peripheral portion of the growing Western European economic system, the American colonies as a peripheral portion of Spain and Portugal, and the Balkans as a peripheral portion of the Ottoman state, then it would be reasonable to expect Spain and Turkey themselves to develop along the same lines as England and Holland—that is, as prosperous mercantile areas with growing towns, an increasingly efficient state, and a growing, prosperous bourgeoisie. The exact opposite happened, in large part because Spain and the Ottoman Empire behaved more like traditional "world empires" than like new "capitalist systems."[17] Basically, neither Spain nor the Ottoman state had true core areas; their entire empires were exploited as peripheral, colonial regions. In this lies the key to the great

[13]Fernand Braudel, *La Méditerranée et le monde méditerranéen à l'époque de Philippe II*, 2nd ed. (Paris: Armand Colin, 1966), **II**, pp. 75–94.

[14]*Ibid.*, pp. 67–68.

[15]*Ibid.*, pp. 17–18.

[16]J. H. Elliot, *Imperial Spain 1496–1716* (New York: St. Martin's Press, 1964), pp. 287–290.

[17]On the failure of Spain and its allies see Wallerstein, *Modern World-System*, pp. 165–221. On the Ottoman Empire see Braudel, *La Méditerranée*, **II**, pp. 131–135 and 471–485.

crisis of the seventeenth century, which devastated the Mediterranean and its allies but left Northern Europe far more prosperous and advanced.[18]

Thus, in both Spain and Turkey, colonies were exploited to finance luxuries, wars, and the maintenance of overextended imperial structures, but not in order to develop core economies. The smaller scope and ambitions of England and Holland permitted these states to use the surplus from peripheral areas for internal economic development.[19]

This development may have seemed to produce short-run benefits for Spain and the Turks, but it led to long-term ruin. Spain became an importer of food as well as industrial goods as its industry and agriculture decayed and internal production increasingly was oriented toward the production of an export good, wool. Precious metals from America paid for the trade imbalance.[20] The Turks suffered a similar fate. There was little indigenous economic initiative, and a growing reliance on technological imports. Control over commerce then fell into the hands of minority Christian populations in the Ottoman Empire and even, to some extent, into British and Dutch hands, as had Spanish long-distance commerce.[21] In other words, by the seventeenth century, Spain and Turkey—themselves former core areas of imperial systems—were becoming peripheral areas of the still growing Western European economic empire. This meant that these countries' peripheral areas were not pushed as far as were the peripheral areas directly attached to the more dynamic capitalist systems growing in northwestern Europe. The process also explains how Spain and Turkey ultimately became simple peripheral adjuncts of the Western European world in the nineteenth century.

The use of the term "empire" may seem confusing to those who view imperial structures in simple political terms. The fact is that the peripheral areas of an empire may be dominated in three ways, and though each way makes some difference, none alters the basic economic relationship between center and periphery. First, there may be direct rule, in which the metropole's agents and personnel form the political elite in the colony. Second, there may be indirect rule, in which a native elite runs things for the metropole, or in which a foreign group, neither native nor from the metropole, runs the colonial polity.[22] Finally,

[18]Eric Hobsbawm, "The Crisis of the Seventeenth Century," *Crisis in Europe 1560–1660*, ed. Trevor Aston (Garden City, N.Y.: Doubleday-Anchor, 1967), pp. 6–29.

[19]That is a theme running through the work of Wallerstein, *Modern World-System*, particularly pp. 224–297.

[20]Elliot, *Imperial Spain*, pp. 290 and 367.

[21]Braudel, *La Méditerranée*, **II**, pp. 133–134 and **I**, pp. 560–578. An interesting sidelight of English expansion into Ottoman waters is provided by British archival sources on Romania from 1427 to 1601. These become particularly dense in the second half of the sixteenth century. E. D. Tappe's search for documents concerning Romania in British archives of that time turned up 25 documents between 1427 and 1550, 30 documents from 1551 to 1580, and 163 documents from 1581 to 1601. E. D. Tappe, *Documents Concerning Rumanian History (1427–1601)* (The Hague: Mouton, 1964), pp. 147–159.

[22]For an example of recent indirect rule and its effect on "native" rulers see Lloyd Fallers, "The Predicament of the Modern African Chief: An Instance from Uganda," *Social Change: The Colonial Situation*, ed. Immanuel Wallerstein (New York: Wiley, 1966), pp. 232–248.

the peripheral area may be dominated by what is now called "neocolonialism" (a term that is new only in the context of twentieth-century Africa and Asia).[23] This means formal political independence for the colony, but economic subservience via the rule of a class of local landowners. Ultimately, the metropole then has considerable political power as well, but does not intervene as long as its indirect agents, the local landowners, are in firm control. This last form of control is perhaps more insidious than the others because there is a *semblance* of independence, and it is more difficult to identify the actual master, the colonial power. While under Ottoman control, Wallachia was ruled indirectly. Later, in the nineteenth century, it attained formal independence, and became a "neocolony." Unlike Bulgaria or parts of modern Yugoslavia, it was never ruled directly by Turkish *pashas*; this had an important consequence, in that the liberation struggle against the Turks in the nineteenth century did not involve an attack on the landowners, who passed as Romanians instead of Turks.

It is within this total framework that the evolution of Wallachian society becomes comprehensible. Without it, events and changes have little logical coherence and seem instead to be a set of tragic blunders that befell an unusually unlucky country.

Taxes and the Ottoman Tribute

After the suppression of temporary independence achieved by Michael the Brave, the annual tribute was raised from 8000 gold ducats a year to 32,000 a year. This was still far less than the 155,000 a year paid in the 1590s before Michael's revolt, but by 1620 the tribute had again been raised, this time to 40,000 a year (60,000 thalers a year). The tribute rose again during the reign of Matei Basarab so that by his death in 1654, it stood at 130,000 thalers (equal, however, to only 65,000 gold ducats because of inflation).[24] The tribute remained steady thereafter, with only minor increases until 1703. But because of the continued inflation, the early eighteenth-century tribute was worth only 54,600 gold ducats. In 1703, the tribute was almost doubled to 230,000 thalers. Thus it remained, but by about 1800 this was worth barely 20,000 gold ducats.[25]

These numbers are misleading however, in that they do not account for the other types of extraction that were added to the original tribute. There were also numerous unofficial bribes, as well as periodic looting expeditions into Wallachia by various Turkish armies and by their Tartar vassals.[26]

[23] For a rich and strongly ideological view of neocolonialism in the twentieth century see the various essays in Rhodes, ed., *Imperialism and Underdevelopment*.

[24] See Bernard Lewis, "Some Reflections on the Decline of the Ottoman Empire," *The Economic Decline of Empires*, ed. Carlo Cipolla (London: Methuen, 1970), pp. 222–225, on the origins and effects of the Ottoman inflation.

[25] M. Berza, "Haraciul Moldovei şi Ţării Romîneşti în sec. XV–XIX," in *S.M.I.M.*, **II**, pp. 37–44.

[26] V. Mihordea, "La crise du régime fiscal des principautés roumaines au XVIIIe siècle," in *Nouvelles études d'histoire* (Bucharest: Académie roumaine, 1970), **IV**, p. 121.

One of the most important new tributes levied in the early eigthteenth century was the grain tribute. This took the form of requisitions by the government in Constantinople of certain variable amounts of wheat, rye, barley, and millet, for which a special low price was fixed by law. Because of the fixed low price, this tribute often amounted to simple seizure of grain from villagers. It was accompanied by a prohibition against selling grain to any but the official agents (to prevent exports to the Austrian or Russian armies on the borders of the Ottoman Empire). As the empire lost control of its two other major grain-producing areas, the Crimea and Egypt, in the second half of the eighteenth century, the Wallachian and Moldavian sources of supply became that much more important. In fact, despite increasing deliveries of grain from the Romanian principalities, the declining Ottoman Empire never solved the problem that also had bedeviled the last days of its Byzantine predecessor—how to keep Constantinople properly fed—and the Turkish capital was subject to periodic famines.[27]

Additionally, numerous gifts were expected from the Wallachian princes, who were obliged to bribe Ottoman officials in order to keep their thrones (and, sometimes, their heads). Thus, in 1709, the total tax receipts of the Wallachian government were 649,000 thalers, and of these, 514,000 were sent in one way or another to the Turks. In 1710, of the total receipts of 547,000 thalers, 430,000 went to the Turks. In terms of gold, this amounted to between 180,000 and 220,000 gold ducats a year for tribute. This was twice as much as the official tribute, and one-third to one-half again as much as the tribute paid in the 1590s.[28]

As the eighteenth century progressed, the number of levies increased. It became common practice for the Porte to put the Wallachian (and Moldavian) throne up for auction to the highest bidder among the noble Greek families in the running, and the winner then had to raise enough taxes during his reign to pay back his debts. Aside from normal taxes, the princes borrowed large amounts from nobles and monasteries. The average reign tended to be short, and the next prince was likely to repudiate the debts of his predecessor, so these loans were risky. From this developed the vying for favors, large-scale bribery, and mixture of financial speculation as part of the political process that characterized the relations between the prince and Constantinople and that also spread into the relations between the nobles, monasteries, and the prince.[29]

Furthermore, there was a tendency for new taxes to yield less and less as time went on, largely because of corruption in the administrative machine and be-

[27] M. M. Alexandrescu-Dersca, "Contribution à l'étude de l'approvisionnement en blé de Constantinople au XVIIIe siècle," *Studia et Acta Orientalia* I (1957): 18–22. On the tremendous inefficiency of transportation and distribution of these supplies and the corruption of the Constantinople bureaucrats, see the rest of this article, particularly pp. 26–37.

[28] Mihordea, "Crise du régime fiscal," in *Nouvelles études*, IV, p. 122.

[29] *Ibid.*, pp. 127–128.

cause of tax evasion. To compensate for this deficit, new taxes were continually being established. The Turks would impose new forms of tribute on Wallachia, and the prince and his nobles would in turn pass these on to the population. The situation was further complicated by the prince's need for an ever larger administration to collect taxes.[30]

By the end of the eighteenth century, the taxes levied on the ordinary villager included: a head tax, levied 4 times a year (but up to 12 times a year when the treasury needed it); a hearth tax, levied twice a year; a tax on cattle, sheep, pigs, vines; a tax on smoke (from the household fireplace), and on cellars; a sales tax on cattle; a tax on pasture grass; a "flag tax" upon the accession to the throne of new prince, and another tax 3 years later if the same prince was still on the throne (presumably to pay off the bribe debts he owed in order to rule for so long); a tax on soap, on all goods sold in a marketplace, and on bridge tolls; a salt tax; and a tavern tax. Numerous others have not even been recorded because taxes were farmed out and the tax farmers collected what they could without always keeping careful receipts. The village community was still responsible, as it had been earlier, for the payment of the head tax, and it was up to the villagers to decide who had to pay what part within the village. There was no regular census, and the tax rolls frequently were falsified by the tax collectors in order to demand more than a village actually owed. In all, about 90% of the government's receipts came from the taxes of common villagers.[31]

Because of the bewildering diversity of taxes, it is difficult to estimate the total amount extracted each year from the villagers. But one fact emerges clearly—the mass of rural inhabitants was ground down by a system of taxation that took much, and in an arbitrary way. Flight and concealment were frequently the only recourses, except for periodic outbursts of violence which were quickly crushed. At the same time, the Turks continued to exert pressure on the prince and nobles to prohibit movement, or at least limit it, in order to be able to collect taxes.

Trade

As noted in the preceding chapter, Wallachian trade patterns changed markedly in the sixteenth century. Aside from the decline of the East–West transit trade passing through Wallachia, there was an increase of direct exports from Wallachia. Manolescu's data show that, with respect to Transylvania, this increase was more relative (to the declining transit trade) than absolute. But there certainly was an increase of direct trade with the Ottoman Empire. Foreigners, mostly Greeks along with some Turks, Albanians, and Armenians,

[30] *Ibid.*, pp. 129–132.

[31] Marcel Emerit, *Les paysans roumains depuis le traité d'Andrinople jusqu'à la libération des terres (1829–1864)* (Paris: Recueil Sirey, 1937), pp. 15–17.

became increasingly important in this trade as of the second half of the century. Some Italians, mostly Ragusans, were also important in this commerce. Sheep was the main export item, and other items included the traditional exports of salt, fish, some wine, honey, and wax.[32]

Michael's wars catastrophically disrupted Wallachian–Ottoman trade. By the early seventeenth century it had declined to such a point that, aside from Bucharest (the main commercial as well as political center), the other trading cities of Wallachia had shrunken back into villages dramatically and had been abandoned by foreign merchants.[33]

The relative stability that followed these wars redressed the situation, and the patterns of sixteenth century trade reasserted themselves. Trade continued with the West, with the Transylvanian cities, and with Venice, but on a reduced scale. Animal, agricultural, and bee products were exported in return for fine cloth, jewelry, and fine artisan goods for the court and the *boieri*. There was also a sporadic commerce with Germany, Austria, and Poland. A small transit trade continued to pass through Wallachia (between the Turks and Western Europe), but again on a smaller scale than in the early sixteenth century. As before, the prince took an active part in these commercial activities; however, an increasing number of foreigners, mostly Christian Ottoman subjects and some Italians, were used as intermediaries.[34]

Although the official Turkish prohibition on trading outside the Empire was far from being totally obeyed (this provision existed for most of the duration of Ottoman rule, but it was particularly in the eighteenth century that attempts were made to enforce it), the major portion of Wallachia's trade was directed toward the Empire. The main Wallachian exports continued to be those of the sixteenth century, and in return Wallachia imported spices, silks, and other Oriental cloths.[35] The renewal of this trade brought back large numbers of Levantines who had been specialists in handling credit arrangements in Constantinople, and who were protected by their connections in the capital of the Ottoman Empire. Toward the end of the seventeenth century, the Greeks, Armenians, Turkish and Spanish Jews, and the few Turks who increasingly populated the cities, especially Bucharest, also brought with them a more Middle Eastern style of life, and there was a marked adoption of these customs (i.e., dress, style of living, etc.) among the Wallachian upper classes.[36]

By the late seventeenth century, the animal export trade had created a remarkable degree of prosperity in Bucharest. Indeed, Wallachia was a rich

[32]Nicolae Iorga, *Istoria comerțului românesc* (Bucharest: Tiparul românesc, 1925), **I**, pp. 181–184, 204–211.

[33]*Ibid.*, pp. 240–257.

[34]*Ibid.*, p. 267; and L. Lehr, "Comerțul Țării Romînești și Moldovei în a doua jumătate a secolului XVI și prima jumătate a secolului XVII," in *S.M.I.M.*, **IV**, pp. 255–260 and 287.

[35]Lehr, "Comerțul Țării" in *S.M.I.M.*, **IV**, pp. 246–247.

[36]Iorga, *Istoria comerțului*, **I**, pp. 300–304. The Spanish- or Ladino-speaking Jews had been in the Empire since their expulsion from Spain in the 1490s.

province. A Florentine secretary of the Wallachian Prince Constantin Brâncoveanu, Anton Marie del Chiaro, wrote:

> The country could not be more fertile or more pleasantly situated. From the Danube to Bucharest (which is in the middle of Wallachia) and from Bucharest to Târgovişte, which is fourteen hours distant from Bucharest by road, nothing is to be seen but an immense and delightful plain, in which not even a small stone is to be found. In every district one sees very fine woods (especially of oaks) laid out with such regularity and kept so clear, that from one end of a wood to the other it is easy to discover if there is anyone there. In this (as in all other kinds of exactitude) it is easy to trace the character of the incomparable Prince Constantin Brâncoveanu. If we desire a clear view of the quality and extent of the country's fertility, it is enough to reflect that droves of horses, pigs, and cattle are sent from Transylvania to the pastures of Wallachia. From Wallachia, Venice is provided with wax and steers, just as the Sultan's kitchen is provided with butter and honey in great quantities.... The greater part of Transylvania is provided with excellent white and red wines, very delicate to the taste and wholesome to the stomach. The horses of Wallachia are much in demand not only from German officials in Transylvania, but also from merchants who come from Poland with orders to procure them.[37]

But the nature of the trade—particularly its centralization in the hands of the prince, a few *boieri*, and their foreign agents in Bucharest—benefited only the capital, and other Wallachian cities consequently remained little more than stagnant villages. In Bucharest, however, the late seventeenth century and the first decade of the eighteenth century was a period of wealth. New churches and palaces were built, especially by Prince Brâncoveanu, who gave his name to one of the few distinctive major architectural styles ever created by the Romanians. (This style—an interesting blend of Byzantine, Turkish, Italian, and Romanian peasant architectures—remained the dominant Romanian style into the 1930s.[38])

The role of the prince and *boieri* in this trade was reminiscent of the role the state had played in the old trading state, except that internal products were far more important than control over the transit trade. In or about 1650, the father of the future Prince Brâncoveanu, and an important *boier* in his own right, owned 12,000 mares, 30,000 sheep, 4000 oxen, 1000 water buffaloes, 4000 pigs, 300 beehives, and a herd of horses in each of the 200 villages he controlled. Each year he sent 1000 oxen to Constantinople for sale. He also owned 1500 Gypsy slaves.[39] His son, who was prince from 1688 to 1714, was even richer. Prince Brâncoveanu's chief commercial agent was a Greek who lived in Bucharest.[40]

[37] Reprinted from his *Istoria delle moderne rivoluzioni della Valachia* (Venice, 1718), translated in Doreen Warriner, ed., *Contrasts in Emerging Societies* (Bloomington, Ind.: Indiana University Press, 1965), pp. 137–138, by permission of Indiana University Press.

[38] Iorga, *Istoria comerţului*, I, pp. 310–312.

[39] *Ibid.*, pp. 258–259.

[40] *Ibid.*, pp. 299–300.

The first half of the eighteenth century was marked by a second intrusion of the West into Wallachian commerce. Austrian expansion into Oltenia placed that part of Wallachia under Vienna's rule from 1718 to 1739. There was an increase of trade with Transylvania, Austria, and Southern Germany, and a corresponding decline of trade with the Ottoman Empire. But this development changed neither the type of trade that had predominated in the seventeenth century (export mainly of animals and animal products), nor the role of foreign merchants who were now increasingly protected by the prince. The new factor of significance was that in the second half of the eighteenth century, there appeared German merchants to join the Levantines (*Lipscani*, or "from Leipzig" in Romanian).[41] But the Turks countered this development by tightening restrictions on trade with the West, and at least until the start of the nineteenth century, commerce with the Ottoman Empire predominated, despite the gradual increase of trade with the West.[42]

In 1714, Constantin Brâncoveanu was executed in Constantinople, and 2 years later his successor also was killed by the Turks. The pretext was that they had tried to ally themselves with the Russians against the Turks, but in the case of Brâncoveanu, the murder may simply have been caused by a desire to seize his great wealth. In 1711, the Moldavian Prince Dimitrie Cantemir had tried to ally Moldavia with Russia, but after the Turkish victory against Peter the Great's army in 1711, Cantemir exiled himself to Peter's court. The Turks then placed a Greek on the Moldavian throne and in 1716, to keep firmer control of Wallachia, they did the same there.[43] The Greek princes, who were to rule until 1821, were called *Phanariots* (after the Greek district of Constantinople, the Phanar). These men came from leading Greek merchant families in the Romanian principalities and Constantinople. From this time on, the competition for the throne took on an unabashedly financial, speculative aspect.[44]

The role of the Levantine merchants, especially the Greeks and Armenians, continued to gain significance during the eighteenth century. As commerce with the West became more important, these merchants spread their activities to the Habsburg Empire.[45] That is not to say that native Wallachian merchants disappeared, however. There continued to be a native merchant class, particularly in the Carpathian Mountain border regions near Transylvania.[46] But, as Iorga has noted, the Phanariot period was one in which both the tax advantages that were given by the Wallachian government to foreigners, and the intercessions

[41] Iorga, *Istoria comerţului*, **II**, pp. 16–17, 36, and 43–45.

[42] *Ibid.*, pp. 101–104 and 116–117.

[43] Andrei Oţetea *et al.*, *Istoria Romîniei* (Bucharest: Editura academiei, 1964), **III**, pp. 218–219 and 433.

[44] W. G. East, *The Union of Moldavia and Wallachia, 1859* (Cambridge: Cambridge University Press, 1929), pp. 4–5.

[45] Iorga, *Istoria comerţului*, **II**, pp. 10–11, 23, 28, 37–38, 65, and 93–95. The Armenians, however, had a more important role in Moldavia than in Wallachia.

[46] *Ibid.*, pp. 42 and 82.

from outside Wallachia in favor of foreign merchants, damaged the native commercial class and put Romanian commerce in both principalities into foreign hands.[47] The process was a long one. It had started in the sixteenth century, but because of (1) Michael's temporarily successful reversal of the situation, (2) the temporary eclipse of Ottoman power, and (3) the decline of the tribute paid by Wallachia to the Turks, at the start of the seventeenth century the role of the foreign merchants was not great. Slowly, their position grew stronger in the seventeenth century so that by the eighteenth, it was considerable. In the period of Phanariot rule the process was accelerated. Thus, by the end of the eighteenth century, foreign merchants were clearly more important than the declining Wallachian merchant class. That the process continued into the nineteenth century does not diminish the fact that it was already well-advanced by 1800.

The pattern of the export trade during the period of Ottoman rule and the Ottoman tribute were the two most important determinants of the evolution of Wallachian rural society and of the power relations between the prince, nobles, and monasteries on the one hand, and the subservient villagers on the other.

Serfs and Free Villagers

Serfdom, decreed by Michael the Brave in the 1590s was not viable in a pastoral society. In the preceding chapter it was shown that shortly after Michael's reign, the process began of freeing the serfs by reselling them their freedom. Thus a class of landless, free villagers was created at the same time that a class of landless serfs came into being—a class virtually of slaves, who could be sold at will by their masters and taken from their villages.

Because animals continued to be the main source of noble and princely wealth, pasturing rights in the various villages controlled by the upper class were more important than actual land ownership. Similarly, labor requirements for raising animals were not nearly so great as for growing cereals. This explains the fact that as lordly power grew and the free communal villages were submerged by economic forces, many of the actual economic techniques of the pastoral communal village (e.g., sharing of pasture, free cutting of forests for wood and to clear temporary agricultural plots, maintenance of large amounts of communal land, transhumance of shepherds with their flocks) continued to exist, even in wholly-owned serfs' villages.[48] Also, since agricultural plots were generally cleared for temporary use and were returned to pasture after the soil was exhausted, there was that much less incentive for villagers to remain in the same

[47] Iorga, *Istoria comerţului*, I, p. 316.

[48] Henri H. Stahl, *Les anciennes communautés villageoises roumaines* (Bucharest and Paris: Académie roumaine and C.N.R.S., 1969), pp. 139–153.

place for long if another lord promised lighter work and tax loads. In the Wallachian case, a very low population density, combined with traditional agri-pastoralist patterns of production, made serfdom an unworkable proposition, at least in the long run.

The continued predominance of old agri-pastoral techniques also explains the fact that though division of communal land into private family plots had begun in the sixteenth century (see preceding chapter), it was not completed until the nineteenth century (except, of course, for the Vrancea, where it was not completed until the twentieth). The actual pattern seems to have been a series of successive partial divisions of land. The area nearest the village would be divided first, and the more distant pastures and forests much later. (In the case of villages not wholly owned by lords, as pointed out earlier it was to the advantage of the lord to preserve the old communal forms under his own control instead of having the land split into family plots.)[49]

In the seventeenth century, the relations between lords and villagers varied between categories of villagers. There were serfs living on land to which they had traditional rights, landless serfs, landless free men, and free villagers with traditional rights to their land. It is therefore necessary to examine each category separately.

Practically all villagers paid a tithe, either to individual lords, to monasteries, to the state, or to a combination of these. Therefore, what distinguished the various types of villagers was the amount of work they were obliged to perform.[50] Serfs were legally required to work for their lords as much as the lord demanded. In extreme cases, this meant that they did no work for their own account (and were thus excused from the tithe) and were total servants of their masters.[51] Presumably, these serfs had no rights of their own to any land, and they (along with Gypsy slaves, who were used as household servants and artisans more than in agriculture or as shepherds) performed all kinds of work, from transporting goods for their masters to taking care of their flocks, farming, building, etc.[52] Many serfs, however, were required to do a lot less. Serfs who lived in villages that were partially composed of free men, or who remained in their original villages and thus had rights to village lands, received the best treatment. Indeed, numerous documents show that the amount of pressure that could be put on these serfs was limited by the resistance of the community, especially if the serfs were owned by monasteries, which seemed generally to have less

[49] Two typical documented cases are the villages of Orodel and Negoiești. C. Stănică, "Hotarul satului Orodel-Dolj," *Sociologie Românească* **II**, no. 1 (1937): 28–29; and Gh. Serafim, "Împărțirea pe moșii și pe trupuri de moșie a satului Negoiești-Mehedinți," *Sociologie Românească* **III**, no. 1–3 (1938): 32–35.

[50] Constantin Giurescu, *Studii de istorie socială* (Bucharest: Editura universul, 1943), p. 199.

[51] *Ibid.*, pp. 187–195; and Șerban Papacostea, "Contribuție la problema relațiilor agrare în Țara Romînească în prima jumătate a veacului al XVIII–lea," in *S.M.I.M.*, **III**, p. 317.

[52] On Gypsy slaves see Marcel Emerit, "De la condition des esclaves dans l'ancienne Roumanie," *Revue d'histoire du sud-est européen* (October–December, 1930).

coercive power than lay lords.[53] Some serfs worked 3 days a year for their masters; some 6, 12, 24, or even 36 days. But because the total was not fixed by law but by local custom, the number was widely variable, depending on the relative power and needs of particular lords.[54]

Though Romanian historians have frequently spoken about the intolerable burden that Ottoman demands had placed on Romanian villagers, and though taxes were in fact quite high, it is interesting to note that insofar as the serfs were concerned, the corvée was low. This does not indicate that the general fiscal burden was light, but it does prove that in a largely pastoral economy, the way of extracting the rural surplus was not through any classical form of serfdom. In eighteenth century Russia, for example, the corvée or *barshchina* amounted to 2 to 3 days a week.[55] Work loads became that high throughout most of Wallachia only in the second half of the nineteenth century.

There were also other kinds of serfs. Those in fishing villages had to fish a certain number of days for their lords as well as pay a fish tithe. From the late sixteenth to the nineteenth centuries, the number of such work days steadily increased.[56] There were also serfs located near salt mines who worked these for their owners.[57]

Serfs owed taxes to the state. They paid a tithe or certain products to their lords, but on others, to the state. Sometimes it was paid in cash, sometimes, in produce.[58] Some serfs paid a head tax, but this was based on their ability to pay—that is, on their own production.[59] Of course, the whole point of free men's selling themselves into serfdom was to escape taxes, and this was generally done by an agreement with the masters, who interceded with the state on behalf of their serfs to reduce or end the tax. If this was not possible, the master assumed the tax burden for serfs who did not pay.[60] The entire situation was rather fluid. Villages and individuals would sometimes sell themselves to escape taxes, then repurchase their freedom and reassume the obligation to pay.

Presumably, those serfs who worked entirely for their masters paid no tax; the rising taxes imposed on *boieri* during the sixteenth and seventeenth centuries

[53] Mihordea, "Crise du régime fiscal," in *Nouvelles études*, **IV**, pp. 154–157.

[54] *Ibid.*, pp. 158–159.

[55] Blum, *Lord and Peasant*, p. 445.

[56] Constantin C. Giurescu, *Istoria pescuitului şi a pisciculturii în Romînia* (Bucharest: Editura academiei, 1964), pp. 70 and 278–279.

[57] A. Ilieş, "Ştiri în legătură cu exploatarea sării în Ţara Romînească pînă în veacul al XVII–lea," in *S.M.I.M.*, **I**, pp. 196–197. But there were also free men and Gypsy slaves who worked in the salt mines.

[58] Giurescu, *Studii de istoria socială*, p. 180.

[59] D. Mioc, "Despre modul de impunere şi precepere a birului în Ţara Romînească pînă la 1632," in *S.M.I.M.*, **II**, p. 105.

[60] *Ibid.*, pp. 80–81 and 110. As will be seen later, this made it vital for the lord to have the ability to gain favors from the central government. If he could not obtain tax advantages for his serfs, he could be obliged to pay high taxes himself unless he found a way to squeeze them out of his villagers. But that was likely to provoke flight, and he would be ruined by having to pay the taxes of those who had fled.

suggest that this was the Wallachian state's way of compensating for the loss of taxes from villagers. This further complicated the social situation, because there were *boieri* who themselves were not able to pay their taxes, were overcome by debt, and who finally sank into the ranks of the free villagers. This made for a rapid turnover of nobles. Those not holding court office (and therefore not having the opportunity to intercede with the state for fiscal advantages) tended to fall out of their class and to be replaced by noble families who held office. Because the prince could appoint office holders from non-noble families and thus create new nobles, the status of *boier* was frequently precarious.[61]

Free men who had inherited rights to land were not subjected to work loads imposed by lords, but they were obliged to pay heavy taxes to the state as well as a tithe on their products. Because taxes were so heavy, at the same time that numerous serfs were repurchasing their freedom, many free villagers became obliged to sell themselves into serfdom to relieve their tax burden. So at this level of society, too, there was a great deal of upward and downward mobility.[62]

An important class of villagers that had not existed prior to the seventeenth century, but which became numerous during that century, was that of the landless free men. Some of the forces that created this class have already been discussed in the previous chapter. Aside from the case in which a lord might give his serfs freedom in return for full rights over their land, there were other ways in which a free man could become landless. For example, a free man might simply flee his village in order to avoid taxes, and thus lose his rights to the use of his village's land. More commonly, a serf might flee and gain *de facto* freedom.[63] This occurred when the population density was low and there was competition among nobles for villagers from whom they could extract a tithe and work obligations.[64]

Since landless free men had no choice but to find a village that would accept them, and since lords were looking for villagers, a lord would accept a free man into his village and not question his origin, in return for which the man would assume the obligation to pay a tithe and give the lord a certain number of work days a year. These could be paid in work, produce, or money. At first the work loads imposed on free men in this category were very light, but as this class became more and more prevalent and serfs rarer, the work load gradually increased. By the early eighteenth century, there was frequently little difference between the taxes and work loads imposed on free men and serfs in lords' villages; the

[61] D. Ciurea, "Quelques considérations sur la noblesse féodale chez les Roumains," in *Nouvelles études*, IV, pp. 86–87. It was the observation of this fact that led the historian Radu Rosetti—see his *Pămîntul, sătenii, şi stăpânii în Moldova* (Bucharest: Socec, 1907)—to propose that all free villagers had once been nobles. (See this work, chap. 3.)

[62] Emerit, *Les paysans roumains*, p. 37.

[63] Giurescu, *Studii de istorie socială*, p. 202.

[64] Stahl, *Les anciennes communautés*, pp. 229–230.

only real difference was that one group was theoretically free, and the other theoretically bound to the land.[65]

The massive growth of the category of free men who owed tithe and work obligations (corvée, Romanian *clacă*) primarily was caused by the increase of oppressive and arbitrary taxes. Many villagers fled their villages in order to gain respite from the burdens of taxation. But after settling in new villages, the pattern would tend to repeat itself, and formerly lenient lords who had previously offered good terms to new settlers would raise the taxes and obligations of older settlers. Some who fled hid in the forests and mountains. Some became bandits (*haiduci*). Many fled across the Danube to Ottoman Bulgaria, or to Transylvania, or to Russia.

There was, of course, no guarantee that conditions in their new homes would be better, and there came to exist floating populations such as that on both sides of the Milcov River which separated Moldavia and Wallachia. These would switch from one principality to the other, depending on the current vagaries of the tax system—sometimes heavier on one side, and then on the other. Some, presumably, learned to avoid taxes by changing country repeatedly.[66] In return, Wallachian lords sought to attract men from Bulgaria, Serbia, Transylvania, Russia, and Moldavia to settle their villages by offering easy terms.[67] The terms would in turn become harsher over time because of the demands of the treasury, starting a new cycle of flights. The new settlers would then be considered in the same category as "landless free men," not because they had no land to work, but because they did not possess the traditional rights of free Wallachian villagers and were dependent on the lord who controlled the areas into which they had moved.

A. M. del Chiaro, whose enthusiastic description of Wallachia in the early eighteenth century was cited previously, also wrote in his *Istoria delle moderne rivoluziono della Valachia*:

> Not, indeed, that the Wallachians lack good qualities and courage to confront the most warlike of nations; but the continuous imposition of exorbitant taxes, which they have to pay many times in a single year, has so degraded them that of the ancient Roman virtues nothing remains but the name. . . .
>
> These continuous oppressions have not only made them cowardly and lazy, but have even reduced them to the desperate decision of abandoning their own nest and seeking refuge, some in the parts of Turkey beyond the Danube, some in Transylvania, where I am certain that the number of Wallachians is greater than it is in Wallachia. And if anyone says to me "How can it be so easy to leave Wallachia and enter other

[65] Giurescu, *Studii*, pp. 203–205.

[66] Papacostea, "Contribuţii la problema relaţiilor," in *S.M.I.M.*, **III**, pp. 247–248; and Mihordea, "Crise du régime fiscal" in *Nouvelles études*, **IV**, p. 131.

[67] Matei D. Vlad, "Mişcări demografice în cadrul colonizării rurale din Ţara Românească şi Moldova (secolele XVII–XVIII)," *Studii şi articole de istorie* **XIV** (1969): 73–82.

> provinces?", I answer that it is not at all difficult for anyone who has the necessary knowledge, especially of some passes through the mountains, which lead into Transylvania, provided he keeps out of the way of the guards (called by the Wallachians *plăiaşi*), since to fall into their hands without a passport from the Prince would certainly endanger his life.[68]

By the first few decades of the eighteenth century, the sharp rise in taxes, the increasing flow of opposing armies into and through Wallachia, and the consequently greater incentive for villagers to flee had virtually eliminated the serf class. Rather, lords increasingly depended on the free men who lived in their villages. Consequently, the amount of work demanded of these men (from here on called *clăcaşi*, the Romanian word that means "men subjected to the corvée") tended to rise. From 1700 to 1718, the normal work load for them was 3 to 4 days a year. From 1718 to 1739, it varied between 3 and 9 days a year (except in Oltenia, which was occupied by the Austrians during this period, and where events took a different turn). From 1740 to 1744, the work load was officially set at 6 days a year, and from 1744 to 1746, when a great reform was decreed, it stood at 12 days a year.[69]

Oltenia 1718–1739: A Premature Experiment in Modern Colonialism

From 1718 to 1739, Oltenia underwent a somewhat different evolution from the rest of Wallachia because of the Austrian occupation. What happened there is of more than passing interest, because it suggests the major difference between Ottoman colonial policies and those of a more advanced European power. Austria, in fact, tried to force Oltenia into a more thoroughly exploited colonial situation, which prefigured the later transformation of all of Wallachia in the nineteenth century.

The primary concern of the Austrians was to maintain their political control over Oltenia, and the local nobility was the only class on which they could rely to maintain that control. The Austrians had neither the manpower nor the knowledge of local conditions necessary to institute a more direct system of rule.[70] At the same time, the Austrians needed a source of food for their army. Oltenia was freed of the Turkish monopoly on cereal sales and a market for cereals was created, chiefly by the presence of the Austrian army.[71] There may

[68] Reprinted from Warriner, *Contrasts in Emerging Societies*, p. 138, by permission of Indiana University Press.

[69] Papacostea, "Contribuţii la problema relaţiilor," in *S.M.I.M.*, **III**, p. 317.

[70] *Ibid.*, p. 277.

[71] *Ibid.*, pp. 243–246.

even have been a certain amount of grain exportation toward the Habsburg Empire.[72]

Intent on rationalizing the administrative system, the Austrians conducted the first census in 1722 and found that 47% of the Oltenian villages were free and had control of their own land. The rest were wholly or partially controlled by nobles and monasteries. The percentage of free villages in the mountain and hill counties was on the order of 60%; in the plains counties it was about 33% (with important variations within each county).[73] The Austrians also tried to regulate the disordered relations between free men without traditional rights to land, the *clăcaşi*, and the lords who controlled the land. In 1721, some categories of *clăcaşi* (those with draft animals of their own who could therefore do more work in a day) were ordered to do 18 days of work a year for their lords. Others were to work 32 days. In 1722, the law was changed and all *clăcaşi* were decreed to owe 52 days a year to their lords.[74] Thus a serious effort was made to transform the Oltenian economy into a more agricultural, cereal-producing economy, capable of generating a significant cereal surplus.

There were even plans to encourage the production of flax for German Transylvanian manufacturers (Transylvania had become part of the Habsburg Empire in 1688),[75] and a merchant company was created in Vienna to encourage trade with "the Orient"—those parts of the Ottoman Empire that Austria was planning to absorb, including the Banat, Oltenia, Serbia, and the rest of Wallachia and Moldavia (which were, at that time, declared to be ancient possessions of the Habsburgs).[76] The result of Austria's planning was the imposition of a heavier work load on the Oltenian *clăcaşi*. In fact, the difference between work loads in Oltenia and the rest of Wallachia during the period of Austrian occupation was about 48 days a year! It was only in the nineteenth century that the work loads imposed on *clăcaşi* increased to such proportions in the rest of Wallachia. Whether or not the Austrians would have succeeded in their planned transformation of free *clăcaşi* villagers into peasant serfs on nobles' estates cannot, however, be known. In 1739, the Turks regained control of Oltenia and the Austrian work rules were abolished.[77]

[72] Andrei Oţetea, "Consideraţii asupra trecerii de la feudalism la capitalism în Moldova şi Ţara Romînească," in *S.M.I.M.*, **IV**, pp. 335–336.

[73] Stahl, *Les anciennes communautés*, p. 23. It must be recalled that historically the Munteninan plains had the lowest proportion of free villages in all Wallachia, far lower than in the Oltenian plains. Muntenia as a whole had fewer free villages than Oltenia. Therefore the 1722 Austrian figures must not be generalized to the rest of Wallachia, because Oltenia is only about one-third of Wallachia. See Stahl's maps, pp. 24, 28, and 32.

[74] Papacostea, "Contribuţii la problema relaţiilor," in *S.M.I.M.*, **III**, p. 317.

[75] Iorga, *Istoria comerţului*, **II**, p. 8; and L. Boicu, "Considérations sur la politique des Habsbourg à l'égard des principautés roumaines (depuis le XVIIIe siècle jusqu'en 1848)," *Nouvelles études*, **IV**, p. 159.

[76] Boicu, "Considérations," in *Nouvelles études*, **IV**, p. 159.

[77] Papacostea, "Contribuţii la problema relaţiilor," in *S.M.I.M.*, **III**, p. 317.

The Reform of 1746 and Rural Society until 1821

In the rest of Wallachia, the growing crisis in villager–lord relations, created by the virtual disappearance of effective serfdom and the constant movement of population fleeing onerous taxes, continued to perturb the state treasury and, ultimately, the Ottoman government, which was losing its source of tribute. Furthermore, the war that had led to the reconquest of Oltenia by the Turks (1736–1739) had left numerous Oltenian villages deserted; the problem of repopulating these villages in order to revive them as a source of revenue was pressing.[78] The Ottomans gave the Prince of Wallachia, Constantin Mavrocordat, the order to remedy the situation by making the tax burden lighter for villagers, in order to induce them to repopulate empty villages.[79]

A series of reforms from 1739 to 1746 resulted, culminating in the formal freeing of the serfs in 1746. (Mavrocordat was later sent to Moldavia to carry out the same reform in 1749.[80]) The reform was not very clear, however, and it continued to be debated until the 1860s because it failed to specify who really owned the land—the villagers or the lords. It was only because the question was not very important in the 1740s that the text of the reform is so contradictory. The substance of the decree said that all serfs were free, and those who had fled could return home as free men without fear of punishment. With their freedom, they would also benefit frow lower taxes. They would, however, have to pay a tithe and a corvée of 6 days a year to their lords (soon increased to 12).[81]

[78] Oţetea, "Consideraţii," in *S.M.I.M.*, **IV**, p. 336.

[79] Papacostea, "Contribuţii la problema relaţiilor," in *S.M.I.M.*, **III**, p. 304, particularly note 4 which refers to the documentary proof that the order for the reform originated in Constantinople.

[80] Oţetea, "Consideraţii," in *S.M.I.M.*, **IV**, p. 339.

[81] The text of the reform decrees is taken from Warriner, *Contrasts in Emerging Societies*, pp. 136–132, by permission of Indiana University Press:

> (a) Decree of the General Assembly of Wallachia for the Liberation of such Peasants gone abroad as may return to their Homes. 1 March 1746. His Highness our enlightened and exalted Lord Io Constantin Nicolae, wishing to draw and gather all the sons of this land who are scattered from their soil, as is his duty as lord, and in accordance with the *hati-sherif* of the mighty Empire, which graciously declared and proclaimed that it is its will, desire and command, that those abroad should be gathered together, took common counsel with us, his whole nobility. It was thought good that the usual rate of tax laid upon the peasants should be lessened for those who have gone abroad, and when first they return to their country, that they may have a dwelling and the wherewithal to live, they should have respite and be free of tax for six years. And after that rate of tax should be kept at five thalers per man per annum in four quarterly payments, and no more; and on whatever estate they settle, they should be unmolested. Only they must work six days a year for the lord of the estate, and give him a tithe of all their crops, as is shown in full in the first papers that were printed. And after this His Highness our learned Lord bethought him for some of the native peasants that have gone abroad who may be serfs of monasteries or of boyars, that the yoke of servitude might hinder them from returning to their country, or that on the other hand, if they trusted to His Highness' call and came back, instead of gaining peace and quiet, they might once more fall anew under the yoke of servitude. His Highness, fearing that this sin might

At the same time, all villagers other than the *moşneni* (the free villagers with traditional rights to their land, formerly called *cneji*) were assimilated into the category of the former serfs as free men who owed a tithe and a corvée of 12 days.[82] This explains the change in terminology. Previously dependent villagers had been serfs, *rumîni*. After the reform, all villagers except the *moşneni* became bound to the obligations of the corvée (*clacă*) and came to be called

Ftn. 81 (continued)

fall upon him since for this nothing had been said in the former papers, took counsel anew with us all, there being present at the Divan the Most Reverend the Metropolitan of Wallachia, Kir Clement. His Highness asked us, which of two things seemed to us more fitting; that some like these should be hindered from returning to their native land, or that coming they should be under the yoke of serfdom as before, for His Highness would bring this to the knowledge of all that he might not remain beneath that sin. To which His Holiness the Metropolitan replied that if they came at His Highness' call and should remain once more serfs, His Highness would have great sin, mortal sin, and in the life to come His Highness' soul would be punished, because His Highness was making himself the cause of their servitude.

And so, lest these men should remain estranged from their country, and His Highness our exalted Lord incur that sin and punishment, if they should be left once more in serfdom, first of all His Holiness the Bishop of Ramnic and we the whole body of nobles, likewise each one separately, spoke our opinion and gave counsel: that whatever serfs of monasteries or of boyars have been estranged from this soil, if they wished to return to their native soil, should settle where they wish, and be free and exempt from serfdom, without further trouble from their masters. And further, whoever wished might come to the Divan to receive a separate paper of his right upon that settlement. This decision seeming good to us all in general, it has been given in writing by this deed which has been signed by His Holiness the Metropolitan and His Holiness the Bishop of Ramnic and the Egumens and by all the nobles of the land. At our prayer His Highness our learned Lord has confirmed it with his princely signature and seal that it be unchanged, and copies of it have been made, printed and confirmed with the Prince's seal, and sent throughout the land.

(b) Decree of the General Assembly for the Liberation of all Peasants 5 August 1746. On the soil of our land we see that many of the ancient customs which have been known to be good and useful, have been thoroughly confirmed by later rulers and are preserved unchanged. But some of these old ordinances we deem to be not only useless, but very harmful to the Christian soul, as has been this ancient custom of serfdom which has remained upon us from our fathers and forefathers until today. For that our brothers in Christ should be beneath the yoke of our servitude is the gravest and greatest of sins, since our Lord Jesus Christ himself in the holy Gospel teaches us, saying: "Love thy neighbour as thyself." But since it is right that we should be subject to this commandment and teaching, we must not put our brothers in Christ beneath the yoke of servitude. Therefore, we too one and all, knowing that this holding in servitude orthodox Christians, who are of one faith with ourselves, is not a Christian thing, but very harmful to our souls, and taking thought for the serfs whom we have held till now under our lordship, they having been sold with their estates in ancient times to our forefathers, have thought it good for the relief of our souls and those of our fathers and forefathers, that wherever men and serfs with their estates to any boyar or monastery, the estates should remain under our lordship as before. But as for the persons of the serfs apart from their estates, whosoever of us shall be willing of his own free will to free them will do well for his own memory; but if he will not do this good deed to his own soul, then those serfs shall have the right to give ten thalers per head in cash and ransom themselves, whether their lord will or no. They shall give the money to their master, and if he will not receive it, they shall come and make complaint to the Divan. For we have all agreed upon this good and spiritual thing and ordained that it be preserved and confirmed among us both by us and by all our race who shall be left inheritors after us....

[82] Stahl, *Les anciennes communautés*, p. 238.

clăcaşi. As will be shown in later chapters, the villagers were not really freed in fact (though they were de jure), and thus in the late eighteenth and nineteenth centuries the word *clăcaşi* came to mean serf.[83]

It is quite clear that the reform of 1746 was not, as has sometimes been asserted, merely the act of an "enlightened despot" imitating Western ways. It was, rather, an attempt to rectify a serious social problem that was damaging the economic and fiscal balance of Wallachia.[84] Here, the appearance of "cultural diffusion" has misled many historians. It might even be said that, despite its magnanimous language, the reform had little to do with serfdom. C. Giurescu has written: "When in 1746 the General Assembly gave serfs the right to repurchase their freedom, it was only completing an evolution that was just about finished. The proof that serfdom no longer existed at that time is that it disappeared immediately without our ever having heard of a single case of repurchase."[85]

Freedom alone, however, meant little. Villagers other than *moşneni* were not given the right to use land unless they paid dues to their lords. They also owed their lords obedience and submission.[86] Though in principle they were free to leave, the act of leaving was hedged with restrictions (e.g., limitation of movement to certain times of the year, after prepayment of taxes) such that in effect the *clăcaşi* were still bound to the land.[87] (Of course, this was no more effective in preventing flight than were the old laws.)

After the reform of 1746, the law was interpreted in many ways and modified a number of times. Sometimes "liberty" was interpreted to mean that the *clăcaşi* had the freedom to choose where they wanted to live; sometimes, as in 1755, it was interpreted to mean that *clăcaşi* were as strictly bound to the land as by the original 1590s law of Michael the Brave.[88] On the other hand, the reform gave the *clăcaşi* inalienable rights to the use of land for which they paid dues, thus ending the practice of selling serfs alienated from their land.[89]

[83] It is useful to recall the changes in terminology mentioned in chap. 3. Originally, the word *cnez* had meant "village chief" and even "noble." In the sixteenth century, with the enserfment of much of the population it came to mean "free man with traditional rights to the land." The term vanished during the eighteenth century and was replaced by *moşneni* (*răzăşi* in Moldavia). The term *rumân* (or *rumîn*), sometimes *vlah* in Slavonic documents, originally meant Wallachian. In the sixteenth century it came to mean serf. In the eighteenth century it disappeared and was replaced by *clăcaşi*. (In Moldavia the original term for serf was *vecin.*)

[84] Oţetea *et al., Istoria Romîniei,* **III**; p. 436. Also, see Pompiliu Eliade, *De l'influence française sur l'esprit public en Roumanie* (Paris: Leroux, 1898), pp. 5–6. The latter takes the view that Western influence made the Phanariots more enlightened and promted the reform. The former emphasizes the element of pressing economic necessity, and is correct.

[85] Giurescu, *Studii de istorie socială*, p. 205.

[86] Valentin Georgescu, "Reflexions sur le statut juridique des paysans corvéeables et la politique agraire de la classe dominante en Valachie dans la seconde moitié du XVIIIe siècle," in *Nouvelles études,* **IV**, pp. 143–144.

[87] Oţetea, "Consideraţii" in *S.M.I.M.*, **IV**, p. 340.

[88] Georgescu, "Reflexions sur le statut," in *Nouvelles etudes,* **IV**, p. 147.

[89] *Ibid.*, pp. 151–152; and Oţetea, "Consideraţii," in *S.M.I.M.*, **IV**, p. 340.

The reform also allowed lords to keep a certain number of servants who were partially or totally exempted from taxes, depending on the type of service they performed. The lords also kept their Gypsy slaves.[90] The reform, further, gave lords monopoly rights over mills, stills, and the sale of alcohol in their villages. These rights were extended and reinforced in the second half of the century.[91] Villagers kept their traditional rights to pasture and forest land, but as of 1774, these began to be restricted and lords were given the right in the villages they controlled to demand payment for wood cut for sale.[92]

But though the position of the lords with respect to dependent villagers was clearly strengthened by the reforms and the modifications that followed them, lords continued to be called "masters of the domain" or "masters of the villages," not "landowners." Indeed, who owned the land? On the one hand, the villager who paid his dues could not be evicted. On the other hand, the lord maintained and strengthened his rights to collect dues.[93] And if the lords did not fully own the land, they certainly drew income from the rights to dues which they did own. In fact, during the last quarter of the eighteenth century, they made insistent demands that the corvée be increased to 24 days a year.[94] The usual explanation is that after 1746, but particularly after the Treaty of Kuciuk-Kanarjik opened up the Black Sea to non-Ottoman ships and thus created the possibility for Wallachian cereal exports to Western Europe, the nobility began to seize demesne land on which to grow cereals. For that, they needed more corvée labor.[95]

That this was not actually the case was shown by Ilie Corfus. Even in the early nineteenth century, the lords had virtually no demesne land to cultivate. The laws of the second half of the eighteenth century and early nineteenth century specified that the corvée obligations did *not* have to be paid in labor, but could be paid in produce or money. The number of corvée days remained stable at 12 days a year (with a few temporary increases that were quickly abolished) while the price owed for each corvée day increased tremendously during this period; this shows that the *boieri* could satisfy their needs for more money and/or marketable produce through direct payment.[96]

[90] Georgescu, "Reflexions sur le statut," in *Nouvelles études*, **IV**; p. 140; and Emerit, "Condition des esclaves," in *Revue d'histoire* (1930).

[91] Oțetea, "Considerații," in *S.M.I.M.*, **IV**, pp. 349–350.

[92] *Ibid.*, p. 348.

[93] Georgescu, "Reflexions sur le statut," in *Nouvelles études*, **IV**, pp. 143–144. Valentin Georgescu and Emanuela Popescu, *La législation agraire de la Valachie (1775–1782)* (Bucharest: Académie roumaine, 1970) show that one problem was that the laws were written in Greek by Greek lawyers steeped in Byzantine tradition. As a result many of the codes try to divide the Wallachian rural classes into Byzantine categories, and this makes it difficult to interpret them because there was little correspondence between late Byzantine society and eighteenth century Romanian society. But the fact that the lords were not full "owners" of the land, even while they were its "controllers", is certain.

[94] Oțetea, "Considerații," in *S.M.I.M.*, **IV**, p. 353.

[95] *Ibid.*, p. 353; and Stahl, *Les anciennes communautés*, pp. 238–239. Both interpretations agree.

[96] Ilie Corfus, *Agricultura Țării Românești în prima jumătate a secolului al XIX-lea* (Bucharest: Editura academiei, 1969), p. 25.

The transformation of the Wallachian rural economy from a primarily pastoral to a primarily agricultural, cereal economy was a slow process which was not completed until the middle of the nineteenth century. But whereas there had always been a mix of agriculture and pastoralism, the balance began to shift toward agriculture during the eighteenth century.

One of the most important changes that made this transformation possible was the introduction of corn (maize) in the early eighteenth century.[97] By the 1740s, it had replaced millet as the main food cereal. Corn had several advantages. In the first place, the Turks did not eat it and thus did not requisition it.[98] Second, it had higher yields than millet[99] and in that respect, it added to the available supply of food and proved to be an inducement to the expansion of cereal cultivation.

By the late eighteenth and early nineteenth centuries, cereal cultivation had spread sufficiently so that it was an important part of the economies of the plains districts, especially those nearest the Danube and near Bucharest. In normal years, by about 1800, most plains districts produced cereal surpluses. The main cereals, in order of importance, were corn, wheat, millet, oats, and rye. The hill and mountain districts, on the other hand, had poor soils for cereal cultivation, and though they did grow some cereals (mostly corn), they remained more pastoral than agricultural (except for those hill districts favored with vines).[100]

Nevertheless, more of the population lived in the hills and mountains than on the plains. As in the past, one of the main reasons for this was that the plains were subject periodically to Turkish plundering raids. This became a particularly severe problem in the eighteenth century because of the decline of the central Ottoman authority over its Balkan provinces. Most of the raids into Wallachia were carried out by insubordinate Danube *pashas* from Bulgaria.[101] Even in the plains districts, population was more concentrated in the forest zones north and west of the open areas.[102] A reconstruction of rudimentary census data from 1810 shows that the hill and mountain districts had about 60% of the population, and the plains 40%.[103] But a rough calculation of the comparative areas[104] shows that the hill and mountain districts had only about

[97] A. M. del Chiaro mentions the existence of maize in his book written in 1718. See Warriner, *Contrasts in Emerging Societies*, p. 138. See also Traian Stoianovich, "Le maïs dans les Balkans," *Annales E.S.C.*, **XXI**, no. 5 (1966): 1028–1040.

[98] I. Claudian, *Alimentația poporului Român* (Bucharest: Fundația Regele Carol II, 1939), p. 97.

[99] Emerit, *Les paysans roumains*, p. 21.

[100] Corfus, *Agricultura Țării Româneşti*, pp. 60–65.

[101] Lewis, "Decline of the Ottoman Empire," in *Economic Decline of Empires*, pp. 232–233, discuss the rise of private armies and the collapse of central authority throughout the Ottoman state in the eighteenth century. See Emerit, *Les paysans roumains*, p. 49, on the raids of the Bulgarian *Pashas*.

[102] Corfus, *Agricultura Țării Româneşti*, p. 61.

[103] Ştefan Ciobanu, "Populația în Țările Româneşti la 1810," *Arhiva pentru ştiința şi reforma socială* **II**(1920); 90.

[104] Calculated from each county's geographical description and area as given in the county sections of *Enciclopedia României* (Bucharest: Imprimeria națională, 1938), **II**.

42% of the land (slightly more or less, depending on the definition of "hilly"). This indicates a population density for the hills and mountains close to twice as high as that for the plains (a little less than twice if Bucharest, with about 5% of the total Wallachian population, is included in the calculation as part of the plains, and a little more than twice if Bucharest is left out of the calculation).

The difference between the plains and the hills and mountains was the basis for a complex system of exchange between them. They could exchange cereals for animals and animal products. The demographic imbalance also created a yearly seasonal migration of hill and mountain people into the plains to cultivate cereals and then return to their villages after the harvest.[105] In November, the herds of sheep would be taken out of the hills toward the Danube plain, and in April they moved back into the hills. During the hot summer months, sheep were pastured in the high Carpathians.[106] This double movement of sheep and people is actually much older than the eighteenth century,[107] and its survival well into the nineteenth century indicates how wrong it would be to classify Wallachian villagers at this time purely as "peasants" attached to the land.

Agricultural techniques, even in the first decade of the nineteenth century, were poor. Plows were made entirely of wood, and only a few had metal tips. Villagers did not generally have enough animals to pull plows (8 to 10 oxen were required), and so they pooled their animals. There was virtually no rotation system, though in the most densely populated hill zones, where land was used repeatedly without rest, there was some manuring. Even there, the quantities of manure available were too small, and yields were very low. There was no manuring at all in the plains, because there was an overabundance of land; after 3 to 5 years of cultivation, fields would lie fallow for 3 to 6 years. In some cases, the fallow period was up to 10 years. In a few plains areas there was a rotation of corn and wheat in alternate years, and this somewhat extended the utility of a given piece of soil. In the steppe a very primitive slash–burn

[105] Corfus, *Agricultura Țării Românești*, pp. 65–66.

[106] There is a description of this transhumance pattern in the book of a Ragusan trader, S. Raicevich's, *Osservazioni storiche naturali e politiche intorno la Valchia e Moldavia* (Naples, 1788), exerpted in Warriner, *Contrasts in Emerging Societies*, pp. 139–140.

[107] Nicolae Dunăre, "Păstoritul de pendulare dublă pe teritoriul României," *Anuarul muzeului etnografical Transilvaniei per anii 1965–1967* (Cluj, Romania, 1969), pp. 115–138. In fact, the otherwise extraordinary homogeneity of Romanian culture and language throughout Transylvania, Moldavia, and Wallachia would be difficult to explain if one neglected the persistence of these transhumance patterns throughout Romanian history. Traian Herseni, in his *Probleme de sociologie pastorală* (Bucharest: Institutul de științe sociale, 1941), goes so far as to suggest that the very essence of Romanian culture is based on the historically ancient shared tradition of pastoralism. Though this is an excessively romantic view to take in explaining modern Romanian culture, it was certainly an important factor in the nineteenth century. Stahl's entire hypothesis about the importance of the communal village tradition is, of course, dependent on the persistence of pastoral habits until the last century or so. For a general discussion of Mediterranean transhumance patterns see Braudel, *La Méditerranée*, I, pp. 78–93. The map on pp. 88–89 shows the transhumance routes between the Carpathians and the Moldavian and Wallachian plains as well as the Transylvanian link.

itinerant cultivation was used.[108] This technology may be compared to that of Western Europe. In France, for example, by the early eighteenth century only a few isolated regions practiced so primitive a system of cultivation (usually in association with pastoralism), and these regions were considered "barbaric" and, economically, "anarchic."[109] Indeed, even in the Middle Ages, most of France followed either the biennial or triennial rotation systems, which were more sophisticated and productive than the irregular system practiced in eighteenth and nineteenth century Wallachia.[110]

Most of the plains villagers were *clăcaşi* and owed a tithe and corvée to lords (who were, it will be recalled, much more powerful in the plains than in the hills and mountains). Migrants from the mountains who cultivated during the summer either were sharecroppers, or else they rented land from the lords who controlled it.[111] There was so much land available in the plains, however, that there was no problem in finding any. The abundance of land was the underlying factor in the perpetuation of old forms of village organization and the vagueness of property laws with respect to land.

Aside from pastoral and agricultural occupations, villagers—especially those in the hills and mountains who had too little land to cultivate—had other occupations. The hills had numerous fruit trees and vines. The most important fruit was the prune from which *ţuica* (Romanian slivovitz) was made. Some of the hill and mountain people were transporters of salt and other goods exchanged between hills and plains, as well as between Wallachia and Transylvania. Also, some of the hill and mountain people hired themselves out as salaried workers in the plains, to help transport agricultural produce or to work in monastery fields. (Monasteries had limited demesne lands to produce their own food.) Others hired themselves out as shepherds for lords or for prosperous villagers who had animals.

Artisanry was also more highly developed in the hill zones. There were potters, carpenters, stone masons, and miners. The other region that specialized in nonagricultural work was along the Danube banks where there were many fishing villages.[112] In other words, despite the low level of agricultural technology, Wallachian village society was quite differentiated and had a complex exchange economy in which money played an important role. As pointed out in preceding chapters, this was already the case from at least the fifteenth century, and records show that village artisanry was a significant factor at least from that time.[113] This explains how it was possible for the corvée owed by

[108] Corfus, *Agricultura Ţării Româneşti*, pp. 66–68.

[109] March Bloch, *Les caractères originaux de l'histoire rurale française* (Oslo: H. Aschehoug, 1931), pp. 27–28.

[110] *Ibid.*, pp. 30–57.

[111] Corfus, *Agricultura Ţării Româneşti*, p. 64.

[112] *Ibid.*, pp. 68–72.

[113] See Ş. Olteanu and C. Şerban, *Meşteşugurile din Ţara Românească şi Moldova în evul mediu* (Bucharest: Editura academiei, 1969), pp. 52–63 and 111–112.

villagers to their lords to be paid in money, and how, in the absence of a significant lordly demesne, there were still ways for lords to extract an income from their *clăcaşi*, either directly or through the sale of products given as tithe or in lieu of the corvée.

The gradual extension of agriculture in the late eighteenth and early nineteenth centuries allowed the population to grow. One estimate for the year 1810 puts Wallachia's population at about 700,000.[114] Estimates of the population made in about 1820 vary around 1 million.[115] (This was twice as many people as at the height of the communal-trade society in about 1400, and more than six times as many people as during the low point reached about 1600.) This was not entirely due to natural population increase, however; despite the arbitrary and harsh rule of the Ottomans, the more Western-oriented Hungarian lords of Transylvania treated their serfs (who were generally ethnic Romanians) more harshly than did Wallachian lords.[116] Throughout the latter part of the eighteenth century there was a considerable net immigration of Romanians from Transylvania into Wallachia. There was also a migratory current from Bulgaria north into Wallachia.[117]

The State, the Nobles, and the Monasteries

After the collapse of Michael the Brave's reign, the anarchic, insolvent Wallachian state, torn by rifts between increasingly powerful nobles and a weakening princely state, may have seemed to be heading toward a sort of political "feudalism" in which the locus of power would become a legal fiction. This did not happen, because of two coordinate conditions. Wallachia's seignorialization was linked to the imposition of foreign rule; that is, Wallachia became a protocolonial society, and the Ottomans wanted to maintain a state structure capable of raising the necessary tribute. At the same time, the Ottomans did not want to destroy the system of indirect rule, and thus the Wallachian state structure had to be preserved in order to avoid the necessity of direct Turkish administration.

It is not totally clear why the Ottomans preserved this system of indirect rule in Moldavia and Wallachia, while in Serbia and Bulgaria they did not. P. P. Panaitescu suggests that until 1600 the Romanian principalities were too strong, and resisted too much to allow the imposition of direct rule. After 1600,

[114] Ciobanu, "Populaţia," in *Arhiva*, **II**, p. 90.

[115] Corfus, *Agricultura Ţării Româneşti*, p. 12.

[116] Serf revolts were much more common and more serious in Transylvania than in Wallachia. There is a substantial Romanian literature on these revolts. In particular, see Miron Constantinescu, *Cauzele sociale ale răscoalei lui Horia* (Ph.D. diss., Bucharest, 1938), on the revolt of 1784.

[117] Vlad, "Mişcări demografice," in *Studii şi articole*, **XIV**, pp. 84–85.

Moldavia and Wallachia ceased to be on the road to further conquests, and so were relatively ignored while the Ottoman Empire pursued more important matters. By the eighteenth century, when Moldavia and Wallachia had again become provinces vital to the empire because they were a source of tribute and food, the Ottoman state structure had begun to disintegrate and Constantinople considered the principalities too important to risk handing them over to potentially insubordinate *pashas*. Thus, while reinforcing its rule by using Phanariot Greek princes, the Porte still preserved a system of indirect rule.[118]

The decline of the power of the central state can be observed in the changing nature and size of the army under command of the prince. As noted previously, the army was originally composed of administrative nobles and lesser administrative personnel under the command of the prince. But by the seventeenth century, this situation had changed—the prince instead relied chiefly on a mercenary army, and the class of *curteni* (civil and military "courtiers") was in decay. In fact, the *curteni* was becoming a class of more independent lords who could not be counted on to provide a military force for the prince. *Dorobanţi* and *călăraşi*, professional soldiers, became the mainstay of the army. The size of the army also decreased drastically. In the sixteenth century, a prince could count on more than 10,000 soldiers. The great Prince Brâncoveanu had about 2000 soldiers in the late seventeenth century. That is to say that by 1700 the prince no longer had an army capable of fighting a war; at best, he had some private guards to control his estates and maintain some semblance of order.[119] This means that it was Ottoman power that kept the state from dissolving into the complete anarchy of political feudalism.

The chief mechanism that kept the nobility dependent on the prince was the need to collect taxes. But the way in which this was done maintained a balance between the nobles and the state such that neither one nor the other could gain complete control. And, while the central state survived, it was unable to replace its nobles with a royal bureaucracy more loyal to the prince and more dependable than the nobles who served it. A description of Moldavia, written in 1787 by the French envoy to that country, Count d'Hauterive (expressed in the form of recommendations to the Prince Alexander Ypsilanti) brings out this fact. Though pertaining to Moldavia, the conditions described were sufficiently similar to those in Wallachia to make the document instructive:

> One must observe what happens when a Hospodar [Prince] is crowned. A crowd of office seekers will gather around him, men who want to collect taxes, ambitious

[118] P. P. Panaitescu, *Interpretări româneşti* (Bucharest: Editura universul, 1947), pp. 145–159. See also Radu Florescu, "The Fanariot Regime in the Danubian Principalities," *Balkan Studies* **IX**, no. 2 (1968): 301–318.

[119] N. Stoicescu, "Contribution à l'histoire de l'armée roumaine au moyen-âge," *Revue roumaine d'histoire* **VI**, no. 5 (1967): 742–763.

> men who want the function of judge, men vain because of their name or because of some old favor who want to be excused from working and want rewards for doing nothing .... All the devices of a complex administration will be put to work to fatten tax receipts which will not always reach the treasury or stay there long. The upkeep of the court, the nation's debts, those of the Prince, his economy, that of his subordinate administrators, the Porte's tribute, disguised under different names and yielding indeterminate sums, will always leave one in the dark as to whether or not they are sufficient, will incessantly exhaust it [the treasury], and all these causes of dispersion, based on the resources of a province ravaged by six centuries of war, of conquests, of barbarianism, of despotism, will make the task of ruling a most difficult function, so difficult that seeing so many causes for oppression, the Prince, unless he be a genius of virtue, will not be able to flatter himself for long that he is governing justly.[120]

D'Hauterive went on to say that Alexander Ypsilanti would be able to face these problems, as he so ably had faced them while Prince of Wallachia (the Turks frequently rotated princes from one principality to the other). In reference to the Moldavian nobility, d'Hauterive wrote:

> I wish I could hide the fact that lately these excellent habits [he is referring to a previous explanation of the Moldavian nobles' fondness for rustic life in their villages—a fondness, he notes, not shared by Wallachian nobles] have changed and the consequences are already all too obvious. The nobles are leaving their rural abode, seduced by the advantages to be gained at court, which they prefer to the honest savings of rural life, less profitable but more sure. They insist on trying to obtain positions which they do not always get, which they do not keep long, which do not pay the debts contracted while trying to gain it, and only bring the short-lived pleasure of distorting their names with yet another hyphen on their signatures.[121]

He added that these new habits (which were probably not so new, in fact, but d'Hauterive yielded to the temptation of comparing his present to the "good old days") made the master hard with his vassals (the *clăcași*), causing them to run away to other countries or to lords who were more lenient. He noted that the nobles in Wallachia had fallen even more deeply into these "sinful" ways.[122]

The origins of tax farming in the sixteenth century have already been described. During the seventeenth and eighteenth centuries, the favor of the princes in appointing men to court positions virtually created a new nobility that also took over the old nobility's power in rural villages. In a state demanding ever more taxes, the crucial factor for a noble was whether or not he could get exemptions and whether or not he could supplement his income with a court or local administrative position.[123] The corrupting influence of this tradi-

[120] le Comte d'Hauterive, *Mémoire sur l'état ancien et actuel de la Moldavie, présenté à S.A.S. Le Prince Alexandre Ypsilanti, Hospodar regnant en 1787* (Bucharest: Carol Göbl, 1902), pp. 168–170.

[121] *Ibid.*, pp. 182–184.

[122] *Ibid.*, pp. 168, 176, 186.

[123] *Ibid.*, and Ciurea, "Quelques considérations," in *Nouvelles études*, **IV**, pp. 86–87.

tion, particularly for the eighteenth century, cannot be underestimated, and it was to leave a legacy that still persists in modern Romania.

After the inception of Phanariot rule, the increased power of the Turks in choosing princes, the temporary nature of the princely appointments, and the connections of the ruling houses with Greek and Levantine commerce transformed the throne into an investment. Each prince had to bribe so many Turkish officials that he frequently spent his entire rule recouping, as d'Hauterive described. The system, in turn, spread to officialdom which gained office in the same way. Furthermore, the princes tended to appoint more and more Greeks to the nobility; these men, living lives of ease in a country that was not theirs, and owing allegiance to the Turks, also regarded their posts as lucrative investments. This was even truer in Wallachia than in Moldavia, as d'Hauterive noted.

In the eighteenth century, nobles commonly lived in the towns, particularly in Bucharest, rather than in the villages they controlled. It even became common for them to rent out the rights to their villages, and to let the "estate farmers" recoup their own investments by extracting, as best they could, the maximum from the *clăcași*. But it was not simply "vice" that prompted Wallachian nobles to live in Bucharest. The countryside was terrorized by runaway villagers mixed in with assorted Turkish deserters, Albanians, Serbs, Bulgars, and Gypsies who lived by brigandage (the *Haiduci*). Outside of Bucharest no one was safe from attack. The estate farmers trying to make quick profits in the villages were ruthless and arbitrary, to the point of frequently violating customary villager rights. While the villagers lived precarious lives, squeezed by bandits, farmers, nobles, and the state, the big *boieri* lived in extravagant Oriental splendor in Bucharest.[124]

During the eighteenth century, repeated attempts were made to rationalize the taxation system in order to limit corruption and loss of revenues.[125] But the problem was too deeply structural to be solvable. Revenues to pay an honest officialdom were insufficient and the entire government, from the prince on down, was put into the position of having to maximize short-term revenues before the incumbent prince was replaced and a new set of officials appointed.

Possibly, if the princes had been truly independent and if they had a more secure power basis, a more solid state bureaucracy might have been built. But given the power of the Turks, an uneasy balance of forces between the princes and their administrative nobility was maintained.

One important consequence of the way in which relations between the state and the *boieri* developed in the eighteenth century was that a strict legal distinction was made between the high *boieri*, who had high court offices, and the petty *boieri*, who had lower posts or none at all. The distinction had in fact existed before, but in 1739 Mavrocordat created two legal categories of nobles,

[124] Emerit, *Les paysans roumains*, pp. 31 and 51; and Corfus, *Agricultura Țării Românești*, pp. 36–37.
[125] Mihordea, "Crise du régime fiscal," in *Nouvelles études*, **IV**, p. 132.

and the high nobles were granted tax exemptions while the others were not.[126] This tended to aggravate the hostility the lesser *boieri* felt toward the more important *boieri*, as there was a direct competition between them for villagers to populate their villages.[127] But the favored position of a few noble families apparently allowed them to extend their control over many villages, such that by the early nineteenth century, a few *boieri* controlled large numbers of villages, while most of the petty nobility controlled only one, or even just a part of a village.[128]

In order to round out the picture of agrarian class relations about 1800, it is necessary to examine the role of the monasteries. So far, these have been mentioned very little, because (1) as a whole, the Orthodox church did not often play an important political role, and (2) monasteries that controlled villages had interests similar to those of the *boieri*. But because monasteries held land in mortmain, by this period they had accumulated control over an enormous amount of land. Furthermore, under Ottoman domination, many monasteries had been "dedicated" to Greek monasteries elsewhere in the Empire (i.e., Athos, Jerusalem, Sinai, Alexandria, Antioch, etc.) in order to secure them against Turkish depredations. These monasteries were headed by Greeks, and large sums were sent annually to the parent institutions outside Wallachia. These monasteries were therefore more interested in making money for the Greek church than in performing services for the Wallachian population, and the hospitals, schools, and chapels they were supposed to maintain more often than not were in ruins.

Aside from the support they received from the Greeks, these monasteries also were increasingly supported during the eighteenth century by the growing political influence of the Russians, who looked on them as potential allies. By about 1800, monasteries controlled about one-third of all the land in Moldavia and Wallachia, and roughly half of this amount was controlled by the "dedicated"—that is, Greek-run—monasteries.[129] The proportion of land controlled by the "dedicated" monasteries may, in fact, have been even higher. In 1810, of 204 Wallachian monasteries, 120 were "dedicated."[130]

This, then, was the way Wallachian society was structured at the start of the nineteenth century. There was a corrupt, avaricious government, run by Greeks with the aid of venal Greek–Romanian nobles. There were foreign-controlled monasteries that controlled large amounts of land. Taxes were high. Most rural folk were virtually serfs. Banditry was rampart. But underneath this, old forms of village organization, based on the traditional agri-pastoral economy, were

[126] Emerit, *Les paysans roumains*, p. 30.

[127] Stahl, *Les anciennes communautés*, pp. 233–234.

[128] Oțetea, "Considerații," in *S.M.I.M.*, **IV**, p. 351.

[129] Emerit, *Les paysans roumains*, pp. 25–27.

[130] Ciobanu, "Populația," in *Arhiva*, **II**, p. 92.

still strong. The period of Ottoman colonialism had fostered a growing export economy and, though the main beneficiaries were the semi-Greek nobility and the Levantine town merchants, life in the villages had begun to change. The economy had become more dependent on cereal cultivation than it previously had been. But all this was just a beginning. In the nineteenth century most of the colonial characteristics of Wallachian society were to become more prominent, because once Wallachia was freed from Ottoman domination and opened to the liberating winds of the Western capitalist economy, its own economy could be "modernized"—that is, colonialized—much more thoroughly.

The changes that followed the end of Ottoman control over Wallachia were largely determined by the changing international context. Therefore, in order to trace the shift from a protocolonial political economy to a truly modern, colonial political economy, the changing international scene must be summarized. Only then can the effects of this change in Wallachian society, particularly rural society, be spelled out.

6

The Transition to Modern Colonialism (1821–1864)

The insistence on the term "colonialism" must be qualified. Except for the few years in which post-1821 Wallachia was directly administered by the Russian army, the real colonial masters of the country were neither in direct control nor even always particularly aware of the details of what was going on inside the country. In fact, Wallachia evolved into something that seems particularly modern: a neocolony, an indirectly controlled state in which there was no single metropole but rather a consortium of overseers. Further, the most proximate great powers, Austria, Russia, and Turkey, were not exactly the most advanced industrial powers in Europe. They had relatively little need for an added agrarian province to serve as an extra supplier of primary products and as a market for their own industrial goods. It was Western Europe that was the more logical metropole for colonial Wallachia, and Wallachia developed in the nineteenth century as a colonial outpost of the more advanced Western economies. In order to see how this happened, it is essential to place Wallachia in the international context of that time. This involves the repetition of a large number of well-known facts studied by diplomatic historians. As such, the discussion of the international scene may seem to disrupt the story of the evolution of Wallachian society, but the diplomatic history of the period is the necessary backdrop to the story of internal social change.

The main actors in this unfolding international scene, at least as far as Wallachia was concerned, were the Russians, the Austrians (later Austro-Hungarians), the declining Ottoman Empire, the more distant but crucial power of Great Britain, and the less powerful but periodically important influence of France. Various combinations of these powers, joined by Germany in the last third of the century, played crucial economic and political roles in all the major events that shaped Wallachia and Moldavia. The other international actors—Bulgaria, Serbia, Sardinia, and Greece—were much less important, and were themselves the pawns of the major powers. The balance of political forces in the Balkans allowed Wallachia and Moldavia to become increasingly independent, at least formally. But the foreign economic influences had a more profound influence in the area than did the somewhat superficial political machinations of the great powers. While international political events were confused and often hard to follow, economic and social change was clearly much more one-directional.

Before beginning the account of the international context in which Wallachia found itself at the end of the Napoleonic Wars, it would be appropriate to review the Balandier model of colonial societies which was specified in Chapter 5, for it is this that gives cohesiveness to the whole story. In a colonial society:

1. The economy is characterized by a quest for raw materials or agricultural products to be used by the industrialized metropolitan economy or economies.
2. Import–export trade is in the hands of the metropolitans, but they may act through the hands of local agents who are frequently "pariah capitalists," that is, foreigners who have adapted to the ways of the colonial masters on the one hand, and to the ways of the natives on the other.
3. There is a large-scale property dispossession of the native peasants, either by native or foreign landowners, in order to extract the agricultural surplus out of the hands of the rural producers. The type of crops grown may change in order to suit the demands of the metropole.
4. The purely indigenous economy stagnates as old forms of economic endeavor dry up and are replaced by metropolitan manufactured imports (the colonial sector, however, grows).
5. A great distance separates the agents of the metropole and the natives who are relegated to the roles of laborer, servant, and peasant.
6. The locus of the colonial or enclave society is the capital and chief trade city in which the elite clusters and develops a way of life quite foreign to traditional native ways. The enclave becomes a cultural as well as an economic adjunct of the metropole.
7. The polity is in the hands of the colonial elite, but the metropolitan power

or powers retain a veto over important acts in order to protect key economic rights.

Because we are now talking about a true colonial political economy, and not a protocolonial political economy, a few of the points suggested in Chapter 5 have been strengthened. In particular, the metropole or metropoles are primarily interested in the colonies to further their own industrial development. They are no longer primarily interested in mere maintenance of military rule, or even in tribute. As long as the economic interests of the industrial metropole can be satisfied without direct rule, the metropole prefers to remain in the political background. This was the case for Wallachia after about 1860. Also, the stimulus to produce an exportable surplus increases, and the property dispossession of the peasants becomes more marked. Labor requirements increase, and the economic power of the world capitalist market penetrates more deeply than the decrees of a traditional empire. As a consequence, modern neocolonies can change much more rapidly and fundamentally than protocolonies, even if they remain formally independent.

After the discussion of international events, the changing political economy of Wallachia will be shown to have followed this general model quite closely.

The International Context

The first great power to take an interest in Wallachian and Moldavian affairs in the seventeenth and eighteenth centuries (other than the Ottoman Empire) was Austria. As explained in the previous chapter, this interest was at once commercial and political. But in the late eighteenth century, and especially in the early nineteenth, Austrian policy abandoned the goal of absorbing the principalities and concentrated instead on maintaining commercial privileges. In large measure, this change was a result of two factors. First, there was the emergence of the "nationalities" issue accompanied by Austria's incapacity to deal with increasing protest against its rule of those Slavic, Hungarian, and Romanian (Transylvanian) territories already within its boundaries. Second, the Napoleonic Wars shifted Austria's center of attention westward and gave it a new nationalities problem after the annexation of northern Italy. After 1815, therefore, Metternich's legitimist policy concentrated on preserving the status quo rather than on trying to force a revision of Balkan boundaries. Furthermore, because Russia was an important ally in this policy, it was deemed preferable to let Russia have a free hand in the Romanian principalities in return for its continued political support in the rest of Europe. But once Ottoman rule had effectively ended in the 1820s, Austria–Hungary became Wallachia's main trading partner. The main export items, as in the past, were animals and animal products. In return, Wallachia imported manufactured goods. Though Austria ceased to interfere directly in Wallachian political affairs, it retained a primary commercial position in Wallachia and Moldavia until the 1870s.[1]

Russia's interest and influence in Wallachian and Moldavian affairs was more direct and powerful. In the eighteenth and nineteenth centuries, Russia conducted a series of wars against the Ottoman Empire whose ultimate goal was control of the Black Sea and of the straits between the Black and Mediterranean Seas. The principalities were on the road to Constantinople and were occupied wholly or in part by Russian armies in 1711, 1736–1739, 1769–1774, 1787–1792, 1806–1812, 1828–1834, 1849–1852, and in 1853. The first major Russian triumph in this series of wars was sealed by the Treaty of Kutchuck-Kainarji in 1774. This treaty between the Russian and Ottoman Empires partially opened the Black Sea, and gave the Russians the right to place a consul in Bucharest. By the Treaty of Bucharest in 1812, Russia's consul was given wide powers of interference in local affairs (and Russia annexed that part of Moldavia called Bessarabia). From the time of this treaty, Ottoman rule became more theoretical than actual. But the final step in this process was the Treaty of Adrianople in 1829, which gave Russia virtually complete control over the principalities (though they continued to pay a token tribute to the Turks and remained officially Ottoman dependencies). The only force that prevented complete Russian annexation of the principalities was general European opposition to such an act, an opposition led by Great Britain.[2]

Russian interest was not directly economic, in that the principalities offered nothing Russia did not already have (except that by mid-century they were a source of competition to the Ukrainian cereal trade and to the port of Odessa). The probability of turning the principalities into a useful market for Russian products was equally insignificant. As Barbara Jelavich has written:

> Although the Russian government was naturally concerned with the internal structure of the Principalities, it was the international position of the provinces which took precedence in the formulation of Russian policy. From 1829 to 1856, the years of the Russian protectorate, the predominant motives of Russian administration had been to establish orderly and effective governments in the Principalities, which would in turn protect Russian interests in the area. An economically flourishing countryside

[1]L. Boicu, "Considérations sur la politique des Habsbourg à l'égard des principautés roumaines (depuis le XVIIIe siècle jusqu'en 1848)," in *Nouvelles études d'histoire* (Bucharest: Académie roumaine, 1955–1970), **IV**, pp. 157–169; Constantin C. Giurescu, M. Gr. Romanşcanu, and Nicholas Georgescu-Roegen, "Comerţul exterior," in *Enciclopedia României* (Bucharest: Imprimeria naţională, 1943), **IV**, p. 465; Ştefan Zeletin, *Burghezia română* (Bucharest: Cultura naţională, 1925), p. 42.

[2]Radu Florescu, *The Struggle Against Russia in the Roumanian Principalities: A Problem in Anglo–Turkish Diplomacy 1821–1854*, Acta Historica II, Societas Academica Dacoromana (Rome, 1962), pp. 63–65; Barbara Jelavich, *Russia and the Rumanian National Cause 1858–1859*, Slavic and East European Series, XVII (Bloomington, Ind.: Indiana University Publications, 1959), pp. 1–3.

> would offer provisions for Russian armies moving toward Constantinople and stable conservative government under Russian domination would insure a strategic bastion on the Danube.[3]

British interest was more complicated. It had been minimal before 1821, but as a result of the Greek revolt against Ottoman rule and the British realization that its vital interests in the Mediterranean would be endangered if the Russians replaced the Ottomans in the eastern Mediterranean, this lack of interest was transformed into a lively concern. Writing about 1821, Harold Nicolson noted that, "In the shape of the Eastern Question a new and lasting controversy, political, strategic and economic, had come to sunder Russia from the West."[4] There is no point in outlining the well-known British effort to keep the Ottoman Empire afloat against Russian pressure throughout most of the nineteenth century. It need only be pointed out that Wallachia was as much a part of this issue, though a less well-known part, as Serbia, Bulgaria, or Greece.

Great Britain also developed an economic interest in the principalities as a result of the Treaty of Adrianople. Because the treaty opened the Black Sea to Western ships, it became possible to export Romanian cereals to Western Europe. At the same time, the Romanian market was opened to Western manufactured products, particularly cloth. In 1837, 379 ships called at the ports of Brăila and Galaţi (the chief ports of Wallachia and Moldavia, respectively). Only 15 of these ships were British, but the principalities exported 563,000 quarters of wheat to Britain in that year. By 1840, 864,000 quarters of wheat were exported to Britain, and by 1848, 132 of the 1132 ships that called at Brăila and Galaţi were British. In 1837, British exports to the principalities were worth 97,405 pounds sterling; by 1848, they were worth 606,694 pounds. By the 1850s, Britain's trade with the principalities was an important (though still secondary) consideration in its attitude toward Russian domination. Though only 2% of Britain's grain imports at that time came from Wallachia and Moldavia, the share of the British market held by the principalities was growing rapidly. In 1853, about one-third of the ships calling at Brăila and Galaţi were either British or bound for Britain.[5]

Nevertheless, it would be wrong to assume that Great Britain's economic interests in the principalities were important enough to explain its policies toward them. From the perspective of Romanian historians (for example, Florescu and Zeletin), 2% of Britain's cereal imports was a large proportion. (The imbalance is familiar—what is a minor component of trade for a big industrial power can be of vital concern to one of its minor economic colonies

[3] Jelavich, *Russia and the Rumanian National Cause*, p. 11.

[4] Harold Nicolson, *The Congress of Vienna: A Study in Allied Unity 1812–1822* (New York: Viking, Compass Books, 1961), p. 269.

[5] Florescu, *Struggle Against Russia*, pp. 262–263; and Zeletin, *Burghezia română*, pp. 45–46.

or neocolonies.) However, from the British perspective, the whole Romanian question was but one part of the rivalry with Russia which was played out on a global scale.[6]

The other great power concerned was France. But for all of its cultural influence ("our great Latin sister") which dated back to the mid-eighteenth century, France played only a secondary role throughout most of the nineteenth century and was important only in the 1850s and 1860s, during the reign of Napoleon III. French trade with the principalities was growing during the nineteenth century, but it never rivaled that of Austria or Great Britain; and its concern with the "Eastern Question" was never as great as that of Russia or Great Britain.[7] France did, however, play an ideological role, most importantly as a source of inspiration for liberal and revolutionary doctrine and as a home for exiled Wallachian and Moldavian revolutionaries and reformers. France's cultural attraction was also important because many sons of the Wallachian and Moldavian *boieri* were sent there for their education.[8]

Though the Ottoman Empire lost effective control over the Danubian principalities in the 1820s, it remained the suzerain in theory, and it periodically interfered in local affairs until a much later date. It continued to receive a small tribute and was part of the diplomatic maneuverings that encompassed the principalities until 1878, when united Romania (consisting of both principalities) was finally declared a fully independent kingdom.[9]

The Organic Regulation and Russian Rule

In 1821 there was a confused anti-Ottoman revolt in Moldavia and Wallachia. One part was led by Greeks, who hoped to stir the entire Balkans against the Turks and recreate a European Byzantium. Another part was led by a minor Wallachian *boier*, Tudor Vladimirescu. Unlike the Greeks, Vladimirescu raised popular enthusiasm for his cause in the villages by promises of reform and liberation from Turkish and *boieri* excesses. He apparently received the support of the lesser nobility, which was hostile to the few dominant big *boieri* families. The revolt broke down into a series of complicated diplomatic maneuverings between Russia, the Ottoman Empire, Austria, and Great Britain. Vladimirescu (who some claim was a Greek agent who got carried away with himself and

[6]W. G. East, *The Union of Moldavia and Wallachia, 1859* (Cambridge: Cambridge University Press, 1929), pp. 26–30.

[7]Florescu, *Struggle Against Russia*, pp. 70–72; East, *Union of Moldavia and Wallachia*, pp. 47–50; Zeletin, *Burghezia română*, p. 46.

[8]Florescu, *Struggle Against Russia*, pp. 223–241; Pompiliou Eliade, *La Roumanie au XIXe siècle* (Paris: Hachette, 1914), II, (1828–1834), pp. 302–347; Dan Berindei, *L'Union des principautés roumaines* (Bucharest: Académie roumaine, 1966), pp. 54–55.

[9]Robert L. Wolff, *The Balkans of Our Times* (New York: Norton, 1967), pp. 84–85.

tried to take over the revolt) was murdered by some Greek officers in his entourage. The Greek leader, Alexander Ypsilanti (a Phanariot noble educated in Russia, whose family was important in the principalities and in Constantinople), was a former Russian general, and he expected Russian help in his revolt. He did not receive it because the Austrians and British pressured Russia into neutrality. Nor was Ypsilanti able to raise popular support after the murder of Vladimirescu. Finally, a Turkish army invaded Wallachia and crushed the revolt. (In Greece events took a different turn, because the revolt had popular support.) The revolt did, however, have a lasting effect: The Turks no longer trusted the Greek princes who had been involved in the conspiracy, and they acceded to Wallachian and Moldavian demands for the reinstallation of native princes.[10]

In 1828 another war broke out between Russia and the Ottoman Empire, and Russia occupied the principalities.[11] In 1829 the two powers signed the Treaty of Adrianople, which opened the Black Sea to the ships of all countries and gave Russia the right to occupy and reorganize Wallachia and Moldavia. Forced grain deliveries from the principalities to the Turks were stopped and Turkish trade monopolies were abolished.[12]

As a result of this new war and the Russian occupation, the Wallachian economy was in a shambles. There were heavy requisitions by the Russian army. A serious famine and plague broke out, and the incidence of brigandage rose.[13] As noted earlier it was in the interest of the Russians to redress the situation and create an economically viable province. The man chosen to do this was the Russian governor, Count Paul Kiselev. He set about reforming the principalities so that they could serve as a source of food for the Russian army. In many ways, his intentions were the same as those of the Austrians when they had occupied Oltenia a century earlier. The main idea was to get the villagers to grow more cerals. Many of the results of his reforms were also similar (see Chapter 5).

A more modern administration was established with a permanent police force, a postal system, and a small standing army. Roads were built and the long-neglected Danube ports were refurbished. The cumbersome Phanariot tax system was simplified by the elimination of many taxes and the consolidation of the treasury into a single administrative body. Grain reserves were established

[10]Andrei Oțetea, "Les grandes puissances et le mouvement Hétairiste dans les principautés roumaines," *Balkan Studies* **VII**, no. 2 (1966): 379–394; Alexandre Despotopoulos, "La révolution grecque, Alexandre Ypsilantis et la politique de la Russie," *Balkan Studies* **VII**, no. 2 (1966): 395–410; Florescu, *Struggle Against Russia*, pp. 85–107; Lucrețiu Pătrășcanu, *Un veac de frămîntări sociale 1821–1907*, 2nd. ed. (Bucharest: Editura politică, 1969), pp. 72–95. Pătrășcanu presents the clearest expression of the current official Romanian interpretation of 1821. Vladimirescu was a hero leading the peasant masses against the *boieri* tyrants. The revolt was the start of modern Romanian history. Many Romanian historians from before 1944 agree with this kind of interpretation.

[11]Andrei Oțetea *et al.*, *Istoria Romîniei* (Bucharest: Editura academici, 1964), **III**, pp. 934–937.

[12]Eliade, *Roumanie au XIXe siècle*, **II**, pp. 39–48.

[13]*Ibid.*, pp. 5–30.

in the villages (perhaps with the future needs of the Russian army in mind). A health service was created to combat epidemics.[14]

But though Kiselev seems to have wanted to improve the lot of the villagers, the Russians were obliged to rely on local elements to support them and run the economy (as had the Austrians before them in Oltenia). This meant relying on the high nobility and the Orthodox monasteries which controlled much of the land. Nor was the favored position of the ecclesiastic and high lay nobility merely a matter of expediency. French liberal ideas notwithstanding, the Russian governor was under the orders of Czar Nicholas. As Barbara Jelavich has noted: "Russian reliance on the conservative boyards, indeed upon a few families of the great boyards as the legitimate power in the state, corresponded with Nicholas's general support of established institutions throughout Europe."[15] Russian policy in the principalities was perfectly consistent with Russian military and political needs, as well as with Russia's ideological predispositions. It is reminiscent of many similar arrangements between a colonial power and a native aristocracy. In many ways, the period of Russian rule was a typical example of "indirect colonial rule" in which a local land-controlling aristocracy profited from the colonial situation. This and the rigors of Russian requisitioning policy explain the passionate hatred Wallachian villagers felt for both the Russians and the high Wallachian *boieri*. It follows that the high nobility and the Orthodox monasteries were pro-Russian, while during the entire period from 1829 to 1864, Romanian nationalist revolutionaries were resolutely hostile to the triumvirate of high *boieri*, dedicated monasteries, and Russian autocracy.[16]

The Russian reforms were embodied in a document called the Organic Regulation whose first published version appeared in 1831. Its main provision simplified and standardized land tenure arrangements in the *boieri*- and monastery-controlled villages. Though Kiselev believed the new arrangements to be more equitable for the villagers, nobles' opinions were taken into account in framing the document. Villagers (the *clăcași*) were guaranteed (1) small allotments of land for their houses and gardens (from 1000 to 1500 square meters), (2) grazing land for their animals (which varied according to the number of animals they owned), and (3) up to 3 additional hectares of arable land for each family. For this, the villagers were to pay the customary 12 days of corvée labor (*clacă*) and also several other days for various other services. The old tithe (*dijmă*) paid to the lords was maintained; but, since it had in fact tended to vary from region to region and to exceed the original amount of 10% of production, the tithe was standardized at 10%. The lordly monopolies on alcohol, mills,

[14]Marcel Emerit, *Les paysans roumains depuis le traité d'Andrinople jusqu'à la libération des terres (1829–1864)* (Paris: Recueil Sirey, 1937), pp. 62–66.

[15]Jelavich, *Russia and the Rumanian National Cause*, p. 11.

[16]See the works cited by Eliade, Florescu, Jelavich, and Emerit.

sale of forest wood, and bridge tolls were affirmed. Under no circumstances were the lords obliged to yield more than two-thirds of the lands they controlled. This meant that in crowded villages some of the villagers' claims under the Organic Regulation were not satisfied. (Later, this provision was somewhat relaxed, but the Regulation firmly supported the principle that lords had the right to do what they wanted with one-third of village lands.) Freedom of movement for the villagers was formally guaranteed, but it was again hedged so much by substantive restrictions as to be virtually worthless.[17]

Because the arbitrary power of the lords theoretically was curbed, because taxes, the corvées, and tithes were standardized and simplified, and because villagers were guaranteed at least minimal use of land, the Organic Regulation was deemed an improvement over the arrangements that had prevailed in the Phanariot period. In reality, the new law marked a great advance in the power of the lords who controlled most of the villages, especially those few high *boieri* families who had concentrated vast numbers of villages under their control during the eighteenth century. First of all, free use of forests and pastures was restricted. (It will be recalled that free use of forests had been partially restricted in the eighteenth century, but under the Organic Regulation this right was further restricted; for the first time, lords were allowed to put an upper limit on the amount of land that could be freely used for pasture.) Second, each day of labor owed by the *clăcaşi* was defined in terms of work that had to be completed, so that it actually amounted to considerably more work than could be accomplished in one day. Because it was common to commute corvée obligations into payments in kind or cash, a large part of the Organic Regulation was devoted to stipulating what payments were owed for each day of commuted labor (there were regional and seasonal variations), for the *boieri* were still more interested in cash dues than corvées. Third, and most important, local administration was left in the hands of lords and their agents, so the provisions of the Regulation were interpreted in each village by the lords' agents. This obviously allowed unfair and quite variable interpretations of the law.

The number of real days of corvée labor owed by the *clăcaşi* has never been properly determined (Bălcescu's work of 1850 remains the basic reference book for this question), but there is general agreement that the 12-day limit was purely theoretical and that the actual number of days owed was considerably higher. Furthermore, it rose continually during the 1830s and 1840s so that by mid-century, it amounted to about 56 real days of labor, instead of 12. Since the price of commutation was also subject to *boier* interpretations, the burden of the corvée was also raised by increasing that price.

[17] Ilie Corfus, *Agricultura Ţării Româneşti în prima jumătate a secolului al XIX-lea* (Bucharest: Editura academiei, 1969), pp. 77–79, 87–89, 96–102; Eliade, *Roumanie au XIXe siècle*, **II**, pp. 84–97; Andrei Oţetea, "Consideraţii asupra trecerea de la feudalism la capitalism în Moldova, şi Ţara Romînească," in *S.M.I.M.*, **IV**, pp. 361–364; Emerit, *Les paysans roumains*, pp. 80–87.

Finally, the Regulation clarified that question of land ownership by stipulating that the lords controlled at least one-third of village lands (except, of course, in the remaining traditional free villages of *moşneni*). Though this was not yet an outright assertion of clear ownership, but still of "control" (the lord continued to be called master of the land—*stăpîn de moşie*—not owner, *proprietar*), the new law certainly gave the lords a firmer legal basis for that control than they had previously.[18]

Radu Rosetti, writing in 1907 about the origins of the disastrous impasse of the agrarian situation, noted that "the Organic Regulation was the triumph of the oligarchy and constituted the culminating point which this oligarchy succeeded in reaching."[19] Rosetti's assertion may have been exaggerated, for, as will be seen, the power of the lords continued to grow. But the high *boieri* families quickly realized the advantages of the new system, and when direct Russian military occupation ended in 1834 it left behind a strongly Russophilic land-controlling elite.[20]

The villagers, on the other hand, quickly saw the disadvantages of the new law and in 1831 there were several scattered rebellions. These were, however, quickly crushed. As usual, the only recourse was flight, and the tempo of emigration from Wallachia by villagers from border areas once again picked up, at least temporarily. Though these movements led to a more gradual application of the new law and to a softening of some of its harsher provisions, the Regulation was not changed in any basic way.[21]

Rural Society under the Organic Regulation

During the three and one-half decades between the Treaty of Adrianople and the land reform of 1864, the Wallachian rural economy shifted from being primarily pastoral to a primarily cereal-growing economy. Though the change had begun earlier (as noted in Chapter 5), it was during this period that the Wallachian villager finally was transformed into an agricultural peasant. A series of major changes resulted from this basic transformation. The most important one was that the nobility became a true landowning class, rather than simply a land-controlling class. At the start of the period, there was little

[18] Dimitrie Gusti, "Chestiunea agrară," *D. Gusti: Opere*, ed. O. Bădina and O. Neamţu (Bucharest: Editura academiei, (1970), **IV**, pp. 43–44; Corfus, *Agricultura Ţării Româneşti*, pp. 93–94, 103–107; Emerit, Les paysans *roumains*, pp. 94–96; Nicolae Bălcescu, *Question économique des principautés danubiennes* (Paris, 1850).

[19] Radu Rosetti, *Pentru ce s'au răsculat ţăranii* (Bucharest: Socec, 1908), p. 269.

[20] Wolff, *Balkans in Our Times*, p. 79. Kiselev favored an indefinite occupation of the principalities and even outright annexation by Russia. But to preserve Austrian friendship in European affairs, the Russian government rejected this. Jelavich, *Russia and the Rumanian National Cause*, p. 11.

[21] Oţetea, "Consideraţii," in *S.M.I.M.*, **IV**, pp. 364–366; Emerit, *Les paysans roumains*, pp. 88–92, 120–125; Rosetti, *Pentru ce*, pp. 76–77.

lordly demesne land; by the end of the period, the situation was beginning to change and lords were drawing an increasing amount of their revenues by actually making the *clăcaşi* work the land, instead of merely paying taxes for the use of land.

Given the rising Western demand for Wallachian cereals and the great power of the lords at the start of the period, it was more or less inevitable that they would turn the changes in the economy to their advantage. There were two corollaries to this change. The first was that the peasants' position vis-à-vis the lords was seriously weakened. Second, the more intensive use of land permitted by the economic shift from animals to cereals increased the food supply and facilitated a veritable population explosion.

The combination of these four factors—the shift to cereal cultivation, the increased power of the lords, the subjection of the peasants, and the rapidly growing population—produced the agrarian crisis of the last four decades of the nineteenth century and the first two decades of the twentieth. All of these factors were related to Wallachia's absorbtion by the European (by then, worldwide) market economy, into which the Ottoman Empire itself was being incorporated. But the basis of noble power, the foreign domination of external commerce, the role played in Wallachia's cities by foreign (mainly Greek) merchants, and the tradition of inefficient, corrupt government which precluded the possibility of meaningful reform, all were established before 1829. The transformation of the rural economy after 1829 intensified these characteristics; it did not create them.

From 1831 to 1835, the average yearly production of Wallachian wheat was about 105 million litres. From 1836 to 1840, it rose to a yearly average of about 120 million litres. From 1841 to 1845, it more then doubled to a yearly average of about 270 million litres. Production fell after that time because of several bad seasons and the social disorders caused by the revolution of 1848.[22] But in the 1850s, it resumed its upward trend.[23]

Corn production also rose correspondingly. At the start of the period, in the 1830s, animal exports were still more important than cereal exports. The balance shifted in the 1840s, and by the 1850s cereal exports clearly were more important than animal exports. This shift also corresponded to the relatively decreasing role of Austria as a market for Wallachian goods and the relatively increasing roles of Great Britain and Western Europe as cereal markets for Wallachian wheat.[24]

From 1831 to 1859, the population of Wallachia increased from about

[22]Corfus, *Agricultura Țării Româneşti*, charts on pp. 302–379. The figures given are transformations of the traditional Wallachian measures into litres and the original data are approximate, so they should not be considered more than simply indicative of trends.

[23]Oțetea *et al.*, in *Istoria Romîniei*, **IV**, pp. 185–186, section by D. Berindei and V. Popovici.

[24]Emerit, *Les paysan roumains*, pp. 216–217, 229; Zeletin, *Burghezia română*, pp. 45–46.

1,500,000 to about 2,400,000, with an average yearly growth of over 2%. But while the growth in the mountain and hill regions was slightly over 1% a year, in the plains it was about 3% a year, suggesting considerable migration from the relatively crowded hills to the newly opened farm lands of the plains.[25] The growth of cereal production was much greater in the plains than in the hills, which were not well-suited to cereal agriculture.[26]

Two points must again be emphasized. First, the changes toward a cereal-growing economy had begun in the eighteenth century, and this explains why sustained population growth began well before 1829. The increase between 1810 and 1831 was anywhere from 50% to 100%; from 1831 to 1859, the population increase was on the order of 50%; and for the period from 1800 to 1860, the population almost tripled. Second, the nobles had been more powerful in the plains than in the hills and mountains since the sixteenth century, and this increased the advantages they reaped from the migration into the plains and the shift from the pastoral to the cereal rural economy.

In 1810 about 60% of the population lived in the hills and mountains (on some 42% of Wallachia's territory). By 1859, only about 52% of the population lived off the plains. Whereas the population density in the hills and mountains in 1810 was about twice as high as in the plains, by 1859 it was only about 50% higher. It seems that the population expansion began in the hills before 1829. After 1829, the growth of the hill regions slowed as many migrated to the plains on a permanent basis, instead of merely migrating seasonally during the growing season (see the previous chapter for an explanation of this movement). This growth was most marked in the Oltenian plain and was less evident in the Bărăgan steppe. The steppe remained a frontier area that still had seasonal, temporary villages that would empty after each growing season as people returned to the hills. Between 1810 and 1829 the hill and mountain counties increased their population about 2% each year, but the rate of increase was more rapid before 1829 than after. During this period the plains counties increased their population at the rate of about 3% per year. But whereas the general increase in the plains for the entire period was on the order of 300%, in the Oltenian plains counties of Dolj and Romanaţi there were increases of 600% to 700%.[27]

[25] C. Rusenescu and D. Bugă, "Territorial distribution and growth of the population between the Carpathians and the Danube, in the 19th and 20th centuries," *Revue roumaine de géologie, géophysique et géographie*, série de géographie 10, no. 1 (1966): 78.

[26] See the charts in Corfus, *Agricultura Țării Românești*, pp. 302–379.

[27] Rusenescu and Bugă, "Territorial distribution," in *Revue roumaine*, pp. 75–84; Vintilă Mihăilescu, "Așezările omenești din Câmpia Română la mijlocul și la sfârșitul secolului al XIX-lea," Academia Română, *Memoriile*, secțiune istorice 3rd ser. **IV**, no. 2 (1924); Ștefan Ciobanu, "Populația în Țările Românești la 1810," *Arhiva pentru știința și reforma socială* **II** (1920); C. Jormescu and I. Popa-Burcă, *Harta agronomică a României* (Bucharest: Carol Göbl, 1907), p. 18. The data from which these conclusions are drawn are at best tentative. Administrative boundaries between countries changed between 1810 and 1831, thus making it impossible to attempt a county-

These rough population data indicate that the Treaty of Adrianople was not the only (though it seems to have been the decisive) spur to the changes that took place in the economy. Before 1829 there had been a kind of anticipatory shift to plains agriculture, but much of the new cereal area was cultivated by migrants who returned to the hills each year. After 1829, however, the opening of new cereal markets in the West and the increased profitability of cereal cultivation prompted a more permanent migratory flow. Again, it is fruitless to speculate what would have happened had international events taken a different course; but it is worth noting that the plains probably would have been developed in any case. The difference would have been in the nature of that development, and it is evident that without the pressures of the international grain market, the relations between lords and peasants would have been different.

The migration to the plains was prompted chiefly by the new economic opportunities there. By migrating, peasants were likely to put themselves at the mercy of powerful lords who could exploit them. But though stories of lords' abuse of peasants abound, the opening of vast areas to cultivation did provide a large new food supply, and this rather than forced recruiting attracted immigrants. While the increasing cultivation of grain was cutting down the available amount of pasture land and the total number of animals, enough of both were left to afford the peasants a reasonably balanced diet. By migrating from the hills to the plains, peasant families could therefore increase their supply of cereals while keeping enough animals to supply their needs. There was little outright starvation at mid-century. Only toward the end of the century did the continuing shift away from animals to cereals, plus the rising population, create a food problem. Pellegra, a nutritional disease caused by excessive reliance on grains and thus by an unbalanced diet, became endemic only in the latter part of the century.[28] The transformation of the 1830s and 1840s therefore set the stage for the later agrarian crisis, without having an immediate impact.

In the 1830s and 1840s, wheat became the most widely cultivated cereal in the plains. But the tremendous increase of surface area cultivated in wheat did not directly result from actions taken by the lords who controlled much of the land. Instead, it was carried out by the peasants themselves. Had the lords really "owned" estates, in the usual sense of that word, they would have used the labor obligations owed to them to develop extensive demesne lands on which to

Ftn. 27 (continued)

by-county comparison. But even aside from this, the census data of the first half of the nineteenth century are based on educated guesses rather than on properly conducted censuses. General trends can be deduced from the data, but a precise enumeration is not feasible.

[28]I. Claudian, *Alimentația poporului român* (Bucharest: Fundația Regele Carol II, 1939), p. 111; and Emerit, *Les paysans roumains*, pp. 270–277, 284–285. On the general relationship between the spread of commercial agriculture, the reduction of nutritional variety, and the consequent spread of pellagra, see Daphne A. Roe, *A Plague of Corn: The Social History of Pellagra* (Ithaca, N.Y.: Cornell University Press, 1973).

cultivate wheat. Most Romanian historians have assumed that this is what happened. But through careful documentary research, Ilie Corfus found that instead the old pattern of noble domination persisted throughout the change in the rural economy. There was virtually no demesne, and even by 1850 almost all of the grain grown in Wallachia was being produced by small peasant holdings. The peasants actually sold their grain directly, in local markets, either to independent merchants or to the lords' agents, and lords received the money due for commuted labor services.[29]

This fact clarifies a theme that runs through Wallachian agrarian history from the sixteenth century until at least 1864 (and, in some ways, into the twentieth century). Even after the Organic Regulation, the lords did not really own land, though they controlled it. This control gave them the right to tax peasants who used the land. If labor dues were raised during the period of the Organic Regulation, this was to raise the lords' incomes from commuted dues, not to mobilize labor in a more direct way.

Lords also perpetuated the eighteenth-century custom of leasing out their estates to "farmers." But these "farmers" (*arendași*) were not agents who managed estates for the lords (because there were in effect no estates to manage), but rather men who leased the rights to collect dues from a lord's villages without directly engaging in cultivation or managing peasant labor themselves.[30] The persistence of this pattern of *boier* power gave the peasants the impression that they themselves owned the land (a point on which they bitterly insisted during the debates that preceded the reform of 1864).

Because of the perpetuation of old patterns of the nobility's control and of a low population density, many of the traditional agricultural techniques—and even some forms of communal village organization—persisted through the major changes in the rural economy. This was particularly the case in the Bărăgan steppe, where many wheat fields were cultivated by seasonal migrants who remained partially pastoral,[31] but it was also true in areas where the cultivators were more sedentary. Old agricultural practices (e.g., no manuring, virtually no crop rotation, primitive plows) survived because there was so much land. Commons continued to take up a major portion of village territories, and many villages were still not divided into private plots at all, even if they were under the control of a lord (and thus officially counted as "private land").[32]

On the surface, the rural economy was transformed because of the increase of cereal, particularly wheat and corn cultivation. The largely pastoral villagers were transformed into peasants. The power of the lords, which was great before 1831, became even greater because the dues imposed on the

[29] Corfus, *Agricultura Țării Românești*, p. 252.

[30] *Ibid.*, pp. 163–166.

[31] Mihăilescu, "Așezările omenești," in *Memoriile*, p. 18.

[32] Henri H. Stahl, *Les anciennes commumautés villageoises roumaines* (Bucharest and Paris: Académie roumaine and C.N.R.S., 1969), pp. 109–112.

clăcaşi were increased. And as pastoralists were transformed into cultivators, the probability that they would flee to other villages because of harsh dues decreased. But the nature of the lords' control over peasants remained unchanged. The *clăcaşi,* serfs in many respects, did not cultivate the lord's land. Ancient forms of communal village life persisted, although admittedly in an attenuated way because the villagers were no longer self-governing or even free. The pattern was finally broken only after 1864, when the lords became full-fledged landowners.

These continued patterns explain the historical controversy that arose in the 1850s and which has persisted to this day. What, exactly, were the Wallachian and Moldavian peasants? Had they been serfs for centuries, reduced to an abject state by generations of servitude? Or were they, as some claimed, free men who owned their land and who were enslaved only under the Organic Regulation? And who were the *boieri*? Were they upstarts who seized control of the land during the Organic Regulation, or were they descendants of a class of landowners who had owned the land for centuries? The answer, of course, is incomprehensible so long as the Western European connotations of "lord," "serf," and "feudal" are applied to the situation. After the Crimean War, a commission of Western European delegates was sent to Romania to suggest an agrarian reform. It is hardly surprising that this commission was unable to clarify the situation and that its suggestions missed the point of what was going on.[33]

The way in which the Organic Regulation was applied had a strong effect on the peasants. The increasing dues they had to pay were not only resented but were felt to be illegal. But the local police, judiciary, and administrative apparatus were in league with the lords and so enforced the frequently arbitrary increases in dues. The lords' agents and the "farmers" who leased the rights to collect dues from the peasants were often cruel and unjust, and because the peasantry felt it owned the land, it was convinced that the system was unfair. But there was little peasants could do about these wrongs.[34]

A certain portion of the peasants, however, remained free. These were the *moşneni,* the descendants of villagers who had never been subjugated by the *boieri.* By 1864, fewer than 5% of the peasants in the eastern part of the Muntenian plain were *moşneni,* and in the western part of the Muntenian plain fewer than 10% of the peasants were free. In the Oltenian plain the proportion of free peasants was between 20% and 25%. In the eastern part of the Muntenian hill and mountain zone, about 30% of the peasants were free. But in the western part of the Muntenian hills and mountains, and in the adjoining Oltenian hill and mountain region, close to 60% of the peasants were still free.[35] In all, about 25% of the peasantry in 1864 was composed of *moşneni.*

[33] Emerit, *Les paysans roumains,* pp. 396–401.

[34] *Ibid.,* pp. 270–280, 291–295.

[35] Henri H. Stahl, "Organizarea socială a ţărănimii," *Enciclopedia României,* I, p. 575.

The Nobles and the Monasteries

Though the Organic Regulation strengthened the position of the major *boieri* families, the much more numerous petty nobility did not fare as well. The Organic Regulation reaffirmed the eighteenth-century law that differentiated between nobles with administrative positions in the state bureaucracy, which entitled the holders to high titles, and the petty nobles who held no such position. The petty nobles were descendants of nobles who themselves held no office. This category was divided into two groups, the *neamuri* and the *mazili*. They were no more than free peasants who claimed noble lineage. There was also a seminoble category of "licensees," originally tradesmen who were granted immunity from forced labor imposed by the state on villagers for state works.

Between 1831 and the 1860s, the number of "petty nobles" vastly increased. Through bribery and the payment of various fees, fraudulent certificates of noble descent could be obtained, and though such certificates conferred few privileges other than immunity from forced labor, a great many men entered the ranks of the petty nobility.[36] The French consul in Bucharest between 1849 and 1856, Eugène Poujade, estimated that in the mid-1850s there were about five times as many such "nobles" as in the early 1840s. There were also 25,000 families of "licensees." Poujade felt that the existence of such a class had nefarious consequences:

> The Organic Regulation had wished to favour the formation of a third estate, and to achieve this aim to which European civilization had tended, it had preserved the guilds and at the same time by establishing municipal councils had made it easy for leading members of the guilds to obtain certain rights. This impulse, given by Count Kisseleff, continued, though slowly, for several years; but soon the industrial class, the budding third estate, slipped back and fell even lower than it had been before the reforms applied by the Organic Regulation. Three causes contributed above all to this retrogade movement. They were: (i) the ease with which peasants were admitted to the number of licensees; (ii) the profusion with which patents of nobility were granted; (iii) the decline of the municipalities. The license was sought after, because it gave exemption from forced labour. Patents of nobility removed from the guilds their richest and most influential members. The decline of the municipalities did away with this useful station in society, where the members of the guilds could rest and console themselves for not attaining nobility. The consequences of this state of things were disastrous for Wallachian society; everyone who rose above the peasant class had himself enlisted in the nobility and removed from this interesting section of the community its natural defenders and supporters. Things have gone so far that the Bucharest guild of wine merchants, whose membership reaches nearly four thousand, numbers perhaps less than 500 retailers with licences. All the others have bought the right of being enrolled in various privileged classes.[37]

[36] Eugène Poujade, *Chrétiens et Turcs* (Paris, 1859), cited in Doreen Warriner, ed., *Contrasts in Emerging Societies* (Bloomington, Ind.: Indiana University Press, 1965), pp. 152–153.

[37] Reprinted from Poujade, *Chrétiens et Turcs*, cited in Warriner, *Contrasts in Emerging Societies*, p. 154, by permission of Indiana University Press.

Poujade exaggerated the potential of the guilds. They never reached the strength that Western European guilds once had, and the stated hopes for the rise of a "third estate" were probably doomed from the start.[38] In fact, it is highly doubtful that the intent of the Organic Regulation had ever been to create a powerful "third estate." Poujade's observations show that the structure of opportunity in nineteenth-century Wallachia was not favorable to the development of a native bourgeoisie. On the one hand, there was the competition of the foreign merchants, and on the other, there was the attraction of government service which conferred high status and real nobility.

The full *boieri* had, along with the prince, a virtual monopoly on political power. But nobles could not transmit their political privileges to their descendants, and thus the grandsons of nobles who could not obtain high office became *neamuri*. Control over land was not yet recognized as full ownership, so it was difficult to transmit it as hereditary property. As a result, there was a constant jockeying among the nobles to insure the appointment of their sons to high administrative positions which would perpetuate noble privileges within the family. As in the eighteenth century, this system encouraged bribery and corruption while also allowing the prince to elevate particular families from common to noble status.

It has been estimated that in about 1850 there were some 400 major noble families in Wallachia and Moldavia (about two-thirds of them Wallachian). Only about 50 of these came from the "historic" nobility; the remainder were more recent, and a high proportion of them were of foreign origin. But the few hundred major families controlled some 75% of all nobility-controlled lands, while the thousands of petty nobles controlled very little land at all. The concentration was even greater than these figures show, for some 15 to 20 families controlled about one-third of all the land in both Wallachia and Moldavia.[39]

This state of affairs made the petty nobility very resentful of the few high nobles who had a near monopoly on political power and the control of vast lands. Many of the petty nobles were educated enough to have notions about Western liberalism and the ideals of the French Revolution, and because of their resentment toward the high nobility many, especially the young, were revolutionary. Poujade noted with näive surprise that, "remarkably enough, it is particularly in the supplementary nobility that revolutionary passions and socialist ideas have found active instruments and docile adherents."[40]

The Organic Regulation perpetuated the institution of the "dedicated monasteries," which the Russians correctly viewed as strong allies because

[38]Municipal government had never developed very far in Wallachia or Moldavia. See Ioan C. Filitti, "Administraţia locală în România," *Enciclopedia României*, I, p. 297.

[39]Emerit, *Les paysans roumains*, pp. 239–240.

[40]Poujade, cited in Warriner, *Contrasts in Emerging Societies*, p. 153.

TABLE 1
Land Distribution in 1864

State property	2%
Various categories of undivided village property	17%
Public institutions (hospitals, charitable institutions, etc.)	3%
Dedicated monasteries	13%
Other monasteries	14%
Individuals	50%

they were Christian Orthodox, and because they were so disliked in Wallachia that they needed foreign protection to preserve them against confiscation.[41]

An official estimate made in 1864 before the land reform shows the distribution of land in Wallachia at the end of the period of the Organic Regulation (see Table 1). (The estimate does not include "unproductive" land—that is, forest and waste land.) The last category includes noble lands and lands of peasants having their own (rather than communal) land. The nobles probably controlled about 40% of all the land, or about 80% of the land controlled by "individuals." Nobles and monasteries together controlled close to 70% of the land.[42]

The changes brought about after the Treaty of Adrianople also changed the nobility's cultural patterns. In 1830, the nobility was still Middle Eastern. Nobles wore long flowing robes and turbans, had little education, and little knowledge of the outside world. But as Wallachia was opened to Western commerce and influence, the high nobility changed many of its ways. Many sent their sons to Western Europe for their education. Their wives adopted Parisian styles of dress. Though they kept their Gypsy household slaves, the nobles began to furnish their palatial townhouses with French tapestries and Viennese furniture. Living in the town, already quite common for nobles in the eighteenth century, became even more common in the nineteenth, and by the middle of the century few nobles lived on their lands.[43] The easing of Turkish rule did not, therefore, change the non-national nature of the Wallachian nobility's culture. Rather, Western cultural habits were grafted to Turkish and Middle Eastern habits. The split between the common rural population and the high nobility was even greater than it had been before. As Emerit has written, "The son of the boier, dazzled by Western life and by the beautiful speeches heard in the liberal cafés [of the West], no longer wanted to know anything about his country's institutions and he could quickly forget the poor Danubian peasant whose hard work let him make these agreeable and instructive trips abroad."[44]

[41] Emerit, *Les paysans roumains*, p. 27.
[42] *Ibid.*, p. 238.
[43] *Ibid.*, pp. 240–245.
[44] *Ibid.*, p. 245.

The Towns

The rapid expansion of foreign trade and the increasing concentration of nobles in the main cities stimulated urban growth. In 1810, Bucharest had about 35,000 people.[45] In 1831, it had a permanent population of about 59,000, and about 10,000 transients. As such it was the largest European city of the Ottoman Empire, aside from Constantinople. By 1860, the population had doubled to 122,000.[46] From 1831 to 1853 Giurgiu, an important Danube River port south of Bucharest, grew from about 700 people to 7400.[47] Brăila, on the Danube near the Black Sea, was once Wallachia's main sea port during the days of the trade state. It had become an insignificant village under Ottoman rule, and by the 1820s it had fewer than 1000 people. But after 1829 it was refurbished by Kiselev and once again became an important port. By 1853, it had 12,000 people. (Galaţi, the main Moldavian port, grew even faster; much of Wallachia's commerce was channeled through Galaţi rather than Brăila.)[48]

A large proportion of the population in the main cities was foreign. Writing in 1878, J. W. Ozanne, an Englishman who lived in Romania, observed, "The middle class in the towns is composed, as I have already said, almost exclusively of the foreign element, of French and Germans and Jews—Polish, Austrian and Spanish [i.e., Sephardic]." The Romanian middle class was composed of doctors, lawyers, military officers, and civil servants, not of merchants.[49]

Though there were some native merchants, the tightening of rules that permitted peasants to leave their lords' lands in the 1840s prevented the emigration of *clăcaşi* from rural to urban areas, and much of the urban population growth was due to foreign immigration.[50] Most of the foreign immigrants were Greeks, Italians, Armenians, Bulgarians, or Ukrainian and Galician Jews. In Giurgiu, most of the wheat transporters were Bulgarian.[51] The Frenchman Colson noted in 1839 that most of the export trade in the port cities was in the hands of Greek brokers, "most of whom inspire no confidence."[52] Iorga wrote disapprovingly of the same Greeks.[53] In 1860, about 1000 of Brăila's inhabitants and 6000 of Bucharest's were Jewish.[54] Though the proportion of Jews was

[45] Ciobanu, "Populaţia," *Arhiva*, **II**, p. 90.

[46] Dan Berindei, *Oraşul Bucureşti, reşedinţă şi capitală a Ţării Romîneşti 1459–1862* (Bucharest: Societatea de ştiinţe istorice şi filologice din R.P.R., 1963), pp. 143, 235.

[47] Mihăilescu, "Aşezările omeneşti," in *Memoriile*, p. 50.

[48] *Ibid.*, p. 50; and Emerit, *Les paysans roumains*, p. 214.

[49] J. W. Ozanne, *Three Years in Roumania* (London, 1878), cited in Warriner, *Contrasts in Emerging Societies*, p. 158.

[50] Corfus, *Agricultura Ţării Româneşti*, pp. 115–121.

[51] Emerit, *Les paysans roumains*, p. 215.

[52] F. Colson, *De l'état présent et de l'avenir des principautés de Moldavie et de Valachie* (Paris, 1839), cited in Warriner, *Contrasts in Emerging Societies*, p. 174.

[53] Nicolae Iorga, *Istoria comerţului românesc* (Bucharest: Tiparul românesc, 1925), **II**, pp. 159–160.

[54] Verax, *La Roumanie et les Juifs* (Bucharest: I. V. Socecu, 1903), p. 55. Verax was the pen name of Radu Rosetti, the historian whose work has been cited earlier. Though he was one of Romania's leading liberal

still fairly small, it was growing very rapidly. By 1876, about 17% of Bucharest's population was Jewish.[55]

To be sure, in Moldavia over 50% of the population of the capital in 1850 was Jewish, and in a number of other cities in northern Moldavia over 60% of the population was Jewish.[56] But even in Wallachia the important position of foreign middlemen created resentment. One of the dominant themes of Romanian liberalism, particularly when it is revolutionary, has always been its antiforeign ideology. In Moldavia this was anti-Semitic; in Wallachia it was more anti-Greek. The matter of foreign middlemen in the cities was further complicated by the fact that many of them were officially protected by Western powers acting through their consuls in Bucharest. The reason for this was that many of the vital trade contacts that Western commercial houses developed were with this foreign urban population. In order to protect these contacts and agents from the Wallachian government's periodic outbursts of discriminatory anger, the Western powers declared a number of merchants to be under their official protection. (This system was common in many Western trading outposts.) Thus, in Bucharest in 1838 about half of the city's Jews were protected by outside powers.[57] Despite his anti-Semitism, Rosetti (Verax) perceived the situation correctly when he wrote:

> Indeed, on their side [i.e., on the side of the Romanians versus the Jews] there was a small merchant class, with a minimal access to capital, conducting a limited and local trade, and especially ignorant of the very names of the Occidental merchandise which would become increasingly demanded in the country to the exclusion of local goods which they had previously handled. They had no idea about where this merchandise was produced, of its real value, of differences in quality. They had no contacts with Western markets.[58]

Naturally, there continued to be native merchants, even in the cities. But the importance of the phenomenon of "foreign merchants" was that these merchants were a highly visible and often crucially located minority. It is

Ftn. 54 (continued)
historians, he was also virulently anti-Semitic, and his book on the Jewish problem in Romania is very polemical. Iorga's opinion was roughly the same, as was that of most Romanian intellectuals. Even the French historian Emerit took a similar position, especially with respect to Moldavia. The origins of anti-Semitism in Romania are, of course, similar to, though more recent than, those in Poland and the Ukraine. In Wallachia, however, nationalist intellectuals reserved their deepest hatred for the Greeks since they were the chief "foreign" middlemen. Again, this situation is reminiscent of many colonial and semicolonial situations. A good account of anti-Semitism in Romania and its consequences in the twentieth century can be found in Eugen Weber's "Romania," *The European Right*, ed. Hans Rogger and Eugen Weber (Berkeley and Los Angeles: University of California Press, 1966).

[55] Dimitrie Sturdza, "Suprafaţa şi populaţiunea regatului României," *Buletin*, Societatea geografică română, XVI, trim. 3 and 4 (Bucharest, 1896), p. 42.

[56] Emerit, *Les paysans roumains*, pp. 159–164.

[57] Verax, *La Roumanie et les Juifs*, p. 50.

[58] *Ibid.*, p. 98.

therefore not surprising that the native Romanian population—from the *boieri* who borrowed from Greek and Jewish moneylenders to the peasants who traded with them—was able to unite on this one issue.

A large part of the population of the growing cities was, however, native. Despite the prohibition on movement, landless peasants did escape to the city, and Bucharest came to be ringed with suburban slums that contained these poverty-stricken people. They performed various petty types of artisan work, or they hired themselves out by the day to perform unskilled labor. Their presence gave large parts of Bucharest the appearance of a poor, overgrown, mud village dominated by isolated, splendid noble townhouses.[59] It was this peasant element that formed the "urban mob" that supported the Revolution of 1848.

The Revolution of 1848

In most respects, Wallachian society of the 1840s and 1850s fits the model of "colonial society" described at the start of the chapter. The economy was increasingly dominated by the growing wheat exports to the West; foreign trade was largely in the hands of an accessory group of non-Western but non-Romanian middlemen; an increasing distance separated the foreign-oriented aristocracy from the peasantry; the peasantry was at least partially dispossessed, in that its rights to the use of land were increasingly hedged by obligations owed to nobles; there was a tendency for the peasant standard of living to stagnate, and in fact it was probably beginning to fall as of about mid-century (at least in terms of diet). The last point is the hardest to substantiate, because there are no data on the peasant standard of living. Because the population was rising at a rapid rate it would seem that there was enough food (though not necessarily an increasing amount of food per capita). On the other hand, the first appearances of pellagra at mid-century suggest that as the wheat export economy entered its boom years, nutritional problems began to appear.[60] As for other indices of the peasant standard of living, virtually all observers of mid-century Wallachia agreed that the general standard was very low. Poujade wrote:

> What then is the situation of the mass of the people in the Principalities, of those who till the soil and on whom, in the last resort, falls the burden of filling the treasury and

[59] Ement, *Les paysans roumains*, pp. 243–244.

[60] See Roe, *Plague of Corn*, for a description of the analogous spread of pellagra in the U.S. South and southern Europe. Also, see S. H. Katz, M. L. Hediger, and L. A. Valleroy, "Traditional Maize Processing in the New World," *Science* 184, no. 4138 (May, 1974): 765–773, for a physiological explanation of how overdependence on corn produces pellagra in cultures that have not learned how to cook it properly.

> forming the militia? Let us take Wallachia. The rural population of this principality is composed of 354,294 peasant families. These peasants pay into the treasury: (i) a tax called capitation, fixed by law at 30 piastres (about 11 francs); (ii) two-tenths extra above the principal to the village funds, in order to compensate the treasury for non-payments in the interval of quinquennial assessments.... The peasant also pays 6 piastres (2 fr. 50) for the roads; 6 piastres for the debts caused by the Russian occupation of 1848; 3 piastres for the dorobanți (county constabulary); 2 piastres for the schools; he also pays some additional centimes for the militia. All these different taxes contravene the basis fixed by the Organic Regulation. It is they which have raised capitation to the high rate which it has reached today and which have overthrown the system of uniform taxation inaugurated in 1830 by Count Kisseleff as the best remedy for the abuses of tax-collecting.
>
> What is worse is that the services which these different supplementary taxes were supposed to help were fictitious or nearly so. For example, the sums collected amounted to 40 million piastres for the roads, 24½ million piastres for the occupation debt, five million piastres for the schools; net result: not a road in order, only three million piastres paid for the occupation, not a school opened!
>
> As for the relations of the peasants with the landlords, they have also been strained, and the situation of the former has been made worse and worse. It has therefore become a matter of urgency to look after the peasant class; it is in all respects the most interesting class in the Principalities....[61]

In the hill and mountain regions, most peasant families lived in wood houses; but in the plains, particularly in the eastern plains, most peasants lived in mud *bordei*.[62] Constantin Golescu (1777–1828), a Wallachian noble, wrote a graphic description of this type of mud house which was half underground:

> These unrighteous practices [i.e., treatment of villagers], unheard of elsewhere in the world, have brought the unhappy inhabitants to such a state, that anyone who enters the so-called villages will see neither church nor house nor fence around the house, nor cart, nor ox nor cow nor fowl nor patch sown for the family's food—in a word, nothing; only some rooms in the earth which are called *bordeie*. Anyone who goes in sees nothing but a hole in the earth, which will hold a man with his wife and children around the hearth, and a chimney of basketwork plastered with dung, protruding from the surface of the ground. Behind the stove is another hole, through which he must escape in haste when he perceives that someone has come to his door; for he knows that it can only be sent to demand payment. And he having nothing to give, will be either beaten, or bound and taken away and sold, for one or two years or more, to a petty boyar or a farmer or whoever it may be, to serve him for those years, so that the money which is paid for those years' [*sic*] of service may be taken to pay his poll-tax. (Again I say: truly, the merciful God is very patient.)[63]

[61] Reprinted from Poujade, *Chrétiens et Turcs*, cited in Warriner, *Contrasts in Emerging Societies*, pp. 154–155, by permission of Indiana University Press.

[62] D. Bugă, "Repartiția geografiă a așezărilor omenești dintre Carpați și Dunăre (Țara Românească) la jumătatea secolului al XIX-lea," *Comunicări de geografie* **VII** (1969): 193–195.

[63] Reprinted from C. Golescu, *Însemnare a călătoriei mele* (Bucharest, 1910), cited in Warriner, *Contrasts in Emerging Societies*, pp. 144–145, by permission of Indiana University Press.

This description is, of course, from the 1820s. But the fact that in the 1850s most of the plains peasants still lived in such houses, and that Poujade noted similar abuses by tax collectors and lords, suggests that there was little (if any) meaningful improvement in the standard of living during the very years when Wallachia was undergoing a remarkable economic expansion.

In 1848, following the revolutions in Austria, Hungary, and much of Western Europe, there was a Wallachian Revolution (an incipient revolt in Moldavia was crushed by a Russian army before it actually got underway).[64] This revolt has since come to be called a "national bourgeois" revolution—that is, one led by nationalist intellectuals and civil servants whose chief goals were (1) the redress of wrongs caused by foreign domination, and (2) the creation of a modern nation–state. Though the social and economic problems of Wallachia naturally concerned the revolutionaries, their main emphasis was nationalistic and political, rather than social or economic. The revolutionaries had come to feel that only by uniting Wallachia and Moldavia into a single Romania could other problems be solved. In the meantime, it was better to subordinate the issues dividing the peasants from the nobles, in order to keep the latter on the nationalist side.[65]

Since the late 1830s, a small group of young Western-oriented *boieri* and intellectuals had been plotting to overthrow the regime of the Organic Regulation. Some looked to England for support against the Russophile government; most hoped that France would intervene in favor of "liberty and progress."[66] In 1840, the plotters staged an abortive coup.[67] But in 1848, supported by the class of petty *boieri*, the Bucharest mob, and a general nationalistic feeling, the Revolution seized the government for a few months. Land was promised to the peasants, but at the same time the new rulers felt compelled to assure the high *boieri* that nothing would be taken from them.[68] The provisional Revolutionary government called for Western help, but the English were more interested in preserving the general European peace than in helping Balkan revolutionaries. The Russians, on the other hand, were occupied in Hungary. The European powers and Turkey therefore decided that a joint Russian–Ottoman occupation force should be sent into Wallachia to re-establish order without unhinging the Balkan balance of power. This was done in 1849, when the Revolution was crushed by joint Russian–Ottoman military

[64] East, *Union of Moldavia and Wallachia*, p. 210.

[65] Cornelia Bodea, *Lupta românilor pentru unitatea națională 1834–1849* (Bucharest: Editura academiei, 1967), particularly pp. 95–115; Dan Berindei, "L'idéologie politique des révolutionnaires roumains de 1848," *Nouvelles études*, **IV**, pp. 207–221; V. Maciu, "Un centre révolutionnaire roumain dans les années 1845–1848: la société des étudiants roumains de Paris," *Nouvelles études*, **III**, pp. 243–275; Pătrășcanu, *Veac de Frământări*, pp. 190–199; Zeletin, *Burghezia română*, pp. 60–62.

[66] Florescu, *Struggle Against Russia*, pp. 163–178.

[67] G. Zane, *Le mouvement révolutionnaire de 1840* (Bucharest: Académie roumaine, 1964).

[68] Emerit, *Les paysans roumains*, pp. 299–321.

action, and the previous settlement between the two empires over the fate of Wallachia was reaffirmed. The Organic Regulation was to remain in effect. Russia would remain Wallachia's "protector"; and the Ottoman Empire would remain the nominal overlord.[69] Thus, the revolutionary government never had a chance to resolve the dilemma of whether to push for a land reform, or court the support of the nobility (which it never really gained in any case) by avoiding reform.

In 1848 little was accomplished in the way of concrete reforms, but in that year the unpopularity of the Organic Regulation was exposed, along with the fact that the regime of the Regulation could be maintained only by foreign intervention. There evidently was considerable support for a nationalistic revolutionary movement, particularly among the younger members of the petty nobility.

In 1851, a partial reform was passed in order to lower the number of corvée days owed by the *clăcași*. Gypsy slaves were freed, though there actually had been a slow movement in the previous decade toward gradual emancipation and, in any case, these slaves were not a significant productive class. But basic *boieri* control over the land was maintained as before; in summary, despite minor face lifting, the essence of the Organic Regulation's system of rules was not modified.[70]

The Union of Wallachia and Moldavia and the Reform of 1864

The Crimean War was fought over a number of issues that revolved around Great Britain's desire to curb Russia's threat to the British Empire, particularly to its "lifeline" running through the Eastern Mediterranean. The fate of the Danubian principalities was one of the important points of the dispute.[71] Romanian grain exports were becoming increasingly important to Britain, and Wallachian and Moldavian markets seemed promising to British industry. Both the French and the British wanted more stable, cooperative regimes in the principalities. But the most important issue was that both countries wanted to limit Russian power on the Danube. After the Anglo–French (and Sardinian) victory against Russia, two sets of issues had to be settled with respect to the principalities. First, should they be united into a single Romanian state? (It was recognized that they shared a common language and rather similar institutions and historical traditions.) Whether or not they were united, what sort or government should they have, and in particular, what should be the role of the *boieri*?

The second issue raised the problem of the "agrarian" question. What sort of

[69] East, *Union of Moldavia and Wallachia*, pp. 19–22.

[70] Emerit, *Les paysans roumains*, pp. 324, 328–333, 355–366.

[71] R. W. Seton-Watson, *History of the Roumanians*, 2nd ed. (Hamden, Conn.: Archon, 1963), pp. 233–235.

law should replace the Organic Regulation? These questions, it was decided, were to be settled by the seven interested powers—Great Britain, France, Austria, Turkey, Russia, Sardinia, and Prussia. The first five of the seven were the most important parties in the discussions to decide these issues. Sardinia followed France's lead on every question in order to maintain its alliance with Napoleon III against Austria; and Prussia was essentially neutral in the discussions, as well as being more removed from the issues in which it had no serious interest.[72]

Great Britain was most interested in the international issues and felt that no substantial internal changes were necessary in the principalities. Rather, the British hoped that the principalities could simply revert to tighter Ottoman control.[73] Austria was more interested than Britain in the domestic problems of the principalities because it ruled a large Romanian population in Transylvania and Bukovina, and because once again it hoped to expand its economic and political influence down the Danube.[74] But Austria had not participated in the Crimean War against Russia, choosing instead to remain neutral, and the only way it could have gained its Danubian ends would have been to give up northern Italy in return. This latter solution, proposed by Napoleon III, was rejected by Austria.

Russia had lost the war and therefore resigned itself to losing its hegemony over the principalities. In an astonishing reversal of its policy, Russia began to support the nationalist liberals in Romania on the question of national unification. This was for the double purpose of annoying the Austrians and of gaining popular support within the principalities.[75] A further consideration in Russia's new position was its desire to gain a friend among the victorious Crimean powers, and Napoleon III had a vague ideological commitment to the Romanian nationalists.[76] The Ottoman Empire simply wanted to regain some of its lost influence in the principalities in order to block future Russian expansion toward Constantinople.[77]

A related issue, which was much discussed but which need not concern us at this point, was whether or not the principalities should be ruled by native or foreign (i.e., Western European) princes. The diplomatic haggling that went on at the various post-Crimean War conferences would have been comical, if the fates of millions of Eastern Europeans had not been decided by considerations of the balance of power between the major powers; and virtually nothing was actually known about the internal conditions and

[72]Emerit, *Les paysan roumains*, pp. 360–364; East, *Union of Moldavia and Wallachia*, pp. 28, 120, 150–152.

[73]*Ibid.*, p. 30.

[74]Dan Berindei, *L'union des principautés roumaines*, pp. 99–100.

[75]East, *Union of Moldavia and Wallachia*, pp. 31–35.

[76]*Ibid.*, pp. 54–79; Jelavich, *Russia and the Rumanian National Cause*, pp. 12–14.

[77]East, *Union of Moldavia and Wallachia*, pp. 35–38.

desires of the people whose fates were being decided and who were being used as international pawns.

According to the Treaty of Paris of 1856, which concluded the Crimean War, two councils—one each from Wallachia and Moldavia—were to be formed in order to decide questions of internal reform. The councils were labelled "Divans ad hoc" and were to be chosen by the population, with each class chossing its representatives. There were representatives of the free and serf peasants (the *moşneni* and *clăcaşi*) churchmen, small nobles, the major *boieri* representatives, and representatives from the cities. The Wallachian Divan never decided anything because it broke up as a result of internal bickering, but the Moldavian Divan actually held sessions in 1857. Because Moldavia and Wallachia were so similar, it is worth examining the debates of the Moldavian Divan because they shed light on existing agrarian relations.[78]

The small delegation of *clăcaşi* expressed a clear and urgent desire to be rid of the corvée and other "feudal" dues. It also claimed that the land belonged to the peasants who cultivated it, and that the land had been put illegally under *boier* control by the Organic Regulation. The *boieri* claimed absolute ownership of the land in all *clăcaşi* villages. While the peasants claimed that the *boieri* were simply "controllers of the land" (*stăpîn de moşie*), the *boieri* themselves claimed that they were "owners" (*proprietar*). (It was during these debates that the historical problem of the origins and development of the nobility first became a point of acute political controversy.) The small free proprietors, the remnants of the *moşneni* (the term for these in Moldavia was *răzăşi*), the small *boieri*, and the cities' representatives joined the side of the *clăcaşi* against the big *boieri*. But the big *boieri* held the balance of power and refused to compromise. The Divan broke up without coming to a conclusive vote on any matter.[79]

A commission of the seven powers was sent to the principalities to observe the proceedings of the Divans and to make recommendations. It contributed little toward a clarification of the situation, but it did conclude that because of the way the Organic Regulation had been applied it had led to a "refeudalization" (the Commission's word) of the principalities.[80]

The main issues, both international and internal, were still not settled by 1858, so another conference was held in that year at Paris. The principalities were placed under a collective guarantee that was to be enforced by the seven powers. Turkish suzerainty was affirmed, but defined very narrowly: The Sultan was given the right to "invest though not reject" the princes of the principalities (though the meaning of this phrase was not particularly clear). The

[78] Rosetti, *Pentru ce*, pp. 282–287.

[79] *Ibid.*, pp. 287–318; Emerit, *Les paysans roumains*, pp. 369–396.

[80] T. W. Riker, *The Making of Roumania 1856–1866* (London: Oxford University Press, 1931), pp. 41, 169–170; 432; Emerit, *Les paysans roumains*, pp. 238–240, 400; East, *Union of Moldavia and Wallachia*, pp. 82–108.

princes were to be chosen for life by assemblies in each of the principalities. Wallachia and Moldavia were declared autonomous in their internal affairs. Some measure of government contact between the two principalities was provided for, but full union was ruled out.[81] The suffrage laws for the new assemblies were extremely restrictive and Wallachia had only 2072 eligible electors. The several hundred richest *boieri* families received about 80% of the seats.[82]

Why did the Paris Conference give so much power to the tiny *boieri* elite and insure the continuation of the social system that prevailed under the Organic Regulation? The diplomatic history of the period sheds relatively little light on this question. Russia, for all its support of the nationalist goal of union, clearly hoped that the Russophile big *boieri* would remain in control.[83] Austria, on the other hand, tended to be anti-*boieri*, because it believed that the *boieri* were pro-Russian. Great Britain was less interested in internal social issues, but in the end consistently supported the *boieri*. The French pressed for social reform (presumably to retain the support of the Francophile liberals). The Ottomans had no fixed position, but hoped to decide the issue themselves. In the end, the following provision (Article 46) was put into the convention signed at the end of the conference:

> The Moldavians and the Wallachians will be all equally liable to taxation and equally admissible to public service in both Principalities. Their individual liberty will be guaranteed .... All the privileges, exemptions or monopolies which certain classes still enjoy will be abolished, and the revision of the law which regulates the relations of the landlords with the farmers will be undertaken without undue delay with a view to improving the condition of the peasants.

But this article was added only to assuage reformist wishes. Article 46 remained a dead letter until 1864.[84]

It was the British view that eventually prevailed. The statement of the British commissioner on the Seven Power Commission of 1857 is revealing, because it shows the British commitment to a distinct ideological position. He claimed that he could not accept "the conversion of the peasant into the owner of the land he now works; for by imposing such a change, the principle of private property would be violated, and in the long run, this would harm the peasant, the owners, and agriculture itself."[85] Thus, though the British were more concerned with international than with internal Romanian issues, their

[81] *Ibid.*, pp. 160–161.

[82] Emerit, *Les paysan roumains*, p. 400.

[83] Jelavich, *Russia and the Rumanian National Cause*, p. 14.

[84] *Ibid.*, pp. 18–19.

[85] Retranslated from the French translation in Emerit, *Les paysans roumains*, p. 398. Rosetti, *Pentru ce*, pp. 322–323 paraphrases the British statement.

position remained consistent with their economic interests as importers of Romanian wheat. It would be tempting to propose (as have many Romanian historians, both pre-Communist and Communist) that the connection between British imperialism and the big *boieri* explains this position. Actually, there is little evidence that there was a direct conscious connection of this sort on the part of the British. The British position was based, rather, on a general ideological reflex which Britain tended to apply quite consistently throughout its imperial zone of influence from South America to India. Any class that seemed akin to the English "gentry class" was favored. And of course, it generally favored large concentrations of land in the hands of men oriented to the world market. But it must not be overlooked that the Romanian case was only a part, and perhaps not even a vital part, of the "Eastern Question." As such, British economic interests in the principalities were less important than global strategic considerations. But once these had been satisfactorily settled, the British ideological reflex based on economic interest could come into play.[86]

There was another reason for the outcome of the Paris Conference. Given the conflicting tangle of big power interests, it was easier to perpetuate the internal social and political system of the principalities as it stood. That, at least, would tend to reduce the chances of protest by other commission powers. On the other hand, any real attempt to carry out reform might have involved an occupying army to enforce the changes. The Paris Conference did not put the major *boieri* oligarchy in power. It follwed the line of least resistance and repeated the actions of the Austrians in Oltenia in the early eighteenth century and of the Russians from 1829 to 1834. It merely sanctioned the continued rule of the oligarchy.

In 1859, the assemblies of Wallachia and Moldavia elected princes. Much to the surprise of the seven powers, the *boieri*, secure in their control of the situation, had been won over to the nationalist cause, and both assemblies elected the same prince, Ioan Cuza. By this act the two principalities were united, and in 1861 they were formally joined into a new Romanian state (which

[86] Barrington Moore Jr., *Social Origins of Dictatorship and Democracy: Lord and Peasant in the Making of the Modern World* (Boston: Beacon, 1967), pp. 343–347, stresses the British attempt to create a landed gentry from the north Indian *zamindar* class, as well as the emergence of a similar class of parasitic landlords in the south despite the supposed differences between the *zamindar* and the *ryotwari* systems. In general, British economic policy favored large landlords in nineteenth-century colonial societies even though the British were not always fully aware of what they were doing and why. The exception occurred where a product of an indirect colony competed with the product of a direct colony, as in the case of sugar from Brazil that competed in the nineteenth century with British West Indian sugar. See Celso Furtado, *The Economic Growth of Brazil* (Berkeley and Los Angeles: University of California Press, 1963), pp. 100–103. In most places the British did not set out to create landlord classes, but the expansion of their economy into primary producing areas strengthened existing landlords. For example, in Argentina in the late nineteenth century, "The [British owned] railroads and the invention of the refrigerator ship not only transformed the pampa . . . but also brought unheard of prosperity to Argentine landowners." (Tomás Robert Fillol, *Social Factors in Economic Development: The Argentine Case* [Cambridge: M.I.T. Press, 1961], p. 43.)

was, however, still theoretically subject to the Ottoman Empire).[87] Faced by this Romanian action which was supported by Napoleon III, the powers accepted it.[88]

Cuza appointed a former nationalist liberal, Kogălniceanu, as his prime minister. Kogălniceanu was one of Moldavia's most enlightened and liberal men, and he won Cuza over to the idea that some kind of agrarian reform was necessary. Both men realized that the crude exploitation of the peasants by the *boieri* was bound to produce an eventual upheaval, and that some change was imperative. It is also probable that Cuza hoped to build up his personal popularity by carrying out a reform, thus strengthening his power base against the *boieri* assemblies.[89]

But the joint efforts of Cuza and Kogălniceanu to alleviate the plight of the peasants were strenuously resisted by the nobles, who successfully blocked all attempts at reform save one: the nationalization of the hated dedicated (foreign-owned) monasteries, which gave the state control of large amounts of land. Otherwise frustrated in their attempt to work with the *boieri* legislature, Cuza and his prime minister overthrew the assembly in May, 1864, held a national plebescite (with universal male suffrage) to approve the action, and decreed a massive land reform that was meant to solve the agrarian problem once and for all.[90] The reform made Cuza the most popular figure in all Romanian history among the peasants; in fact, faded old pictures of his portrait are still found, 100 years after the event, in many a Romanian peasant house. But no decree could change the fact that the Romanian economy was becoming increasingly colonial, with the *boieri* and foreign interests jointly aligned against the reform measures. Though these measures finally freed the peasants form the last legal vestiges of "feudalism," they did so only to bind them to the landowners' power far more thoroughly than they had ever been bound when they were serfs. The land reform of 1864 marked the opening of the most bitter chapter in the history of peasant–lord relationships.

[87] Riker, *The Making of Roumania*, pp. 249, 339–341; Berindei, *Union des principautés*, pp. 159–191.

[88] East, *Union of Moldavia and Wallachia*, pp. 162–168.

[89] Emerit, *Les paysans roumains*, pp. 440–447.

[90] Constantin C. Giurescu, *Viața și opera lui Cuza Vodă*, 2nd ed. (Bucharest: Editura, științifica, 1970), pp. 164–181, 199–224, 252–254.

7

The Developed Colonial Political Economy and the Agrarian Crisis (1864–1917)

In the latter part of the nineteenth century, Wallachia (united with Moldavia in the new Romanian state) became a fully modern colonial society. This does not mean that it was modernized, in the usual sense of that word, but rather that it took its place as a fairly important peripheral portion of Western Europe's industrial economies by its provision of primary products (mostly cereals), and that its economic, political, and social structure was largely determined by its international economic position. It would be as wrong to call late nineteenth-century Romania a "traditional" society as it would be to call mid-twentieth-century African societies "traditional." (That was the whole point of Balandier's critique of standard anthropological definitions of modernity.)[1] Certainly, these societies were not industrial, and many traditional social forms and attitudes remained, but they had undergone change because of the influence of the industrial world.

"Modernity" usually has been defined in certain descriptive terms that fit industrialized societies. Modern societies are said to be highly centralized, and

[1] George Balandier, "The Colonial Situation: A Theoretical Approach," *Social Change: The Colonial Situation*, ed. Immanuel Wallerstein (New York: Wiley, 1966), pp. 34–61.

their citizens are supposed to be much more mobilized than the citizens of traditional polities. Modern societies are said to be oriented to scientific thought and technological progress; traditional societies, on the other hand, are supposed to be filled with superstition, and they tend to remain stagnant technologically. Modern economies are characterized by producers who produce largely or almost entirely for the market, so that virtually no one is self-sufficient; the reverse is said to be true in traditional societies. Modern societies are supposed to have a high rate of savings and investment, but traditional societies do not. Modern capital is highly liquid, and can thus be channeled in the most productive direction; traditional capital is not liquid, and thus the potential for economic change is low. All of these differences produce social differences as well, and these, in turn, cause further economic differences. (Authors disagree on the causal order, but rarely on the association between social and economic changes.) Modern societies are achievement-oriented, not ascriptively stratified. Work is separated from family life. Norms are universalistic, not particularistic. In short, rationality dominates.[2]

By these criteria, Wallachia was not yet modern in the late nineteenth century. At best, it was in transition. A growing share of production was being sold in the market, and even exported abroad, but there was little or no industrialization, and most villagers still consumed most of their production. The state was becoming more centralized, but decision making and political participation was concentrated in the hands of the very small landowning elite and the small state bureaucracy, which was effectively controlled by these landowners. There was a growing railway network, and in Bucharest and the main port cities there was an increasing number of people with Western educations and an understanding of Western science and technology. But the Wallachian peasantry was technologically backward compared to Western peasants, and the rural economy was characterized by technological stagnation.

But if Wallachia was not yet modern, it was certainly not traditional. For one thing, the entire orientation of the economy—to cereal exports—was a nineteenth-century phenomenon. The very peasant class that was supposed to be the bearer of tradition was a nineteenth-century creation, since before that time rural villagers were more pastoralist than agricultural. New lands were being colonized and brought under the plow. The population was increasing very rapidly.

Nor will the notion of a dual society hold up.[3] In being partly modern (in the

[2]The leading writers who have put forward such views are Talcott Parsons, *The System of Modern Societies* (Englewood Cliffs, N.J.: Prentice-Hall, 1971); Samuel P. Huntington, *Political Order in Changing Societies* (New Haven: Yale University Press, 1968); Gabriel Almond and G. Bingham Powell, *Comparative Politics: A Developmental Approach* (Boston: Little, Brown, 1966); Wilbert E. Moore, *Social Change* (Englewood Cliffs, N.J.: Prentice-Hall, 1963); and various works by Alex Inkeles, Daniel Lerner, and Reinhard Bendix.

[3]For a discussion of these terms, see Manning Nash, "The Multiple Society in Economic Development: Mexico and Guatemala," *American Anthropologist* 59 (October, 1957): 825–833. Nash uses the term "multiple" rather than "dual," but the idea of plural cultures' existing within a single state is well brought out.

cities) and partly traditional (in the countryside), Wallachia may seem to have been a good example of what has been called a dual society in transition. But first of all, this social dualism actually was very old, dating back to the communal-trade political economy, when it was much more pronounced than in more modern times. Second, the colonial society was not functionally dual because the cities and the elite depended totally on rural production, while the peasantry was under the control of landowners and the cities. In the fourteenth or fifteenth century, Wallachia *was* a true dual society; the Ottoman conquest changed this, and the coming of age of the modern colonial society ended the dualism once and for all. The difference between the elite and urban way of life and the rural way of life was but two sides of the same coin, and one could not have occurred without the other.

Even the term "transitional" is suspect. Certainly, Wallachia was in transition. In fact, it had been in transition many times before, particularly in the sixteenth century. But it was not in transition toward the type of society that prevailed in Western Europe. It was not becoming industrialized; rather, it was becoming more of a colony. Even the reform of 1864 led in that direction, because the freeing of land from traditional bonds and its transformation into fully private property helped both the landowners and the export economy, while furthering the subjugation of the peasants. All this can be verified by looking at: (1) patterns of international trade; (2) the changes in class structure; (3) the changes in rural society; and (4) the nature of the agrarian crisis that resulted at the start of the twentieth century.

The Open Economy

A colonial or neocolonial economy is open. As Dudley Seers has pointed out, this means that it is highly dependent on exogenous forces—namely, the market—for its primary agricultural or mineral exports. In return, it imports a large number of industrial goods, from luxury items that cannot be produced locally to consumer goods that can be produced more cheaply abroad.[4] The alliance between local landowners who extract the main export goods and the industrial trading partners of the colony make a change in this pattern difficult, because those in power profit from the situation. Profits are exported either in the form of actual repatriation (or investment), flowing from the colonial to the metropolitan countries, or in the form of purchases of industrial goods. Thus, whatever the investments made, they are designed to strengthen the colonial pattern, not to change it. Railroads are built, leading from the

[4]Dudley Seers, "The Stages of Economic Growth of a Primary Producer in the Middle of the Twentieth Century," *Imperialism and Underdevelopment*, ed. Robert I. Rhodes (New York: Monthly Review Press, 1970), pp. 163–180.

hinterlands to the main commercial cities, port facilities, and the like. But what little industry develops beyond this is either controlled by foreigners or is of only marginal significance; at best, it specializes in the mildest form of import substitution, not in creating a diversified industrial structure.[5]

A quick look at Romanian trade figures supplied in Tables 1 and 2 shows the pattern that prevailed. (Unfortunately, it is impossible to separate Wallachian from Moldavian statistics after 1860. But given that Wallachia comprised two-thirds of the new state, and that social and economic conditions were virtually the same in both parts, this does not pose much of a problem.) Though the pro-

TABLE 1
Exterior Commerce of Wallachia and Moldavia from 1832 to 1913 in Gold (Constant) Lei[6]

	Imports	Exports
1832	18,000,000	21,000,000
1840	20,000,000	35,000,000
1850	28,000,000	47,000,000
1860	63,000,000	116,000,000
1865	68,000,000	112,000,000
1875	100,000,000	145,000,000
1885	268,000,000	248,000,000
1895	305,000,000	265,000,000
1905	338,000,000	457,000,000
1913	590,000,000	670,000,000

TABLE 2
Composition of Romanian Exports as Percentage of Value of Categories[7]

	Cereals	Wood	Petroleum[8]	Other
1882	80.9	2.1	0.7	16.3
1892	88.3	1.1	0.7	8.9
1902	78.1	5.2	0.1	16.4
1912	75.8	3.8	10.3	10.1

[5] *Ibid.*; Dudley Seers, "Rich Countries and Poor," *Development in a Divided World*, ed. Dudley Seers and Leonard Joy (Harmondsworth, England: Penguin, 1971), p. 18; Oscar Braun, "The External Economic Strategy: Outward- or Inward-looking?", in *Development in a Divided World*, p. 172.

[6] C. C. Giurescu, M. Gr. Romaşcanu, and N. Georgescu-Roegen, "Comerţul exterior," *Enciclopedia României* Bucharest: Imprimeria naţională, 1943), **IV**, pp. 463–465.

[7] *Ibid.*, p. 466.

[8] The Ploeşti oil fields became important in the early twentieth century and provided a new primary product for export.

portions of the categories of imports are more difficult to calculate, the overwhelming percentage consisted of manufactured goods (see Table 3). Thus, most of Romania's trade was with industrialized states. As Great Britain turned

TABLE 3
Percentage of Imports from Various Countries as Percentage of Value of Total Imports[9]

	1882	1892	1902	1912
Great Britain	16.9	22.8	19.5	13.8
Austria–Hungary	50.0	23.4	24.6	21.8[10]
France	8.6	8.1	6.0	6.1
Germany	11.3	29.8	28.3	37.7
Belgium	1.0	5.4	1.8	3.2
Turkey	3.8	3.7	3.3	2.3

TABLE 4
Percentage of Exports to Various Countries as Percentage of Value of Total Exports[11]

	1882	1892	1902	1912
Great Britain	39.9	42.2	11.0	6.7
Holland	2.0	0.6	3.6	8.1
Austria–Hungary	30.5	11.0	11.8	14.8
France	10.9	3.9	3.0	7.8
Germany	2.3	11.7	5.3	6.6
Italy	1.9	7.1	5.4	18.8
Belgium	0.2	15.1	54.5	23.8
Turkey	5.1	5.3	2.0	4.0

[9] Giurescu, Romaşcanu, Georgescu-Roegen, "Comerţul exterior," *Enciclopedia României*, **IV**, p. 466.

[10] Austria–Hungary's attempts to absorb Romania's economy ended in 1885. Basically, Austria–Hungary was not sufficiently industrialized, and Romanian food imports conflicted too strongly with the interests of the Hungarian landowners. Whereas before this data Transylvania was industrializing by exporting manufactured goods to Romania and importing Romanian food, the opposition of the Hungarian landowners caused a reversal of the policy that encouraged this. The result was a customs war between Austria–Hungary and Romania from 1885 to 1891. Trade between the two countries fell off sharply, and Transylvanian industry was ruined. This set off a strong migratory trend from Transylvania to America and spelled the end of Austrian economic power in Romania. Austria–Hungary's place was taken by Germany which became the chief provider of Romanian manufactured imports.

[11] Giurescu, Romaşcanu, and Georgescu-Roegen, "Comerţul exterior," *Enciclopedia României*, **IV**, p. 466. The import and export statistics in the statistical anuaries of the pre-World War I years list imports under categories such as "wood and wood products," "metals and metal products," etc., so that it is not clear what proportion of the imports were finished and semifinished goods. But when it is shown that in the decade before World War I most such goods came from England and Germany, it becomes clear that these two countries were not exporting raw lumber or minerals to Romania. The reverse conclusion can be drawn from exports to industrial countries from Romania.

to new sources of cereal imports at the end of the nineteenth century, relying more heavily than before on America, Romania began exporting more to other food-deficit countries of Western Europe (see Table 4).

As can be seen from Table 5, the quantity of cereal exports which had been growing since the late eighteenth century continued to grow rapidly, particularly wheat and corn. Other cereal exports also grew, but not as rapidly.[12]

The surface covered by cereals also grew very rapidly, as Table 6 shows. On the average, about half of all wheat produced was exported. The proportion of corn exported was less than this, but it was still a major part of production.[13]

In most twentieth-century colonial or neocolonial societies, very rapid

TABLE 5
Average Yearly Wheat and Corn Exports in Metric Tons[14]

	Wheat	Corn
1880–1884	334,000	610,000
1885–1889	593,000	610,000
1890–1894	748,000	802,000
1895–1899	678,000	454,000
1900–1904	751,000	787,000
1905–1906	1,722,000	320,000

TABLE 6
Average Yearly Number of Hectares of Wheat and Corn[15]

	Wheat	Corn
1862–1866	697,000	980,000
1867–1871	877,000	1,085,000
1872–1876	1,065,000	1,385,000
1866–1890	1,282,000	1,766,000
1891–1895	1,435,000	1,794,000
1896–1900	1,561,000	1,993,000
1901–1905	1,681,000	2,090,000
1906–1907	1,869,000	2,006,000

[12] *Anuarul statistic al României, 1909* (Bucharest, 1909), p. 159.
[13] *Ibid.*, pp. 145–147, 159.
[14] *Ibid.*, p. 159.
[15] *Ibid.*, p. 146.

urbanization has occurred.[16] This was not the case in Wallachia, perhaps as a result of both the low population density in nineteenth-century Romania and the availability of large amounts of new land until the turn of the century. Population growth will be examined below, but at this point it is worth noting that most of the population remained rural; while the cities grew, only the main city, Bucharest, grew much more rapidly than the hinterlands. This can be used as a further indicator of the direction of development—not toward an industrial, urban economy, but rather toward a rural, cereal-export economy. A county-by-county breakdown or rural and urban population demonstrates this point.

In 1876, 88% of the Wallachian population was rural. Only Ilfov, containing Bucharest, and Brăila, containing the main Danube port, were less than 80% rural. By 1899 only Ilfov was less than half rural, while Brăila was 61% rural. During that time, only Ilfov showed a high degree of urban growth, going from 36% to 52% urban. Aside from these two counties, the rural population fell by an insignificant proportion, from about 92% of the total in 1876 to 90% in 1899.[17]

By any statistical test, then, Wallachia and Moldavia fit the model of the open economy. There was growth—indeed, rapid growth—but only in the production of cereals and in the main enclave of the colonial political economy, Bucharest. That growth deeply affected rural life and was in turn affected by rural changes.

The Effects of the Reform of 1864

The terms of the reform of 1864 ended corvée and tithe obligations and finally established full private property rights over the land. Former corvée peasants (*clăcaşi*) received title to their houses and garden plots and to varying amounts of farm land, according to the number of oxen they possessed. As in the Organic Regulation, the *boieri* did not have to relinquish more than two-thirds of the corvée village lands, and they received firm title to at least one-third of the land. Forest lands were not included, and remained the property of the lords, except for forests that had belonged to unappropriated (*moşneni*, or free) villages. The farm land meted out to the former serfs was declared inalienable for 30 years in order to promote stability and to prevent land speculators from buying out the peasants.[18]

[16]See Kingsley Davis, "The Urbanization of the Human Population," *An Urban World*, ed. Charles Tilly (Boston: Little, Brown, 1974), pp. 160–175.

[17]Dimitrie Sturdza, "Suprafaţa şi populaţiunea regatului României," *Buletin*, Societatea geografica română **XVI**, trim. 3 and 4 (Bucharest, 1896), p. 64; *Anuarul statistic, 1909*, p. 23.

[18]*Lege rurală cu proclamaţiunea Mariei Sale Domnitorului a Principatelor Unite Române* (Bucharest: Imprimeria Statului, 1864), pp. 8–11.

There were four categories of former serfs who received different amounts of land according to the number of oxen and cows they possessed. Those with at least four oxen and one cow received 5.5 hectares. Those with at least two oxen and one cow got 3.9 hectares. Those with at least one cow got 2.3 hectares. Those with less received house and garden plots (on the average of about .2 hectares).[19]

In actual fact, the distribution of land was very uneven and varied significantly from county to county. The best way of comprehending the effects of the reform is to combine the land given after the reform of 1864 with that given after the amendment of 1878, which distributed land to the young families that had not yet formed as of 1864. The county-by-county distribution sheds a good deal of light on the nature of agrarian society in each area.

The percentage of serfs who actually received land was different in each county. In most of the hill and mountain areas, more than 90% of the former serfs received some land, either in 1864 or in 1878. But in the plains areas, in which there was a far larger proportion of serfs but in which the lords were also much more powerful, the percentage of former serfs who benefited from the reform varied from about 50% in parts of the Bărăgan to a high of 85% in the county of Olt. A table of Wallachian counties, classified by geographic characteristics, shows the wide variance between the two main types of regions.

The mean percentage by county of peasants who were serfs before 1864 was 72%, and the percentage of serfs who received land in 1864 and 1878 was 82%; therefore, a table of "high" and "low" categories can be constructed.[20] Tabulating those counties that had 72% or fewer of their peasants in serfdom before 1864 as "low serf" and those counties where 82% or fewer of the serfs received land from the reforms as "low reform" counties, and then dividing the counties by their respective geographic characteristics, yields Table 7. (See Map 2.)

[19] *Ibid.*, p. 8.

[20] The statistics on the percentage of serfs who received land from the reforms of 1864 and 1878 are taken from C. Jormescu and I. Popa-Burcă, *Harta agronomică a României* (Bucharest: Carol Göbl 1907), table 13, pt. 2. Their figures agree very closely with those given in an earlier estimate of the distribution in Leonida Colescu, *La loi rurale de 1864 et statistiques des paysans devenus propriétaires par l'application de la loi de 1864* (Bucharest, 1900), p. 5. The statistics on the percentage of peasants in each county who were serfs before 1864 are based on questions asked during the census of 1912. They are thus based on the memory of peasants about their families 50 years earlier. This makes the numbers at least somewhat questionable; however, the fact that the distinction between *moşneni* (free) and *clăcaşi* (serf) remained so important in the peasants' minds (they remain important even today) suggests that these numbers are at least roughly correct. The results of the inquiry of 1912 are reported in Henri H. Stahl, "Organizarea socială a ţărănimii," *Enciclopedia României*, I, p. 575. The division of counties into hill and plains counties follows the conventional division made by Romanian geographers. But it is possible to validate the division by seeing what percentage of each county was cultivated about 1900. All of the counties listed as plains counties had at least 50% of their total surface under cultivation at this time except for Râmnicu-Sărat which had 49%. None of the hill counties had more than 40% of its land under cultivation. See Jormescu and Popa-Burcă, *Harta agronomică*, p. 152.

TABLE 7
Relationship between Geography, Serfdom, and the Effects of the Reform of 1864, by County

	Hill and mountain		Plains	
	High reform	Low reform	High reform	Low reform
Low serf	6	1	1	0
High serf	1	0	0	8

Seven of the eight hill and mountain counties were "low serf"; only one of the nine plains counties was "low serf." On the other hand, seven of the eight hill and mountain counties were "high" on reform, and only one of the nine plains counties was in that same category.[21]

It is fairly easy to explain these differences. In the hills, the lords had always been somewhat weaker than in the plains (as is reflected by the lower number of serfs), and they were not able to manipulate the local administration quite as easily as did the plains lords. There thus were fewer exceptions made to the reform law. At the same time, because there were relatively fewer serfs to satisfy, it was easier to accommodate them. But the first reason, rather than the second, was more important. Given the relative abundance of land in the plains (which were, shown in the last chapter, more lightly populated), only the local power of the lords and the corruption of the local administration can explain why the distribution was not more equitable in that region, especially in the vast spaces of the Bărăgan (Ialomiţa and Brăila). Indeed, later developments verify this contention; the Bărăgan eventually became an area of heavy immigration.

Under the system of peasant–lord relations that evolved after 1864, the lords saw the advantage of giving plots to the peasants, and most of the immigrants did receive land. But the fact that the advantages to be reaped by the lords were not obvious in the first years of the reform explains why relatively large numbers of serfs initially were kept from enjoying the benefits of the new law. In addition to this, wherever possible the lords gave the serfs the worst of the village lands; they measured plots fraudulently; they often gave the peasants lands to which there were no paths, so that the peasants would have to pass through lords' lands to reach their fields (for which they naturally had to pay the lord); and the lords soon began to buy up peasant lands, even though this was illegal, by using various legal ruses. The tradition of administrative corruption that had developed throughout the period of Ottoman rule, and which had been per-

[21] It would be tempting to explain every deviant case. But in view of the fact that the data are not that precise, and that the breakdown by county hides some of the differences, both geographic and social, within counties, this would be counterproductive. Nevertheless, when the data are grouped in this way, most cases do fall into the categories that are hypothesized.

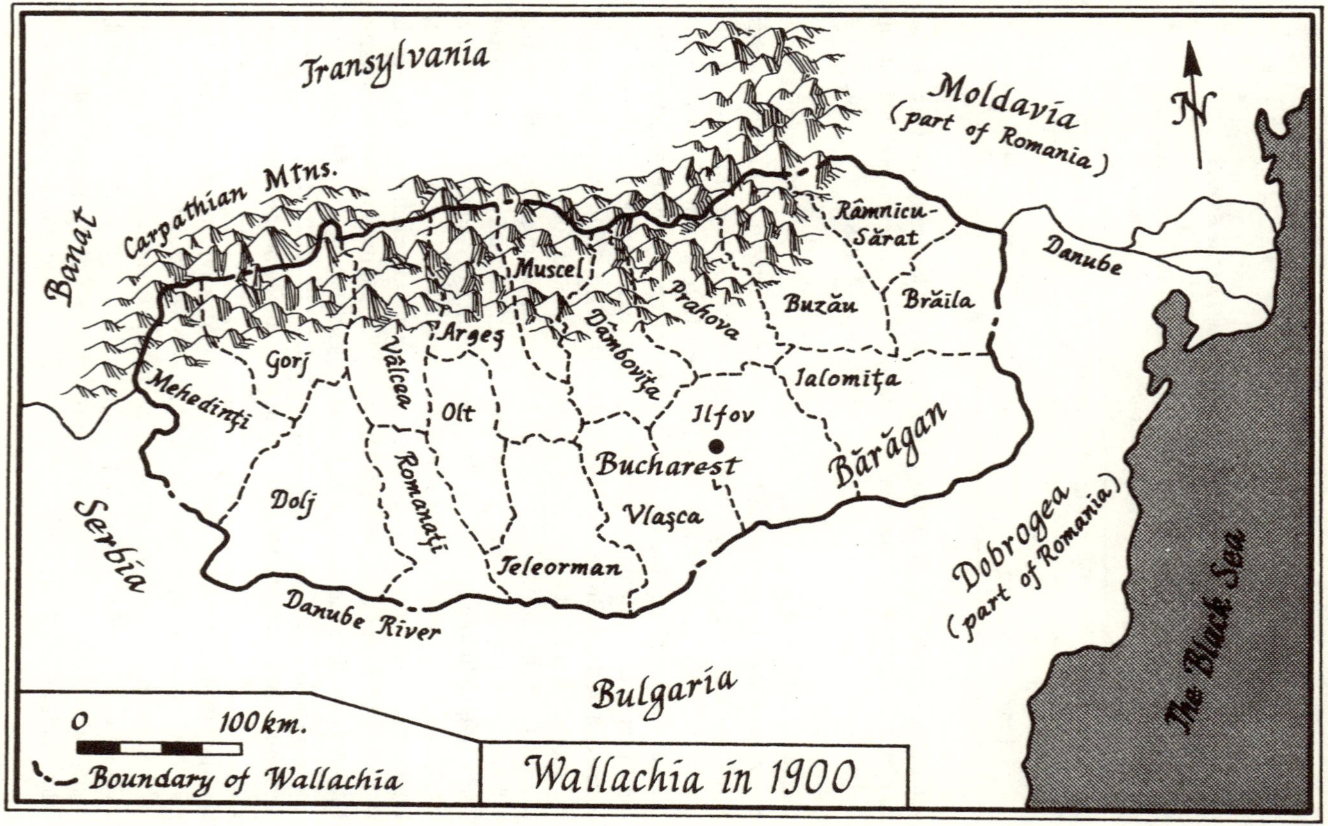
Transylvania
Moldavia
(part of Romania)
N
Carpathian Mtns.
Banat
Râmnicu-
Sărat
Danube
Muscel
Prahova
Buzău
Brăila
Argeş
Dâmbovița
Gorj
Vâlcea
Ialomița
Mehedinți
Olt
Ilfov
Bărăgan
Bucharest
Romanați
Dolj
Vlaşca
Serbia
Teleorman
Dobrogea
(part of Romania)
Danube River
The Black Sea
Bulgaria
0
100 km.
Boundary of Wallachia
Wallachia in 1900

Map 2

petuated under the Organic Regulation, greatly weakened the power of the central government to counteract these evasions of the law.[22]

It has been estimated that, in general, the richest category of peasant serf received enough land to form viable units of production. This was truer in the extensively cultivated cereal areas of the plains than in the more diversified hill regions.[23] But only a minority of the beneficiaries of the reform had enough animals to be in this "rich" category of serfs. In the hills, the proportion of prosperous serfs was even smaller than in the plains, so that many more of the beneficiaries found themselves on inadequate holdings. Conversely, because a larger portion of the plains serfs received no land at all, the plains had a larger portion of landless ex-serfs. In either case, the result was the same—many of the freed serfs could not survive without either working for the lords in the plains and in those hill areas which had estates, or emigrating to the plains in search of estate lands that needed labor. In order to get an idea of how many ex-serfs were in this position, it is essential to distinguish between the hill and plains areas. Whereas 5 hectares was the bare minimum size a peasant needed to be self-sufficient in the plains, somewhat less land was needed in the hills because these often had some vineland, fruit trees, and more available pasture for animals in the nearby mountains. It will be assumed that, in the plains, only the richest category of ex-serf received enough land. In the hills, it will be assumed that the first two categories of ex-serfs received enough land.

In the hills, on the average, 48% of all serfs did not receive enough land. This amounted to 27% of all peasants. In the plains, 80% of all serfs received insufficient land. This amounted to about 67% of all peasants.[24] (These percentages are calculated by averaging data from the county level.)

This does not yet give a fair indication of the proportion of peasants with inadequate holdings, because many of the hill *moşneni* (free peasants before 1864) also had inadequate holdings.[25] Assuming that at least one-third of the *moşneni* did not have enough land (this is somewhat less than the proportion of serfs in the hills with inadequate holdings—and there is no good reason to assume that the *moşneni* were any more prosperous than the ex-serfs; most accounts suggest they may have been, on the average, somewhat poorer) *at least* 40% of the hill counties'

[22]Marcel Emerit, *Les paysans roumains depuis le traité d'Andrinople jusqu'à la libération des terres (1829–1864)* (Paris: Recueil Sirey, 1937), pp. 509–513.

[23]Dimitrie Gusti, "Chestiunea agrară," *D. Gusti: Opere*, ed. O. Bădina and O. Neamţu (Bucharest: Editura academiei, 1970), **IV**, p. 49.

[24]Jormescu and Popa-Burcă, *Harta agronomică*, p. 38. Again, these figures are not as precise as they seem to be. The authors give the percentage of the receiving serfs in each of the four categories of wealth. By multiplying this by the percentage of serfs who received any land at all one gets the percentage of all serfs in each category of receivers. Taking this and adding the percentage of ex-serfs who received no land at all gives the total percentage of ex-serfs left with insufficient land.

[25]Emerit, *Les paysans roumains*, pp. 248–250; G. Vâlsan, "O fază în popularea Ţărilor Româneşti," *Buletin*, Societatea geografica română, XXXIII (Bucharest, 1912): 201–226.

populations were on inadequate holdings. Because the plains had far fewer *moşneni* than the hills, the numbers given need only be augmented slightly to show the total proportion of plains peasants on inadequate holdings—on the order of 60% to 80% of the peasants in most of the plains districts.

Nor do the simple statistics of land distribution explain the whole situation. Before the reform, the forests and pastures had been communal (though, as noted earlier, increasing restrictions on the use of forest and pasture lands had been imposed by the lords throughout the nineteenth century). After the reform, the larger part of these areas became the property of the lords. In the plains, it was in the interest of the lords to clear such areas for cereal cultivation. So the availability of pasture was sharply decreased, and as a result the poor peasants no longer had enough pasture available to them. This is reflected by the rising incidence of pellagra (due to the disappearance of protein sources). Corn became the only source of food among many of the peasants. But whereas the peasant corn dish *mămăligă* traditionally had been eaten with dairy products and some meat, by the late nineteenth century the intake of animal products had fallen.[26] The over-all number of animals did not decline between 1860 and 1900, but neither did it rise, while during that period the rural population increased by more than 50%.[27]

One other aspect of the reform virtually guaranteed that peasant misery was to follow. The reform gave expropriated land to the freed serfs, but it obliged them to pay back their corvée and tithe obligations. The lords received state bonds that were to be repaid from the peasants' dues over a 15-year period. The burden of repayment was too heavy for most peasants, and the debt was never fully repaid but refloated through a series of state bonds. Thus, payments by the peasants continued.[28] As might be expected, substantial numbers of those who gained land in the reform lost it because of their inability to pay off the debts incurred through the reform. At least some of this land found its way back into the hands of the lords.[29] Though there are no statistics on actual land turnover that resulted from peasant indebtedness, by about 1900 well over one-third of the cultivated lands in the eastern Wallachian plains belonged to large landowners rather than to the peasants.[30] This does not, however, explain the insi-

[26] Ioan Claudian, *Alimentaţia poporului român* (Bucharest: Fundaţia Regele Carol II, 1939), pp. 110–111; A. D. Xenopol, "Starea economică a ţaranului român," *A. D. Xenopol, Opere economice*, ed. Ion Veverca (Bucharest: Editura academiei, 1967), p. 314.

[27] Jormescu and Popa-Burcă, *Harta agronomică*, p. 219.

[28] Colescu, *La loi rurale de 1864*, pp. 27–30.

[29] An account of the events after the reform of 1864 can be found for certain villages. The post-World War I Romanian sociologists collected accounts about the past from old village men and women. One such account, taken from the village of Iteşti, indicates that between the demands for repayment of debts, taxes, and the lord's demands on their labor, peasants had a hard time keeping their land. C. I. Floareş, "Amintire cu privire la situaţia dinainte de împroprietărire a unui sat de foşti clăcaşi," *Sociologie Românească* **II**, nos. 7–8 (1937): 362–364.

[30] Jormescu and Popa-Burcă, *Harta agronomică*, p. 140.

dious way in which the peasants were turned back into serfs. To understand that process, it is necessary first to understand the development of agrarian relations after the reform.

The Overthrow of Cuza and Kogălniceanu

The coup that led to the reform of 1864 was resented by the *boieri*, who initially did not realize that they could turn the consequences of the reform to their advantage. At first, they had hoped to receive foreign help to redress the situation to their liking, but Russia was busy repressing a Polish revolt, Austria and Prussia were engaged in a war with Denmark, and Napoleon III supported Cuza. The Ottoman Empire, supported by Great Britain, was anxious to intervene against Cuza, but Cuza traveled to Constantinople and persuaded these powers that his coup was not meant to harm their interests, and thus was able to pass his reform.[31]

The reform had unexpected results. Cereal production dropped very sharply in 1865 and 1866. The peasants felt that they no longer needed to cultivate those amounts of grain that had gone to pay for corvée and tithe obligations, but only enough to satisfy their own needs. Thus, for Wallachia and Moldavia together, the area cultivated in wheat fell by more than 50% between 1864 and 1865, and the area cultivated in corn fell by slightly more than one-quarter.[32] This seemed to confirm the lords' worst fears, and it also increased the antipathy of the liberal–nationalists (i.e., the leaders of the revolt of 1848 and their followers) for Cuza.

The liberals had never been particularly pro-peasant, but had merely fought for national unity and independence. By 1865, both aims had been achieved, and Cuza was viewed as a demagogue willing to ruin the national economy by expropriating the *boieri* and showing a dangerously radical tendency to favor the peasants. The oppostion of the liberals was crucial in at least one respect: With their old connections in Paris, they were able to persuade Napoleon III to drop his support of Cuza. Faced by joint *boieri*–liberal oppostion, and stripped of all foreign support, Cuza could rely only on the peasantry. But the reform had not altered the balance of political forces. That could have been done only by arming the peasants, which would, however, have brought immediate foreign intervention. In 1866 there was a coup against Cuza, and rather than trying to fight back, he went into exile.[33]

By the time of his overthrow, Cuza apparently had recognized that the reform of 1864 was insufficient to establish a prosperous and independent

[31] Emerit, *Les paysans roumains*, pp. 502–503.

[32] *Ibid.*, p. 521.

[33] Constantin C. Giurescu, *Viaţa şi opera lui Cuza Vodă*, 2nd ed. (Bucharest: Editura ştiinţifică, 1970), pp. 252–391.

peasantry. He had been planning to extend the reform before he was forced to abdicate. After Cuza's overthrow, despite a number of minor adjustments over the next five decades, the law of 1864 remained essentially unchanged.[34]

The political system established after 1866 favored a perpetuation of the inequities written into the reform law of 1864. A monarchy was established by the nationalist–liberals, whose main goals still were to establish a fully independent Romania and to legitimize its existence through Europe. (It was only in 1878 that the last theoretical remnants of Ottoman domination were removed and Romania became a fully independent kingdom.) A Hohenzollern prince, under the name of Carol I, was chosen to replace Cuza; he was to rule for 50 years.[35]

In theory, the government was controlled by a parliamentary regime, but the right to vote was so restricted that the landowners held the real power. As late as 1911, 45% of the members of the Chamber of Deputies and 48% of the members of the Senate were listed as landowners. In fact, the actual proportion of landowners in parliament was higher, because quite a few of those listed as having other professions were really landowners as well. (For example, about one-quarter of the members were listed as lawyers, and many of these were landowners, as were some of the other members listed under a variety of professions.)[36] Political control alternated between the "liberal" and the "conservative" parties, but both were largely controlled by landowners and their ideologies differed slightly, if at all. Romanian politics in the late nineteenth century was filled with intrigues over foreign alliances. There was a pro-German party favored by the king, a pro-French party, and a great deal of discussion about whether to join the Central Powers or the Entente. And, though the peasant question came up again and again, the peasants were almost totally powerless.[37]

Agrarian Relations after 1866: Neoserfdom

The new government imposed work loads on the peasantry in order to force the ex-serfs to repay their debts. The army was used to enforce this new regulation,

[34] Emerit, *Les paysans roumains*, p. 525.

[35] R. W. Seton-Watson, *History of the Roumanians*, 2nd ed. (Hamden, Conn.: Archon Books, 1963). Seton-Watson goes into great detail to explain the intrigues associated with Romanian politics. The key issue seems to have been the Great Powers' fear that Romania might become a "revolutionary" state (p. 325). Thus, England's agreement that Cuza had to be overthrown was crucial (p. 313). The political form that emerged after 1866 satisfied the powers and kept Romania safely away from potentially radical experiments and, not coincidentally, as a state firmly committed to being a grain exporter to the West. Those familiar with the literature on "neocolonialism" in the twentieth century will not, of course, be surprised by this reasoning.

[36] Mattei Dogan, "L'origine sociale du personnel parlementaire d'un pays essentiellement agraire, la Roumanie," *Revue de l'institut de sociologie*, nos. 2–3 (Brussels, 1953): 168–169.

[37] Paul Lendvai, *Eagles in Cobwebs* (New York: Doubleday, 1969), pp. 333–335.

and the peasants were obliged to work on estate lands. Thus, a new form of the corvée was established, assuring the lords of a cheap labor force.[38] This was not, however, the only source of labor. Those peasants without sufficient land to support themselves had no recourse but to work the lands of the big owners. A sharecropping system developed that was rather similar to the prereform arrangement. Peasants cultivated the lords' land, in return for which they were allowed to work plots for themselves. The lords did not own the means of production, either the animals or the tools necessary for agriculture; rather, the peasants used their own.

The difference between the new system and the old one was one more of form than of substance. Before the reform, the land had been controlled, but not owned outright, by the lords. After the reform, land was owned by the lords; but for all practical purposes, peasants continued to work demesne land as if little had changed. This meant that the technological level of agriculture remained primitive, and that for the peasant little or no change had occurred, or rather no change for the better. On the contrary, the new arrangements were far more onerous than the old ones because they demanded more work by the peasants on the lords' lands.[39] The proof of the worsening situation (aside from the drop in nutrition reflected by rising pellagra rates) was that in 1882, the parliament felt compelled to pass a law that assured the peasants the right to work on their own land rather than on the lord's at least 2 days a week. This was believed to be the minimum required for survival.[40] In other words, by the 1880s it was common for the peasants to spend two-thirds of their working time on the lords' lands. This was clearly far in excess of the yearly 12 days of corvée required before the Organic Regulation, or even in excess of the estimated 56 days a year that peasants gave lords in the mid-nineteenth century.

Though the agrarian system remained basically the same between 1866 and World War I, a number of minor changes were made. As mentioned earlier, new households received some land in 1878. At that time, some 27,000 peasant families received an average of 5.2 hectares.[41] In 1881 and 1889 there were further distributions. The distribution of 1881 was quite small and included only some 4250 Wallachian peasant families, but in 1889 about 81,500 families received land. The numbers of recipients in 1889 was particularly large in the plains areas, where fewer peasants had received land after 1864.[42] As a result of these distributions, most ex-serf families eventually received some land. This was possible because the state held large reserves of land obtained at the time of

[38] Constantin Garoflid, "Regimul agrarîn România," *Enciclopedia României*, I, p. 578.

[39] The system was best described by Constantin Dobrodgeanu-Gherea, an early Romanian socialist, in *Neoiobăgia* [neoserfdom], 2nd ed. (Bucharest: Viaţa românească, n.d.), pp. 106–130.

[40] Garoflid, "Regimul agrar," *Enciclopedia României*, I, p. 578.

[41] Colescu, *La loi rurale de 1864*.

[42] Jormescu and Popa-Burcă, *Harta agronomică*, table 13, pt. 2.

the expropriation of the dedicated monasteries. But the land distributions met with few objections, because they were felt to relieve peasant discontent while not seriously endangering the position of the large owners.

As will be shown later, by the 1880s it was obvious that the land was becoming relatively overpopulated, and that even when the peasants owned their small plots of land, they would still have to work for the large owners in order to survive. In 1882, military supervision of forced labor was abolished. In 1893, the laws obliging peasants to work on estate lands were again relaxed (both these measures were passed by conservative governments). Despite the relaxations of restrictions, the peasants' situation worsened. In all of Wallachia and Moldavia, the average peasant holding in 1864 was 4.6 hectares. In 1896 it was down to 3.4 hectares, and in 1905 it was officially down to 3.2 hectares. (In fact, it was lower, because the censuses often lumped more than one family into a single household unit.)[43] By the late nineteenth century, the population had risen sufficiently to make forced labor useless.

The argument presented previously that serfdom is suited to conditions of low population density (to provide a labor force for a landed elite) is readily applicable to the relaxation of formal restrictions on peasant freedom in the last decades of the nineteenth century.[44] With a higher population density, the agrarian system could move into what Arthur Stinchcombe has called a "family-size tenancy" system. Briefly, this is a system in which

> the operative unit of agriculture is the family enterprise, but property rights in the enterprise rest with rentier capitalists. The return from the enterprise is divided according to some rental scheme, either in money or in kind. The rent may be fixed, with modification in years of bad harvest, or share.[45]

Such a system, according to Stinchcombe, tends to be politically insecure because of five factors. First, because the issue in the conflict between peasant and rentier is relatively clear, "the lower the rent of the rentier capitalists, the higher the income of the peasantry." Second, the peasant bears a disproportionate share of the risks involved in the enterprise because the rentiers shift risk away from themselves. Third, there tends to be little social contact between the rentiers and the peasants. The former tend to live in the cities, and "the urban rentier, with his educated and often foreign speech, his cosmopolitan interests, his arrogant rejection of rustic life is a logical target of the rural community. . . ." Fourth, "the leaders of the rural community, the rich peasants, are not vulner-

[43] Garoflid, "Regimul agrar", *Enciclopedia României*, I, pp. 578–579.

[44] See n. 7, chap. 5; Maurice Dobb, *Studies in the Development of Capitalism* (New York: International Publishers, 1963), pp. 66–67.

[45] Arthur Stinchcombe, "Agricultural Enterprise and Rural Class Relations," *Class, Status, and Power*, 2nd ed., ed. R. Bendix and S. M. Lipset (New York: Free Press, 1966), pp. 182–190.

able to expulsion by the landowners. . . . The rich peasant shares at least some of the hardships and is opposed in his class interests to many of the same people as are the tenants." Finally, the tenant farmer is aware of the fact that he could manage a farm without the aid of the owner; in fact, he does manage the land he works, and production is not based on large units.[46]

This system fits the Romanian agrarian system between 1866 and World War I. Even before the reform of 1864, Wallachian and Moldavian rural society had developed many of the characteristics described by Stinchcombe. The aristocracy had become largely urban and was letting its lands be managed by "farmers" (*arendași*) who rented the right to collect peasant dues. The adoption of foreign cultural habits (Greek during the Ottoman domination, and French increasingly during the nineteenth century) had done much to split the aristocracy from the peasant masses. The peasants bore not only most of the risks of production, but also all of its capital costs. The landowners therefore were viewed as usurping and useless parasites rather than as a protecting, paternalistic, "feudal" nobility. The only elements that had been lacking before the nineteenth century to transform the system into a true "family-size tenancy" system were (1) the existence of a readily marketable crop (as was shown above, pastoralism did not readily lend itself to this type of system), and (2) a population density sufficiently high to make forced labor unnecessary. Under the Organic Regulation, the wheat-exporting economy developed sufficiently to create an imperative demand for fixed labor; but it was not until the 1880s that the population density reached a high enough level to satisfy the other requirement for the transformation, which explains the transition by way of a forced labor system.

But Stinchcombe's explanation leaves out the dynamic elements of the situation, even though he notes that such systems are politically unstable. This is a doubtful generalization since, in some places (for example, China) family-sized tenancy systems persisted for centuries—perhaps millenia.[47] The key is the existence of a dependent peasantry that produces a surplus for market-conscious landlords, and a rapidly growing demand for the surplus commodity. Whether these elements jointly produce a tenancy system or a more direct form of serfdom depends on the population density and the technology—that is, on the availability of labor; it does not depend on a shift in the type of political economy.

In that sense, Dobrodgeanu-Gherea's term "neoserfdom" is more appropriate.

[46] *Ibid.*, pp. 185–187. The only statement made by Stinchcombe that does not fit Romania is that such a system requires "high productivity." In cases where wheat and maize are the main crops, he suggests that a "historical, rather than economic explanation is appropriate . . . ."

[47] At least this is the view of Hsiao-tung Fei, *China's Gentry* (Chicago: University of Chicago Press, Phoenix Books, 1968), pp. 108–126. He feels that the introduction of Western manufactured goods destroyed an old tenancy system in which peasants relied on handicraft activities to balance their budgets. When handicrafts declined but rents did not, the tenurial system cracked.

The Wallachian peasants were not simply tenants; they were almost serfs bound to accept unequal contracts. This type of development has been very common in areas newly opened to a capitalist market in agricultural products. In much of Latin America, particularly in Peru, Bolivia, and Mexico, the nineteenth-century liberal revolutions transformed land into private property and established legal systems that recognized the right to "free" contracts. The Indian peasantry then went through a period of "neoserfdom."[48] Elsewhere, for example in large parts of southern Europe, the growth of the market and the liberalization of property and contract laws produced similar results.[49] Whether peasants were held by some form of tenancy agreement or by some other contractual agreement made relatively little difference.

Population Changes

As might be expected, the areas in which population grew most quickly were the plains counties, where cereal production was most important.

The median Romanian county grew by 53% between 1859 and 1899. The average hill county grew by 42%, and the average plains county by 77% during this period.[50] These growth figures are for whole counties, not just for rural areas. But, since it was shown perviously that outside of Ilfov (Bucharest), cities grew only slightly faster or no faster at all than their hinterlands, these estimates of population increase are quite close to the simple rural increase. Of eight hill and mountain counties, only one grew faster than the median county growth. Of nine plains counties, only two grew more slowly than the median. The most rapid growth was in the Bărăgan steppe (Brăila and Ialomiţa). In general, people migrated rather heavily from the hills to the plains, and Romanian migrants from Hungarian Transylvania added to this migration. The growth of the plains—particularly the Bărăgan steppe where the landlords were most powerful—shows that it was not lack of land that prevented more equitable distribution at the time of the reform of 1864. The plains' growth also shows that the need for labor was rapidly increasing in the best cereal areas, and that much new land was being cleared.

The availability of new land prevented the kind of disproportionate urban growth seen in many underdeveloped countries in the twentieth century. There was actually no general overpopulation at all, only relative overpopulation from the point of view of the peasant who did not own enough land. But the situation was changing very rapidly as a result of the large population increase, so that by the 1890s the landlords could easily procure sufficient labor. As

[48]Doreen Warriner, *Land Reform in Principle and Practice* (London: Oxford University Press, 1969), pp. 7–10.
[49]E. J. Hobsbawm, *Primitive Rebels* (New York: Norton, 1959), p. 67, 79–80.
[50]Jormescu and Popa-Burcă, *Harta agronomică*, p. 18.

shown earlier, this ended the period of legally forced corvées. But because the ending of legal corvées coincided with the filling of the land, the peasants did not benefit, and the trend of population growth signaled a period in which the position of the peasants vis-à-vis the lords was bound to decline because of the increasing abundance of labor. A land reform in 1890 or 1900 would have given the peasants enough land; a generation later, overpopulation was becoming absolute, not relative, and it was too late for land reform to restore the balance.

The issue of very rapid population growth in colonial political economies is complex and not fully understood. Generally, growth is ascribed to a fall in death rates, while traditionally high fertility rates do not change. But Hla Myint has argued that the introduction of the capitalist market has greatly influenced the process by opening new lands for cultivation. This in turn has stimulated population growth, possibly by eliminating traditional restraints on fertility and certainly by producing more food.[51] Stephen Polgar has argued that the interests of the landlords and colonial masters should be taken into account, for obviously they could only profit from rapid increases in the rural labor supply, which of course would force down wages. Thus, in Java, from 1830 to 1900, the population increased at an annual rate of 2%; in Taiwan, under Japanese rule, the population doubled in 40 years in the twentieth century; Egypt's population grew from 2.5 million to 9 million in the nineteenth century; and Mexico's population grew from 5.8 million to 16.5 million from the beginning of the nineteenth century to 1910.[52] As far as Wallachia is concerned, the population grew from fewer than a million at the start of the nineteenth century to 3.8 million in 1899.[53]

There is no way to untangle the reasons for this growth. The opening of new lands was one major reason. The shift from pastoralism to farming vastly increased the food production. Did the landlords have anything to do with this growth? Did the act of migration break down traditional restraints on fertility? Did the average age at marriage change, or the number of births per couple? Those questions must remain unanswered until Wallachian demographic statistics have been studied much more carefully by historical demographers. But there is no question about the magnitude of the population increase and its social and economic effects in the countryside. Nor is there any doubt that it was linked to the general change from a protocolonial to a fully colonial political economy.

[51]Hla Myint, "The Peasant Economies of Today's Underdeveloped Areas," *Subsistence Agriculture and Economic Development*, ed. Clifton R. Wharton (Chicago: Aldine, 1969), pp. 100–101.

[52]Steven Polgar, "Population History and Population Policies from an Anthropological Perspective," *Current Anthropology* 13, no. 2 (April, 1972): 207.

[53]C. Rusenescu and D. Bugă, "Territorial distribution and growth of the population between the Carpathians and the Danube, in the 19th and 20th centuries," *Revue roumaine de géologie, géographie, et géophysique*, série de géographie 10, no. 1 (1966): 79.

Rural Society and Economy in 1900

Late nineteenth-century Wallachia was not a stagnant society. The economy and population were growing, and as a result, the distribution of landholding and the pattern of rural production were somewhat different by 1900 than they had been at the time of the 1864 reform. But change did not occur uniformly throughout rural Wallachia, and there were, as there had always been, significant regional differences. The nature of these differences reveals a great deal about the nature of the changes in the late nineteenth century. A number of rural censuses were taken between 1896 and 1905, and the county-by-county data are available. These censuses depict the situation at the turn of the century.

Generally, in the plains, the large landowners were more powerful than in the hills and mountains, coinciding with the suitability of the land for cereal cultivation, particularly wheat. But the landowners' power also coincided with the old pattern (from the sixteenth century) in which lords had been more powerful in the plains and free peasants (*moşneni*) more common in the hills. Also, the hills were still relatively more populated and land more scarce, so that there were more very small holdings there than in the plains. But factors other than geography were at work, because in some plains counties the lords were relatively weaker than in others, and in some hill counties they were relatively quite powerful. Where lords were very powerful, there was virtually no middle peasant class—no kulaks with enough land to be free of the need to sharecrop large estates. Where lords were relatively weak, however, there was a significant middle peasant class. (These were peasants holding between 7 and 50 hectares, easily more than enough for a family, but not enough to join the ranks of the landowners.) The relative influence of purely geographic factors and of historical ones in the general pattern is shown in Table 8.

A series of rank order correlations between the columns shows the interrelation between the variables. (Spearman's rank correlation formula was used, with all correlations reported significant at the .01 level or better.)[54] Where large landowners owned a large proportion of the land, middle peasants owned a small proportion of the land; the correlation is −.85. Where large landowners owned a large proportion of the land, there were few very small holdings of less than 2 hectares; the correlation is −.78. This again proves that if lords did not provide enough land for a fair distribution after the reform of 1864, this was not for lack of land. In the following decades, landlords and also the state did distribute land in order to stimulate immigration, so that by 1900 there were few very poor peasants in the plains counties dominated by large estates. Large landlords wanted a work force, however, and it was not in their interest to allow the development of a significant class of prosperous middle peasants who

[54] For a simple explanation of how to calculate and use a rank order correlation coefficient, see Paul G. Hoel, *Elementary Statistics* (New York: Wiley, 1966), pp. 255–257.

TABLE 8
Proportion of Land Held by Large Landowners, Middle Peasants, and Poor Peasants and the Influence of Geography and History, circa 1900[55]

	Percentage of land held by large owners (1000 hectares +)	Percentage of land held by middle peasants (7–50 hectares)	Percentage of land held by poor peasants (2 hectares –)	Percentage of peasants free in 1864
Hill and mountain counties				
Argeş	13	15	48	62
Buzău	26	9	43	33
Dâmboviţa	9	6	44	23
Gorj	3	18	47	63
Mehedinţi	22	10	37	38
Muscel	4	12	67	39
Prahova	14	6	55	30
Vâlcea	0	24	34	63
Plains counties				
Brăila	68	0	2	0
Dolj	24	6	25	25
Ialomiţa	50	3	4	8
Ilfov	30	2	11	1
Olt	20	10	32	37
Râmnicu-Sărat	37	4	36	19
Romanaţi	15	9	29	22
Teleorman	46	4	17	8
Vlaşca	40	4	11	8
Median	22	6	34	25

might be self-sufficient. The number of such peasants was therefore kept down rather effectively. By and large, the preceding correlations coincide with geography, and the difference between the hills and the plains is quite apparent.

But the historical influence is also clear. The number of free peasants in 1864 correlates very highly with the extent of landholding by the middle peasant class in 1900 ($R = .97$). This explains a seeming discrepancy in three plains counties with good cereal lands—Dolj, Olt, and Romanaţi; all three of these should have had very powerful landlords in control of much of the land, but large estates actually controlled less than 25% of the land. This was because in those counties, the lords had never managed to eradicate the free peasant class as fully as in some other plains counties. The interference of the free peasants prevented the extension of large estates. The incidence of free peasants in 1864 and the extent of large estates in 1900 correlate –.85.

[55] Jormescu and Popa-Burcă, *Harta agronomică*, tables, pt. 3. For free peasants, see no. 20, this chapter.

Two other counties were highly deviant. Mehedinţi and Buzău, both hill counties, had a large concentration of estates relative to other hill counties, as well as large concentrations of middle and poor peasants. The explanation for this is geographic. Both counties, though mostly in the hills, also have large plains areas suitable for wheat cultivation. Thus, the deviance of the counties reflects their split geography, part plain and part hill.

In general, historical and geographic—economic influences combined in the same direction. Lords had long been more powerful in the plains, and it was there that cereal cultivation expanded most rapidly. Free peasants had generally been more concentrated in the hills, and there cereal cultivation did not expand rapidly. What would have happened if Wallachia's main cash crop in the nineteenth century had been a hill and mountain product? It is unlikely that the expansion of large estates would have taken place so quickly or so easily. As it was, a great deal of political and social tension resulted from the growth of the colonial economy into the rural hinterland; had the main produce come from the hills, however, the degree of tension would have been much higher.

Because the heart of the colonial production system was in the cereal-growing areas where landlords were the most powerful, a better understanding of the workings of that system requires a closer look at peasant—lord relations. Only then can the full magnitude of the late nineteenth-century agrarian crisis become apparent.

The sharecropping system that developed in the estate areas took on various forms, but the essentials were fairly uniform. The general rule was that peasants worked a lord's land with their own tools, and in return they were allowed to cultivate some of the lord's land for their own benefit. The proportion of land cultivated for the lord compared to that cultivated for the peasants varied from area to area, and even from village to village. It ranged from a ratio of 1 hectare for the lord to 3 for the peasants, to a ratio of 1 : 1. However, the peasants had to fulfill their obligations to the lord before being allowed to work their allotted plots. This meant that whatever the ratio of lands, the peasants were obliged to satisfy the landowner's demands before they could satisfy their own during the busiest times of the growing season, sowing and harvesting especially, when time was of the essence.[56] There were also standard sharecropping contracts in which the lord simply took a portion of the harvest, instead of having his land worked directly.

A survey taken in 1906 on 196 estates showed that in 90% of the cases, these two different kinds of sharecropping arrangements netted the lords at least one-third of total peasant production. In 60% of the cases, the lords got at least

[56] Sample contracts from 1906 were collected by G. D. Creangă, *Contracte de învoeli agricole în vigoare pe anul 1906* (Bucharest: Carol Göbl, 1907). See also Vasile Liveanu *et al.*, *Relaţii agrare şi mişcări ţărăneşti în România 1908–1921* (Bucharest: Editura politică, 1967), p. 31.

half of peasant production. For all of Romania, about 60% of the contracts drawn up between peasants and lords were sharecropping contracts of the two types described; 30% of the contracts were money contracts rather than direct sharecropping contracts; and the remaining 10% of the contracts were based on different types of arrangements. In Moldavia, contracts tended to be based on money rents; in Wallachia, they tended to be ordinary sharecropping contracts such as the ones described. In actual fact, the money contracts often worked out in the same way as the sharecropping contracts. Peasants who owed money rents generally had to borrow from the lords or their agents, and they paid it back in work and produce.[57] In any case, it was a typical "family-size tenancy" system. The fact that peasants also owned some of the land worked in favor of the system, in that it helped stabilize them on the land.

A brief look at the average size of the peasants' holdings in 1896 shows the extent to which they were dependent on the landowners for their livelihood. In all of the hill and mountain counties, the average peasant holding was smaller than 3 hectares (except in Vâlcea, which had virtually no large landowners). In the plains counties, holdings were between 3 and 4 hectares, except in Ilfov (4.05 hectares), Ialomiţa, (4.72 hectares), and Brăila (5.05 hectares). But in the eastern plains, where holdings were larger, the land also received much less rain and larger holdings thus were essential for survival, so that even there very large numbers of peasants had insufficient holdings.[58] Another way to view this is to take all the peasants who held up to 10 hectares (this includes those with no land), and to then look at the proportion of these peasants who held various amounts of land (Table 9). Generally, it may be assumed that those who held less than 5 hectares in the plains, and those who held less than 3 in the hills, could not survive on their own plots.

The camouflaged retention of the pre-1864 arrangements not only perpetuated peasant servitude, but it also kept agricultural techniques from evolving in that the peasants had neither the capital nor the economic freedom necessary for experimentation with new techniques. That the peasants bore the capital costs of cultivating estate lands is evident from the results of the agricultural census of 1905. At a time when most of the work was still being done with animal traction (the short-lived tendency of the big landowners to adopt more advanced machinery, and to invest in their own tools in the period between 1900 and 1915, will be discussed later), the peasants owned 425,000 of the plows in use in Wallachia while the landowners or their agents owned 18,000. In other words, the peasants owned 96% of the plows, even though they owned less than 45% of the land.[59] It should be noted that the same census found that,

[57] Liveanu *et al.*, *Relaţii agrare*, pp. 30–31.

[58] Jormescu and Popa-Burcă, *Harta agronomică*, table 11, pt. 3.

[59] *Statistica maşinilor şi instrumentelor agricole interbuinţate în 1905*, Ministerul agriculturei, industriei, comerţului, şi domenilor (Bucharest, 1907).

TABLE 9
Peasants with Insufficient Land, circa 1900, by County[60]

County	Percentage of peasants holding up to 3 hectares	Percentage of peasants holding 3 to 5 hectares	Total percentage without enough land
Hill and mountain counties			
Argeş	67	24	67
Buzău	57	26	57
Dâmboviţa	62	29	62
Gorj	67	23	67
Mehedinţi	58	23	58
Muscel	82	13	82
Prahova	74	18	74
Vâlcea	55	26	55
Plains counties			
Brăila	5	34	39
Dolj	42	44	86
Ialomiţa	15	63	78
Ilfov	24	56	80
Olt	50	38	88
R.-Sărat	46	29	75
Romanaţi	42	47	89
Teleorman	27	60	87
Vlaşca	23	57	80

[60] Jormescu and Popa-Burcă, *Harta agronomică*, table 1, pt. 3. It is difficult to prove that the limits of 5 hectares and 3 hectares are perfectly reasonable. Doreen Warriner estimated that in this type of agriculture (rather primitive extensive cereal cultivation with no rotation of crops) about 70 people can live on 100 hectares of land. This means that a family of 4 would need more than 5 hectares, and a family of 5 about 7 hectares. In fact, in the county of Dolj in the 1930s she found that a family of 4 could just barely manage on 3.3 hectares, and that as a general rule .9 hectares per person was the lowest limit. Given the fact that in the late nineteenth century families tended to be larger than in the 1930s, a limit of 4.5 to 5 hectares does not seem unreasonable. To set the limit at 3 hectares for the plains would certainly be to set it too low. If the limit were set at 4 hectares, the percentage of peasants with insufficient land in the plains would have been:

Brăila	11% (too low because Brăila was very dry and peasants probably needed more than 5 hectares to survive)
Dolj	65%
Ialomiţa	19% (the same applies to Ialomiţa as to Brăila)
Ilfov	54%
Olt	75%
R.-Sărat	60%
Romanaţi	65%
Teleorman	57%
Vlaşca	55%

In any case, more than 50% of the plains peasants needed to work on more than they had, except possibly in the Bărăgan where that number may have been lower (though not as low as indicated by these figures because the area was so dry). See Doreen Warriner, *Economics of Peasant Farming*, 2nd ed. (New York: Barnes & Noble, 1964), pp. 116–120.

We might note that taking peasants who owned less than 10 hectares does not include all of the peasants. But because, depending on the county, from 95% to 99% of all peasants were, in fact, in this category, the numbers given in the table are a fair reflection of the numbers of peasants with insufficient land.

by this time, various types of machines were being bought by the big owners; however, there were only about 35 machine-driven plows in all of Wallachia. The most common type of advanced machine was a thresher.[61]

It is not surprising, therefore, that until 1900, wheat and corn yields remained low despite the very rich land. Rotation was still not practiced, and though the agricultural census of 1905 showed that wooden plows were being replaced by metal ones, agricultural technology was only slightly more advanced than it had been in the early nineteenth century.[62] Table 10 demonstrates this fact. For all practical purposes, there was no change in yields between the 1860s and the 1890s.[63]

TABLE 10
Yields in Hectoliters per Hectare
(Average per Year)[64]

Years	Wheat	Corn (maize)
1862–1866	11.8	12.7
1867–1871	11.0	13.7
1872–1876	9.1	12.4
1886–1890	13.3	12.3
1891–1895	14.0	12.8
1896–1900	11.4	12.7

[61] *Statistica maşinilor.*

[62] See Warriner, *Economics of Peasant Farming,* pp. 116–120, for a description of agricultural technology in the 1930s.

[63] For purposes of comparison, 1 hectoliter equals 2.84 U.S. bushels, 1 hectare equals 2.47 U.S. acres. Thus 10 hectoliters per hectare equals 11.5 bushels per acre. Because the hectoliter, like the bushel, is a measure of volume rather than of weight, the weight of produce per hectare must be calculated differently for each crop. One bushel of wheat is equivalent to 60 pounds (U.S.) and one bushel of maize equals 48 pounds. The conversion of volume units to weight units, however, is not always precise because impurities in the grain add volume. This is particularly true in a more backward agricultural society. In fact, the weight to volume ratio was calculated each year and for each county by the Romanian Ministry of Agriculture, and it varied somewhat over time and from place to place. But, roughly, 1 hectoliter of wheat weighed 78 kilograms and 1 hectoliter of maize weighed 62 kilograms. With these measures the Romanian yield can be compared to American and European yields.

	U.S. yields in bushels/acre			Romanian yields in bushels/acre	
	Wheat	Corn		Wheat	Corn
1880s	13.2	25.6	1886–1890	15.3	14.1
1900s	13.9	25.9	1896–1900	13.1	14.6

Work in man hours per acre, Romania and U.S., 1900 (the Romanian data are calculated at 7 hours per day)

	Wheat	Corn
U.S.	15	112
Romania	59	118

[64] *Anuarul statistic, 1909,* pp. 146–147. The average yields are for Wallachia, Moldavia, and the Dobrodgea together. The Dobrodgea was added to Romania in 1878 and was lightly populated, and yields in Wallachia and Moldavia were comparable so that these statistics are a fair representation of Wallachian yields.

That the landowners frequently leased out their lands to "farmers" (*arendaşi*) who managed the estates for them hardly made matters better. These *arendaşi* were the most bitterly hated figures in the peasant world. They tended to be landowners themselves, often smaller landowners who could not retire to the cities to enjoy their lands, or professional speculators and usurers. Until the first decade of the twentieth century, these men were not true estate managers, in the sense of directing the actual production of crops, but rather dues collectors who leased the rights to peasant dues from the landowners. In Moldavia, the first few years of the twentieth century saw the formation of huge "trusts" of such farmers who were on the verge of taking over a major portion of the land, but in Wallachia this tendency never developed.[65] State and monastery lands (the nondedicated, Romanian-owned monasteries had never been expropriated), as well as the lands belonging to various hospitals, to the universities, and to a number of other public institutions, were all run in the same way and were leased out to farmers.

Much has been made of the fact that many of the farmers were "foreign," mostly Jews in Moldavia and Greeks in Wallachia. Indeed, the foreign farmers were the most hated of all, and their presence (which incidentally was not recent, since foreign merchants had been a prominent feature of trade for several centuries) gave rise to much xenophobic sentiment, both among the peasants and among the wealthy landowners who used these foreigners. But though this group played a crucial role in Moldavia, where Jews constituted a large proportion of the farmers, it cannot be said that foreign *arendaşi* were equally important in Wallachia, despite the propaganda that cited foreigners as the main cause of discontent and peasant anger.[66] The foreigners were, however,

Ftn. 64 (continued)

Thus, U.S. yields in wheat were about the same as Romanian wheat yields, but the amount of labor put into each acre of wheat in the U.S. was about one-quarter that in Romania. With maize, the labor imput was about the same, but U.S. yields were about 60% higher. *Anuarul statistic, 1909*, pp. 296–297; and *Historical Statistics of the United States: Colonial Times to 1957*, U.S. Bureau of the Census (Washington D.C., 1961), series K 83–97. Romanian wheat yields can be compared to British yields. Counting the average Romanian yield as 13 hectoliters per hectare equaling 1000 kilograms per hectare, the following comparison can be established:

Year	England, wheat yields in British tons/hectare
1650	.74
1750	1.01
1850	1.80

One thousand kilograms equals 1.1 British tons. Thus, Romanian yields in 1900 were a bit higher than British yields in 1750, but much lower than those in 1850. C. Clark and M. Haswell, *The Economics of Subsistence Agriculture*, 3rd ed. (New York: Macmillan, 1967), p. 87.

[65] Radu Rosetti, *Pentru ce s'au răsculat țăranii* (Bucharest: Socec, 1908), pp. 502–504.

[66] Eugen Weber, "Romania," in *The European Right* (Berkeley and Los Angeles: University of California Press, 1966), pp. 502–509.

a highly visible and significant minority of the farmers, and the practice of distributing estates to the farmers was a very real focus of peasant grievance.

In all but two mountain counties, 50% to 70% of the arable land in holdings of 50 hectares or more was leased out to farmers. But outside of the Bărăgan Steppe, far less than one-third of the leased lands was controlled by foreign farmers.[67] Romanian farmers controlled most of the leased estates of the absentee landlords.

A New Bourgeoisie?

The evidence presented makes it quite clear that Wallachia continued to be an open economy, dominated by a tiny landowning class even after its union with Moldavia and its full entrance into the Western market system. Yet Romanian social theorists long debated the question of whether or not late nineteenth-century Romanian society was evolving into a "bourgeois" state. That some argued this point (most notably Ştefan Zeletin, in his book on the Romanian bourgeoisie and on the rise of the liberal party) and concluded that Romania was actually evolving in the direction of a liberal Western and industrial state, suggests a need for further clarification about the class structure at the end of the nineteenth and in the early twentieth centuries.

There is no doubt that some of Wallachia's cities underwent considerable growth in the second half of the nineteenth century; Bucharest grew from 122,000 people in 1860 to about 280,000 in 1899, and Wallachia's main port of Brăila grew from 12,000 in 1853 to about 60,000 in 1899.[68] But the only other city to experience this kind of growth was the oil center of Ploeşti, which grew from about 15,000 people in 1853 to 45,000 in 1899. In 1899, only two other Wallachian towns had more than 20,000 people.[69] By 1899, only three counties in Wallachia had populations that were less than 85% rural, and these were the counties of Ilfov (50% of the population lived in Bucharest), Brăila (35% of the population lived in the city of Brăila), and Prahova (20% of the population lived in Ploeşti and a few other small towns in the oil region).[70]

The three major Wallachian cities grew as administrative and commercial centers oriented to the needs of the open economy, so their growth hardly suggests any kind of industrial development. Indeed, all the evidence points in the opposite direction: the late nineteenth century was characterized by the

[67] Jormescu and Popa-Burcă, *Harta agronomică*, table 9, pt. 3.

[68] Vintilă Mihăilescu, "Aşezările omeneşti din Câmpia Română la mijlocul şi la sfârşitul secolului al XIX-lea," Academia Română, *Memoriile*, secţiune istorice ser. 3, **IV**, no. 2 (1924); p. 50; E. de Martonne, *La Valachie, essai de monographie géographique* (Paris: Armand Colin, 1902), pp. 319–329. The numbers in these two works differ somewhat.

[69] Mihăilescu, "Aşezările omeneşti," in *Memoriile*, p. 50.

[70] *Anuarul statistic, 1909*, p. 40.

decline of artisan industry and its replacement by manufactured imports.[71] At the same time, the old pattern persisted in which a major portion of Romania's foreign trade was handled by non-Romanians. In 1899, 8% of Brăila's population was Greek, and about 11% was Jewish.[72] About one-sixth of Bucharest's population was Jewish, and about one-seventh was Protestant or Catholic (and thus was foreign, because the majority of Wallachians was Orthodox).[73] In all, about 100,000 of Ilfov's population were listed as "foreign" in 1899, and almost all of these foreigners lived in Bucharest.[74] This means that about 35% of the city's population was foreign.

Another indicator of the state of the urban economy was that two-thirds of the capital invested in the few Wallachian industrial enterprises was owned by foreigners.[75]

Given the continuation of this old pattern, in which foreigners controlled much of Romania's commerce and in which there were no signs of industrialization, but only signs that the Romanian economy was becoming ever more colonial, what was the basis of those theories that proclaimed the emergence of a new bourgeoisie? Radu Rosetti believed that by the end of the nineteenth century, the old nobility virtually had vanished; it had lost its estates to usurers, to speculators, and to other "new men" capable of taking advantage of the growth of the market economy.[76] Zeletin also thought that the "old nobility" had been in decline since 1828, and that by the early 1900s it had been replaced by "Big Finance," a clique of politician–speculators who controlled the National Bank created in 1880.[77] It is, of course, impossible to trace the fluctuating fortunes of the various landowning families from 1800 to 1900 (the one attempt to publish such an analysis in the early twentieth century was partially censored by the government of that time).[78] But the historical evidence presented earlier shows that in every period of Wallachian history there had been rapid turnovers within the ranks of the elite. Zeletin and Rosetti's observations show only that the process of change within the ranks of the elite was continuing.

Being a noble had always been a matter of being adept at financial manipulations. Before the nineteenth century, the dues of villagers had provided income, since at least the late sixteenth century. During the nineteenth century this gradually changed, and by 1900 the peasants were being used, to produce

[71] G. Zane, *Industria din România în a doua jumătate a secolului al XIX-lea* (Bucharest: Editura academiei, 1970), p. 234.

[72] de Martonne, *La Valachie*, p. 331.

[73] *Anuarul statistic, 1909*, pp. 32–33.

[74] *Ibid.*, pp. 28–29.

[75] de Martonne, *La Valachie*, p. 318.

[76] Rosetti, *Pentru ce*, pp. 432–439.

[77] Ştefan Zeletin, *Burghezia română* (Bucharest: Cultura Naţională, 1925), pp. 153–159.

[78] In the tables that accompany G. D. Creangă's work, *Proprietatea rurală în România* (Bucharest, 1907), the names of the owners of estates were blacked out by the printers on orders of the government.

cereals on the landowners' lands, however, the basis of economic power had not changed. The financial manipulations of the elite perhaps assumed a more modern form through the creation of a national banking system, but in retrospect it is obvious that this was not very different from the dealings of the Greek nobles in the eighteenth century.

The other alleged component of the "new bourgeoisie" was the administrative elite created by the new Romanian government.[79] But here again, this was nothing new. In the eighteenth century, as previously, administrative power had always been intimately associated with control of the land. Indeed, I have argued that the nobility originated as an administrative elite, and that the connection between administration and control over villagers had never been broken. The apparent changes in class structure were thus perfectly consistent with the development of the cereal-exporting economy, and also with the perpetuation of the colonial society that had first begun to emerge under Ottoman rule. Rather than heralding a fundamental change in class structure, the phenomenon observed by Rosetti and Zeletin indicated a remarkable *absence* of change.

This is not to suggest that there was no change at all. On the contrary, the evidence presented previously, in the discussion of agrarian relations after 1866, shows that the position of the peasants deteriorated—and the power of the landlords solidified—because of the change from loosely defined to strongly

TABLE 11
Wallachian Distribution of Land in 1896[80]

Type of owner	Number	Percentage of all owners	Amount of land owned in hectares	Percentage of total land owned
Peasant owners (0 to 10 hectares, includes landless)	628,754	97	2,023,459	42
Medium owners (10–100 hectares, includes richer peasants and small landlords)	16,389	2.5	361,451	7
Larger owners (more than 100 hectares)	3,289	0.5	2,459,294	51
Total	648,432	100	4,844,204	100

[79] Rosetti, *Pentru ce*, p. 435. See also Hugh Seton-Watson, *Eastern Europe Between the Wars*, 3rd ed. (Hamden, Conn.: Archon Books, 1962), pp. 124–125. For an anti-Zeletin position see Şerban Voinea, *Marxism oligarhic* (Bucharest: Editura I. Brănişteanu, 1926).

[80] Jormescu and Popa-Burcă, *Harta agronomică*, table 11, pt. 3.

defined property rights over estate lands. A virtual demesne developed, cultivated by tenants instead of by serfs.

When Wallachia had been a part of the Ottoman economic sphere, it had had a weakly colonial economy because the Ottomans were relatively undemanding (at least in terms of the potential agricultural wealth of Wallachia, inefficiently demanding may be a better term). In the nineteenth century, as Wallachia was incorporated into the world capitalist system, it developed a strongly colonial economy that was relatively much more demanding. A greater surplus had to be extracted from agriculture. By the late nineteenth century, this change had produced a different economy. Many of the old noble families failed to keep up with the changes, but it is absurd to conclude that the power of the landowning class had therefore diminished. Table 11 reinforces this point. About 3300 families owned half of Wallachia's lands, which surely does not suggest that the power of the landowners was diminishing.

Agricultural Innovations

At the end of the nineteenth century, Romanian agriculture began to change. Mechanization was beginning to make some slight inroads; some crop rotation was introduced; and even peasant equipment began to be upgraded, often with loans from landowners and the estate farmers.[81] Why this happened is not really clear. The growing competition of American wheat had something to do with the change. Perhaps even more importantly, the great expansion of wheat and maize cultivation had taken place on largely virgin lands throughout the nineteenth century; as was shown in the previous chapter, this had been particularly true on the eastern plains of Wallachia, and had resulted in a very careless form of slash and burn cultivation. Using such a primitive technology entailed seriously diminishing returns once the virgin land had been used up.[82] It is probable that the landowners and estate farmers realized this by the 1890s, and in order to guarantee their incomes, they began to make investments.

By 1905, about two-thirds of the landlords who owned more than 100 hectares in the plains and who managed their own lands had invested in some form of mechanical (steam-driven) devices on their estates. About 40% of the estate farmers on the plains had done the same. In the hill areas, the proportion of investments naturally was much smaller, but even there some progress was noticeable. To be sure, most of the work continued to be performed as before—by the peasants using their own equipment—but at least there was some change, and that change was accelerating in the first decade of the twentieth century.[83]

[81] Constantin Garoflid, *Agriculture veche* (Bucharest, 1943), p. 157.
[82] Warriner, *Economics of Peasant Farming*, p. 118.
[83] *Statistica maşinilor, 1905.*

The elementary technological change resulted in significant increases in crop yields. As shown above, productivity had remained essentially static between the 1860s and the 1890s, so that the increases in the 1900s stand out markedly as not owing merely to chance (see Table 12). The 1901–1905 average

TABLE 12
Yields in Hectoliters per Hectare per Year[84]

Years	Wheat		Corn (maize)	
1896–1900 (average)	11.4		12.7	
1901	15.6		19.4	
1902	18.1		11.1	
1903	16.2	15.9	13.7	11.6
1904	11.0		3.3	
1905	18.6		10.6	
1906	19.8		22.1	
1907	8.7		10.5	
1908	10.7	14.2	13.8	15.5
1909	11.8		11.6	
1910	20.0		18.4	
1911	17.1		18.7	

for wheat was 15.9 hectoliters per hectare—the highest 5-year average in Romanian history up to that time. The 1906–1910 averages were lower, but they still exceeded the average for any other preceding 5-year period except for 1901–1905. Productivity records were frequently broken during this decade as wheat productivity reached new highs in 1901, 1902, 1905, 1906, and 1910. Corn productivity hit record highs in 1901 and 1906.

It is obvious that some kind of change was occurring. In the long run, it probably would have revolutionized Wallachian and Moldavian agrarian society: Peasants would have been thrown off the land as a result of increased mechanization, and the landlords would have completed a long evolutionary process from dues collectors to rational capitalist producers. Any secondary effects this might have produced must, however, remain purely speculative. The change came much too late, and the political pressures that had built up in the nineteenth century exploded in the twentieth. The evolution of the landlords into rational capitalists was first shaken by a serious peasant revolt in 1907, and was then brought to a complete halt by the political aftermath of World War I.

[84] *Anuarul statistic, 1912,* p. 49.

The Revolt of 1907

In March, 1907, the peasants revolted. The revolt began in northern Moldavia and at first was specifically anti-Semitic, for most of the estate farmers there were Jewish. But the revolt then spread into Wallachia, where there were few Jewish estate farmers, and it took on a general antilandlord and antifarmer character as the peasants demanded land. The army was called out, and within a month the revolt was put down. The best estimates suggest that 11,000 peasants, or 2 of every 1000 rural inhabitants, were killed.[85]

The revolt of 1907 was the central traumatic event of Romanian agrarian history up to that time, and it left a deep imprint on agrarian relations for the following four decades. Even today, the revolt is considered a central event, and the Communist Party has encouraged greater study of this event than of any other in Romania's history before 1944.

At the time, the revolt unleashed a flood of writings to explain the phenomenon; it also brought attention to the fact that there was a serious agrarian crisis because of the poverty and subjection of the peasants and the great wealth of several thousand big landowning families. Ten years later, faced with the Bolshevik Revolution in Russia and the danger of its spread into Romania, the government heeded the lesson of the revolt of 1907 and decreed a sweeping land reform that fundamentally changed agrarian relations in Romania. In fact, though the effects were somewhat delayed, the revolt of 1907 destroyed the old system.

As the most analyzed event in Romanian agrarian history, the revolt of 1907 has been explained in a variety of ways. For Rosetti, it was the inevitable climax to a century of gradual peasant enslavement.[86] The wheat export economy and the cupidity of the landowners and estate farmers had combined to produce a disaster. Most of the good analysts agreed with Rosetti, whether they were to the left or the right of the political spectrum. C. Dobrogeanu-Gherea, a socialist, who agreed with Rosetti, termed the system that had evolved "neoserfdom."[87] The conservative landowner C. Garoflid also agreed with the essence of this explanation.[88] Those who disagreed claimed that the revolt had been caused by foreign agitators (whose existence was never proved), and many who did agree with Rosetti's analysis placed most of the blame for Romania's social problems on the Jews.[89]

[85]Henry Roberts, *Rumania: Political Problems of an Agrarian State* (New Haven: Yale University Press, 1951), p. 3.

[86]Rosetti, *Pentru ce.*

[87]Dobrodgeanu-Gherea, *Neoiobăgia.*

[88]Garoflid, "Regimul agrar în România," *Enciclopedia României*, I, pp. 577–585.

[89]This was Rosetti's opinion as well in his anti-Semitic diatribe written before the revolt, Verax, *La Roumanie et les Juifs* (Bucharest: Socecu, 1903). There he predicted that the Jews would bring ruin to Romania. In fact, it was the spread of capitalist relations he disliked, and the Jews were only one of the many instruments of this spread.

There was actually nothing very unique about the 1907 Romanian peasant uprising. In many respects, it was similar to uprisings that have occurred in rural societies subjected to the abrupt introduction of a demanding capitalist colonial political economy. Hobsbawm has explained such uprising in terms of the expansion of the capitalist market into less-developed rural regions. Hobsbawm noted:

> The irruption of modern capitalism into peasant society, generally in the form of liberal or Jacobin reforms (the introduction of a free land-market, the secularism of church estates, the equivalents of the enclosure movements and the reform of common land and forest laws, etc.) has always had cataclysmic effects on that society. When it comes suddenly . . . its effect is all the more disturbing.[90]

Eric Wolf has taken up the same theme, but specifically applied to colonial societies in the twentieth century. He emphasized that the sudden creation of a large-scale market in land must have profoundly unsettling effects on peasants long used to considering land as community or family property, the utilization of which is subject to many social ties and requirements. Because impersonal market forces strip the land of these social obligations, and consequently render life insecure for many peasants, "capitalism necessarily produces a revolution of its own."[91]

It is the newness and abrupt rise of demand that unsettles the society, for this new demand for a cash crop destroys the security of more traditional forms of land tenure. In Wallachia, the free communal villages began to break up in the sixteenth century, but the old agri-pastoral communal techniques did not change until the nineteenth century. Forest and pasture remained largely common until the nineteenth century. Dues remained low until the nineteenth century. Most importantly, land did not become fully private–that is, a commodity to be bought and sold at will—until the reform of 1864 created private property rights over all the land and gave the lords control of the very best lands. The new political economy, pushed by the demand of the world market, was therefore most strongly resented in those areas where old forms had strongly persisted until 1864, and later until the turn of the century.

If it were possible to measure the persistence of old social forms and attitudes, the strength of capitalist demands, and the intensity of the rebellion by village, or at least by county, Hobsbawm's and Wolf's theories about the nature of peasant unrest might be tested for this case. This would facilitate an understanding of the nature of the rebellion of 1907, and also would show the importance of regional differences.

At the county level, there is a good measure of the power of the growing

[90]Hobsbawm, *Primitive Rebels*, p. 67.

[91]Eric Wolf, *Peasant Wars of the Twentieth Century* (New York: Harper and Row, 1969), pp. 277–278.

capitalist market: the percentage of the arable land devoted to wheat. There are also detailed accounts of the rebellion on a county-by-county basis, allowing the construction of a scale that roughly indicates the relative intensity of the rebellion in each county.

The persistence of old social forms is harder to measure, but an indirect measure is available at the county level. It can be assumed that, where the rural population was more literate, old social forms had disintegrated further than where the population was less literate. Additionally, in more traditional areas far more boys than girls were sent to school, so the male/female literacy ratio also indicates the persistence of traditional social attitudes. The higher the ratio, the less changed the county. If the ratio of literate males/females is divided by total literacy, there results an excellent measure of the persistence of a traditional social outlook. Thus, a county with equal male/female literacy and a high literacy rate would have a low "traditionalism" score. In fact, with perfect literacy, the score would be *1*. For example, if the number of literate males were 10 times as high as the number of literate females, and the overall literacy were on the order of 20%, the "traditionalism" score would be 10 divided by 1 divided by .20 = 50. In other words,

$$\text{Traditionalism} = \frac{\dfrac{\text{Literate males}}{\text{Literate females}}}{\text{Over-all literacy rate}}$$

Literacy rates by sex and county are available for the rural population in 1899.

It is expected that counties high on "traditionalism" (at least in terms of general social outlook, as measured by the literacy scores), and high with respect to the strength of the market in the key colonial product, wheat, should have rebelled most strongly. The prediction is really that those counties that had changed considerably because of the introduction of market forces, but in which the social outlook had *not* changed quickly because the introduction of these forces was relatively recent and the population was still attached to old ways, should have been the source of most of the political agitation. In other words, what is being predicted is that the interaction between the market indicator and the traditionalism indicators, when combined, would produce a score predicting the intensity of the rebellion in each county. The usual way of producing this kind of interaction term is to multiply its component parts. In effect, each score alone predicts little, but combined they increase the predicted score according to their joint strength.[92]

The rebellion took place mostly, but not exclusively, in the plains. However,

[92]On multiplicative interaction effects see Hubert Blalock, *Theory Construction* (Englewood Cliffs, N.J.: Prentice-Hall, 1969), pp. 156–162.

some plains counties experienced a low degree of rebellion. In general, the rebellion took place wherever the landlords were relatively strong; again, this was not exclusively the case, for in some counties with very strong landlords there was no rebellion, while in counties with relatively weaker landlords, there was a great deal of violence. Thus, the varying intensity of rebellion cannot be explained either by simple geographic factors or purely on the basis of the preponderance of large estates.

Counties labelled "0" experienced almost no rebellious activity in 1907. Those labelled "1" experienced localized, minor outbursts of rebellion. In counties labelled "2," the rebellion was relatively widespread, but was contained to specific, limited parts of the county. In counties labelled "3," the rebellion was very widespread and also very violent; in these counties entire peasant armies roamed about, attacking estates and engaging in pitched battles with government troops sent out to quell the rebellion.[93]

Using the available information, Table 13 has been constructed to show the expected rebellion score (the strength of market forces multiplied by the traditionalism score), and to compare this with the actual rebellion score (ranging from 0 to 3). The two columns can then be correlated to test the validity of the explanation. The prediction works perfectly for the five most rebellious counties, and for three of the least rebellious counties.

Ilfov might well have rebelled, at least weakly, if not for the presence of Bucharest with its concentration of armed government forces in the center of the county. Here, the overwhelming presence of the military from the start had a strong inhibiting effect.

The fact that Gorj behaved contrary to the prediction is due to a flaw in the indicators. The traditionalism score is so high that it counterbalances the very low market score.

Five of the seven counties intermediate on the actual rebellion score ("1" and "2") had a correspondingly intermediate predictive score. The two other counties, Prahova and Râmicu-Sărat, were on the high end of the group with low predictive scores.

Over-all, the predicted and actual rebellion scores can be correlated by using a rank-order technique. Ranking the predictive scores is straightforward. To rank the actual scores involves many tie scores. All counties with a "3" score were ranked "third" (i.e., the mean of 1 + 2 + 3 + 4 + 5). All counties with a score of "2" were ranked "seventh and one-half" (i.e., the mean of 6 + 7 + 8 + 9). All counties with a score of "1" were ranked "eleventh" (i.e. the mean of

[93] For accounts of the revolt see Rosetti, *Pentru ce*, pp. 614–621; Philip G. Eidelberg, *The Great Rumanian Peasant Revolt of 1907: Origins of a Modern Jacquerie* (Leiden: E. J. Brill, 1974); and especially Andrei Oţetea *et al.*, *Marea răscoală a ţăranilor din 1907* (Bucharest: Editura academiei, 1967), which is largely devoted to a lengthy county-by-county description of events. The coding of the intensity of the revolt is based on this work and on Rosetti.

TABLE 13
Predicted versus Actual Intensity of Rebellion[94]

County (hill or plain)	Percentage of arable land in wheat (1900–1904)	Combined literacy score (1899)	Product of (1) × (2)	Actual intensity of rebellion
Olt (P)	41.9	122	5112	3
Teleorman (P)	48.2	102	4916	3
Romanaţi (P)	47.7	79	3768	3
Vlaşca (P)	46.0	80	3680	3
Dolj (P)	45.1	66	2977	3
Argeş (H)	24.2	80	1936	2
Buzău (H)	33.9	49	1661	2
Dâmboviţa (H)	28.6	49	1401	1
Gorj (H)	12.5	112	1400	0
Mehedinţi (H)	39.3	33	1297	2
Ilfov (P)	40.9	31	1268	0
Vâlcea (H)	15.2	83	1262	1
Prahova (H)	25.4	35	889	1
R.-Sărat (P)	30.5	29	885	2
Ialomiţa (P)	36.5	21	767	0
Brăila (P)	30.6	16	490	0
Muscel (H)	6.8	24	163	0

10 + 11 + 12). All counties with a score of "0" were ranked "fifteenth" (i.e., the mean of 13 + 14 + 15 + 16 + 17).

The correlation between the rank of the predictive scores and the actual scores is +.84, a highly significant coefficient (at the .001 level). This strongly confirms the general explanation of the rebellion, despite the presence of several slightly anomalous counties. In essence, the Hobsbawm–Wolf explanation holds very well. The rebellion was the consequence of the rapid penetration of Western capitalist forces into a society still largely imbued with a less modern outlook toward social customs. As such, the rebellion was an attack on the fundamental nature of the colonial political economy, and its reverberations ultimately destroyed that political economy.

Reform Legislature after 1907

Fear of a new revolt prompted talk of reforms after the revolt. Though the Conservative Party tended to hold the view that the large landowners should

[94] Literacy scores are based on *Anuarul statistic, 1909*, pp. 34–35. The percentage of wheat lands in each county is from Jormescu and Popa-Burcă, *Harta agronomică*, p. 152. For a more technical, and statistically more sophisticated, analysis, see Daniel Chirot and Charles Ragin, "The Market, Tradition and Peasant Rebellion: The Case of Romania in 1907," *American Sociological Review* 40 (August, 1975): 428–444.

be left in full possession of their lands, the Liberal Party (which was as much of a landlord party—it had led the government that represessed the revolt) was more flexible. Between 1908 and 1914, under the leadership of Ionel Brătianu, the Liberal Party gradually moved toward a program favoring some kind of reform that would give the peasants enough land to defuse potential violence, but would preserve the landowners' wealth.[95] Even within the Conservative Party, a group led by Constantin Garoflid suggested that some sort of reform was inevitable.[96] In both parties it was hoped that if reform came, it would only expropriate a minimal part of the big owners' lands; however, calculations of the amount of land needed to satisfy even a small proportion of the peasants indicated that far more land would have to be expropriated to have any effect. Though the Liberals came to be considered the party of reform because they represented banking and financial interests as well as landowners, it is clear that both parties hoped to avoid reform as far as possible. But a group of political realists in both parties also realized that the situation eventually would explode again, and so tried to devise some satisfactory compromise. Apparently the main difference between the two parties was that the Liberals had a few more political realists, and because its leadership had been successful in financial and banking affairs as well as in landowning, the party had somewhat more confidence that it could transform government compensation from confiscated lands into a new source of wealth. In any case, the difference between the two parties was quite relative, and it was the fear of Communism that finally led to the actual reform of 1917.

Between 1908 and 1917, a number of minor reforms was passed. A little land was distributed to a few peasants; attempts were made to set up village cooperatives; the most blatantly exploitative types of tenancy contracts between landlords and peasants were made illegal (in particular, the contracts that demanded that the peasants must finish their work on the lord's land before they could work on their own were made illegal); and the large trusts of estate farmers, who federated to control huge amounts of land, were banned. In actuality, however, most of these reforms had little effect. Work contracts continued to be made as before; the feeble attempts at encouraging peasant cooperatives yielded few results; and the amount of land distributed was too small to make a difference. Trusts of estate farmers were, however, effectively banned (these trusts were more threatening to the landowners than were the peasants). But the lack of immediate reform does not negate the facts that (1) the landowners and government were worried, and (2) they realized that ultimately, some change would have to be made.[97]

[95] Z. Ornea, *Țărănismul* (Bucharest: Editura politică, 1969), p. 31.
[96] Liveanu *et al.*, *Relații agrare*, pp. 111–113.
[97] *Ibid.*, pp. 107–136.

World War I and Its Aftermath

The Politics of World War I and Romania's role in that war are not really worth reviewing in depth for the purposes of this study. The king and a number of politicians were pro-German; the Liberal Party remained loyal to its 1848 Francophile position. No action was taken until 1916, when it seemed as if the Entente would win. Then, fortified by the promise that it would receive Transylvania as a prize, Romania attacked Austria–Hungary. The Romanian army was decisively beaten by a German army, and Wallachia was occupied by the Germans. The Romanian army then retreated to Moldavia, where it was reinforced by the Russian army. The Moldavian front remained essentially stagnant for the rest of the war, but with the Russian Revolution of 1917, the Romanian government realized that the Russian troops' revolutionary enthusiasm threatened what was left of Romania.[98] The king of Romania proclaimed a land reform to quiet agitation within the ranks of the largely peasant army.[99] As Eastern Europe collapsed into chaos in 1918, the peasants in Russian-held Bessarabia, in Austrian Bukovina, and in Hungarian Transylvania began to seize land. The peasants in these areas were largely Romanian-speaking, and the Romanian government foresaw the likelihood of ideological infection from these areas, particularly because it was preparing to annex the three regions. The decision to push on with the reform, and the granting of universal suffrage in 1919, prevented revolution from spreading to Romania, and also insured the inevitability of a tremendous change in agrarian relations.[100]

Though the reform took over 10 years before it was completed, the landlord-dominated rural society was destroyed and the peasantry freed. Before World War I, the big landlords (owning more than 100 hectares) owned slightly more than 50% of all of Wallachia's land; in 1935, they owned about 10% of all the land. Even in the counties where they had been most powerful (Brăila, Ialomiţa, and Ilfov), they retained only 14% to 15% of the land. With very few exceptions, the giant estates of more than 1000 hectares vanished.[101]

That the reform created an economic disaster was not so much the fault of the politicians and landowners as of demography. By 1920, the population had grown to such an extent that even after massive redistribution, the average peasant family still had too little land. By 1940, the problem had worsened

[98] Seton-Watson, *History of the Roumanians*, pp. 475–520.

[99] David Mitrany, *The Land and the Peasant in Rumania: The War and Agrarian Reform 1917–1921*. (New Haven: Yale University Press, 1930), p. 101.

[100] For details of the political disputes that went on between 1917 and 1921 over the land reform, see Seton-Watson, *History of the Roumanians*, p. 551; Mitrany, *Land and Peasant*, pp. 111–119, 165–167; Robert L. Wolff, *The Balkans in Our Times* (New York: Norton, 1967), p. 99.

[101] *Enciclopedia României*, **II**. Land holding statistics are distributed throughout the volume within the separate articles about each county.

because of further population growth. Ultimately, the only solution was massive industrialization to drain the excess rural population off the land. And, though the leading economic experts of the 1920s and 1930s perceived this, it was only after 1944 that the Romanian government carried out such a program.[102]

[102]See, among others, Roberts, *Rumania*; Warriner, *Economics of Peasant Farming*; and A. Golopenția and M. Georgescu, *60 Sate românești* (Bucharest: Institute de științe sociale, 1941), II, pp. 9–41 on the problems between the wars. See John M. Montias, *Economic Development in Communist Rumania* (Cambridge: M.I.T. Press, 1967) for an analysis of the solutions applied by the Communists.

8

Social Change in Peripheral Societies

Wallachia has always been a rather small and unimportant country, and its union with Moldavia to form modern Romania hardly changed this. Though part of Europe, it has generally been considered an exotic and peripheral part of the continent. There are certainly more people who have heard of Dracula than people who could place his homeland on a map. One is tempted to conclude, as did Barrington Moore, that such "small societies" are hardly worth studying. He wrote:

> The fact that smaller countries depend economically and politically on big and powerful ones means that the decisive causes of their politics lie outside their own boundaries. It also means that their political problems are not really comparable to those of larger countries.[1]

But given the above, and also taking note of the fact that the "large" countries of one era may not be the large ones of the next, questions still remain. In what ways are "smaller" countries different, and how do they behave?

[1] Barrington Moore Jr., *Social Origins of Dictatorship and Democracy: Lord and Peasant in the Making of the Modern World* (Boston: Beacon, 1967), p. xiii.

One approach taken by cultural anthropologists stresses the utility of studying small and unimportant societies. Such studies can yield insights into the general nature of human organization, and they often can serve as living "museums" which teach us how modern societies may have originated. The study of exotic societies permits a well-founded development of evolutionary theories of Parsons, Lenski, and other "neoevolutionary theorists." But if the start with assumptions drawn from "exotic" ethnographic monographs. This is as true for Marx (via Morgan) as it is for Spencer, Durkheim, or the more recent theories of Parsons, Lenski, and other "neoevolutionary theorists." But if the story of Wallachia is to be used in this way—to augment the empirical range of evolutionary theories—then this particular study is an unqualified failure. Because Wallachia has always been a peripheral society, but nevertheless always involved in a larger world context, it provides few clues that might enlighten us about the general nature of human evolution. It was never isolated enough to qualify as a living "museum"; outside forces have influenced it too strongly to allow statements about any "natural" course of change.

The very fact of its being peripheral to, but always connected with, larger developments and international forces is the most interesting aspect of Wallachian social history. There have been numerous other peripheral societies in the same position in the past, and there are many today. It is precisely in the study of such societies that grand theory, along the lines of either Barrington Moore or the evolutionary thinkers, has always failed. Some generalizations about the nature of change in peripheral societies may be extracted from Wallachian social history.

Any conclusions must be divided into three categories that correspond to the main types of political economy that prevailed between 1250 and 1917. The three dominant types were:

1. the communal-trade society from before the formation of an independent state in the thirteenth century until the collapse of old trade routes and the imposition of a high tribute in the sixteenth century;
2. the protocolonial society subservient to the Ottoman Empire from the sixteenth century until the start of the nineteenth; and
3. the modern neocolonial, grain-exporting society tied to the Western capitalist market from the 1820s until World War I.

The changes from one type of political economy to another never followed logically from internal developments within the old stage. "Internal contradictions" in one period cannot explain the transition to the next period. No inherent logic explains the changes, because they were caused primarily by the changing international context. This is the most important aspect of peripheral societies. (It might be argued that the same holds true for "central" societies as well, but this is not the place to pursue that point.) The effects of international forces, however, were at least partially moderated by domestic, endogenous qualities of the prevailing political economy.

The communal-trade society was internally based on lightly taxed and free rural villages, and the state was based on its control of trade routes. In this dual society, the state and elite had relatively little influence on the mass of the population. But this situation could survive only so long as a heavy internal tribute was not extracted from the rural producers. All states dependent primarily on trade routes share this precarious stability. In times of change, control of the rural population—that is, raising a surplus from rural production—becomes problematic. The collapse of a trading state will therefore unleash predictable form of class warfare among the rural population, the state, and the old administrative nobility which the state no longer can support.

In Wallachia, the imposition of Ottoman hegemony during the sixteenth century determined the outcome of the class struggle. The nobility won, but a weak state was preserved to act as a central tribute-raising agency. The outcome of the typical three-sided struggle depends, however, on the particular forces at work. Without Ottoman intervention, the rural population or the central state might have won. In the first case, the state would have disintegrated, and Wallachia would have devolved into an anarchic condition in which small groups of villages would have become virtually independent tiny states. If the central state had won, on the other hand, a relatively strong nation–state might have emerged, ruled by an absolute prince. In many ways, Wallachia was ready for this kind of transformation in 1500. The population was linguistically and religiously homogeneous, and Wallachia was a geographically coherent unit with great potential wealth. But international forces decreed a different outcome, and Wallachia never became a "Sweden of the Balkans," despite Vlad the Impaler's and Michael the Brave's attempts in that direction.

The transition to a protocolonial economy and society was somewhat blunted by the largely pastoral nature of the rural economy. The *çiftlik* system of "plantation estates," which developed through much of the Ottoman domain, never spread to Wallachia because agriculture was not that important and because the Ottoman economy and polity exerted too little power to effect so great a transformation. So the serfdom imposed in the 1590s was never very effective. This demonstrates the limitations of the generalization about the effects of high new demands on a free, rural, and low-density population. Slavery or serfdom is the usual outcome of such demands in such circumstances, as is evident in other East European and many Latin American examples. But in Wallachia, the transition was only partial because of the relative weakness of the Turks and because of previous domestic circumstances.

The changes that took place in the nineteenth century reveal the great power of capitalist market forces. Certainly, Western Europe never exerted as much direct political power over Wallachia as had the Ottomans. But its economic influence was sufficient to revolutionize rural life by creating a large class of serf cultivators. This change was, however, greatly facilitated by the fact that the political supremacy of the Wallachian landowning class was well established long before 1829. In no other Balkan case (particularly not in Serbia or Bulgaria) did the nineteenth century produce such a blatantly colonial society.

Externally-forced changes will take place more or less easily and rapidly according to the nature of the previous political economy. In Wallachia's case, the nineteenth-century economic transformation was enormous, but the political transformation was slight. Had there been no noble class in power at the start of the modern neocolonial period, the economic change probably would have been much slower, and the rural population would have resisted much more successfully. In fact, without the previous control of the nobility, the Wallachian economy would never have become as export oriented so quickly. As it was, the change ultimately produced a violent political reaction from the peasants, and in the aftermath of World War I there was a decided regression from the colonial pattern that had prevailed before the war.

The colonial typology established in the study is of great utility, but it should not be exaggerated. A number of unusual circumstances made Wallachia an extreme example of modern neocolonies; if the political history of pre-nineteenth-century Wallachia had been different, the nineteenth-century colonial pattern would also have been different and certainly less extreme.

This study also offers some negative conclusions about peripheral societies—conclusions that attack some aspects of general theories of social change. By itself, the much-abused notion of cultural diffusion is a relatively meaningless concept. Wallachia's intensive contacts with the West after 1829 did not produce meaningful improvements in the technology of agricultural production. Farming spread, but yields did not increase; a good rotation system was not introduced, and it was not until the first decade of the twentieth century that some mechanization was begun.

But then, after the land reform of the post-World War I years, there was a technological regression to nineteenth-century levels. In the nineteenth century, there was no large-scale urbanization and almost no industrialization to speak of. There was no trend toward a more democratic society, at least until the Russian Revolution of 1917 panicked the Romanian elite. Rather, the whole evolution of nineteenth-century Wallachia was in a direction opposite from that of the West at that time. Serfdom was aggravated, the cultural distinction between the elite and the peasantry widened, and the standard of living of the rural population either stagnated or declined. On the other hand, the elite did absorb Western ideas, particularly the idea of linguistically-based nationalism. From about 1900 until 1914, the landowners began to import Western farm machinery. Some modern administrative reforms were made, particularly during the period of Russian occupation.

What this points to is that the notion of diffusion must be used carefully. Different classes adopt foreign ways differently and highly selectively to further their interests; they will avoid foreign ideas and techniques that seem to oppose their interests. Also, dominant powers select only certain of their traits for export. England, for example, had no interest in seeing Wallachia evolve into a parliamentary regime in the nineteenth century. That would have upset grain exports by overthrowing the prevailing system of land tenure. Thus, cultural diffusion is an important process, but it can be understood only in terms of each society's class structure and international position.

It has been claimed that the abolition of serfdom in the 1740s was a product of spreading Western enlightenment, but careful study shows that it was the result of domestic economic conditions and the pressure of the Ottoman Empire. It has also been claimed that the land reform of 1864 was the product of Western liberalism, but the effects of the reform were such as to make this claim dubious. About no time in Wallachia's history can it be said that a foreign idea or technology seeped in without some kind of resistance, and this resistance can always be explained by the specific interests of various classes, rather than by a generalized love of "tradition."

General evolutionary laws of human development do not work well for peripheral societies. This is certainly true of the Marxist stages of history. It is also true of the more recent evolutionary theories, such as that of Gerhard Lenski, who posits a set of universal stages based on technological progress.[2] There were major technological changes in Wallachia, from a primarily pastoral to an agricultural society, and then from slash-and-burn to permanent cultivation. But Lenski's generalizations about horticultural, agrarian, and industrial societies are irrelevant in a discussion of Wallachian social history except at a very abstract level. In fact, it could be argued that Lenski's ideas are of little use in understanding social change in *any* colonial or semicolonial society, because such change is heavily dominated by exogenous factors.

As for the evolutionary theories proposed by Talcott Parsons,[3] these have so little empirical grounding as to be virtually meaningless. Parsons may be right or wrong, but this can hardly be demonstrated with case studies. All he really puts forward is a way of distinguishing between "primitive" societies (i.e., less differentiated, less bureaucratic, less universalistic, less democratic, more ascriptive), and "modern" societies. But Wallachia was never "primitive" or

[2]Gerhard Lenski, *Power and Privilege: A Theory of Social Stratification* (New York: McGraw-Hill, 1966); Gerhard Lenski and Jean Lenski, *Human Societies* (New York: McGraw-Hill, 1974).

[3]Talcott Parsons, "Evolutionary Universals in Society," *American Sociological Review* 29 (1964): 339–357. Also see other works by Parsons, including *The System of Modern Societies* (Englewood Cliffs, N.J.: Prentice-Hall, 1971).

"modern." The best that can be gained from this kind of theory is that contemporary Romania has evolved so that it is now more "modern" than in the past. How, why, and when this happened would have to be left in the air by those trying to confirm or even use Parsons' theory. Why did the nation—state not emerge in the sixteenth century? Why did the introduction of modern market forces reinforce serfdom, instead of producing a great surge toward industrialization? Why did the national bureaucracy become weaker from 1400 to 1700? Why was serious industrialization delayed until the Russian occupation after World War II? In short, Parsons' evolutionary theory, and other such theories, may be helpful for those examining all of mankind over all of history. But such theories provide few insights into the process of change in specific societies, particularly in peripheral societies.

With respect to general theoretical orientations, this study reaffirms Weber's classical wisdom. There are no universal stages or causal master keys. The only useful approach is to develop ideal types. These must be derived from empirical historical data. Of most significance are those features peculiar to individual types.[4] It has been my contention that a fruitful (though not the only) way of establishing ideal types is through the study of political economies. This facilitates the study of social change in any given society, while also allowing modest generalizations about other societies sharing important typological similarities.

[4]Guenther Roth, "The Genesis of the Typological Approach," *Scholarship and Partisanship: Essays on Max Weber*, ed. Reinhard Bendix and Guenther Roth (Berkeley and Los Angeles: University of California Press, 1971), pp. 257–258.

References

1. General Works

Almond, Gabriel, and Powell, G. Bingham. *Comparative Politics: A Developmental Approach.* Boston: Little, Brown, 1966.

Balandier, Georges. "The Colonial Situation: A Theoretical Approach," *Social Change: The Colonial Situation.* Edited by Immanuel Wallerstein. New York: Wiley, 1966.

Baron, Samuel H. *Plekhanov, the Father of Russian Marxism.* Stanford: Stanford University Press, 1963.

Beckford, George L. *Persistent Poverty: Underdevelopment in Plantation Economies of the Third World.* New York: Oxford University Press, 1972.

Bendix, Reinhard, and Roth, Guenther. *Scholarship and Partisanship: Essays on Max Weber.* Berkeley and Los Angeles: University of California Press, 1971.

Blalock, Hubert. *Theory Construction.* Englewood Cliffs, N.J.: Prentice-Hall, 1969.

Bloch, Marc. *Les caractères originaux de l'histoire rurale française.* Oslo: H. Aschehoug, 1931.

Bloch, Marc. *Feudal Society.* Chicago: University of Chicago Press, 1961.

Blum, Jerome. "The Rise of Serfdom in Eastern Europe." *American Historical Review* **LXII**, no. 4 (July 1957): 807–836.

Blum, Jerome. *Lord and Peasant in Russia from the Ninth to the Nineteenth Century.* New York: Atheneum, 1964.

Boxer, C. R. *Four Centuries of Portugese Expansion, 1415–1815.* Berkeley and Los Angeles: University of California Press, 1972.

Bovill, E. W. *Caravans of the Old Sahara.* London: Oxford University Press, 1933.

Braudel, Fernand. *La Méditerranée et la monde méditerranéen à l'époque de Philippe II.* 2nd ed. Paris: Armand Colin, 1966.

Bureau of the Census. *Historical Statistics of the United States: Colonial Times to 1957.* Washington, D.C., 1961.

Chapman, Anne C. "Port of Trade Enclaves in Aztec and Maya Civilizations," *Trade and Market in the Early Empires.* Edited by Karl Polanyi, Conrad M. Arensberg, and Harry W. Pearson. New York: Free Press, 1957.

Chirot, Daniel. "Urban and Rural Economies in the Western Sudan: Brini N'Konni and Its Hinterland." *Cahiers d'études africaines* **VIII**, no. 4(1968): 547–565.

Chirot, Daniel. "The Growth of the Market and Servile Labor Systems in Agriculture." *The Journal of Social History* **VIII**, no. 1 (Winter 1975): 67–80.

Clark, C., and Hasswell, M. *The Economics of Subsistence Agriculture.* 3rd ed. New York: Macmillan, 1967.

Coquery-Vidrovitch, Catherine. "Recherches sur un mode de production africain." *La Pensée* 144 (1969): 61–78.

Davis, Kingsley. "The Urbanization of the Human Population," *An Urban World.* Edited by Charles Tilly. Boston: Little, Brown, 1974.

Dobb, Maurice. *Studies in the Development of Capitalism.* New York: International Publishers, 1963.

Domar, Evsey. "The Causes of Slavery or Serfdom: A Hypothesis." *The Journal of Economic History* **XXX**, no. 1 (March 1970): 18–32.

Elliot, J. H. *Imperial Spain 1496–1716.* New York: St. Martin's Press, 1964.

Fallers, Lloyd. "The Predicament of the Modern African Chief: An Instance from Uganda," *Social Change: The Colonial Situation.* Edited by Immanuel Wallerstein. New York: Wiley, 1966.

Fei, Hsiao-Tung. *China's Gentry.* 2nd ed. Chicago: University of Chicago Press, 1968.

Fillol, Tomás Roberto. *Social Factors in Economic Development: The Argentine Case.* Cambridge: M.I.T. Press, 1961.

Finley, M. I. "Was Greek Civilization Based on Slave Labor," *The Slave Economies: Historical and Theoretical Perspectives.* Edited by Eugene D. Genovese. New York: Wiley, 1973.

Frank, Andre Gunder. "The Development of Underdevelopment," *Imperialism and Underdevelopment.* Edited by Robert I. Rhodes. New York: Monthly Review Press, 1970.

Furtado, Celso. *The Economic Growth of Brazil.* Berkeley and Los Angeles: University of California Press, 1963.

Genovese, Eugene D. *The World the Slaveholders Made.* New York: Vintage, 1971.

Grousset, René, and Léonard, E. G. *Histoire Universelle,* I. Paris: Gallimard, 1956.

Grousset, René. *L'Empire des Steppes.* Paris: Payot, 1960.

Hobsbawm, Eric J. *Primitive Rebels.* New York: Norton, 1959.

Hobsbawm, Eric J. *Karl Marx: Pre-Capitalist Economic Formations.* New York: International Publishers, 1965.

Hobsbawm, Eric J. "The Crisis of the Seventeenth Century," *Crisis in Europe 1560–1660.* Edited by Trevor Aston. Garden City, N.Y.: Doubleday-Anchor, 1967.

Hoel, Paul G. *Elementary Statistics.* New York: Wiley, 1966.

Huntington, Samuel P. *Political Order in Changing Societies.* New Haven: Yale University Press, 1968.

James, C. L. R. "The West Indies in the History of European Capitalism," *The Slave Economies: Historical and Theoretical Perspectives.* Edited by Eugene D. Genovese. New York: Wiley, 1973.

Katz, S. H., Hediger, M. L., and Valleroy, L. A. "Traditional Maize Processing Techniques in the New World." *Science* 184, no. 4138 (17 May 1974): 765–773.

Kula, Wittold. *Théorie économique du système féodal: pour un modèle de l'économie polonaise, 16e–18e siècles.* Paris and The Hague: Mouton, 1970.

Laslett, Peter, ed. *Household and Family in Past Times.* London: Cambridge University Press, 1972.

Lenski, Gerhard. *Power and Privilege: A Theory of Social Stratification.* New York: McGraw-Hill, 1966.

Lenski, Gerhard, and Lenski, Jean. *Human Societies.* New York: McGraw–Hill, 1974.

Lewis, Bernard. *The Arabs in History.* New York: Harper Torchbooks, 1966.

Lewis, Bernard. "Some Reflections on the Decline of the Ottoman Empire," *The Economic Decline of Empires.* Edited by Carlo Cipolla. London: Methuen, 1970.

Lichtheim, George. "Marx and the 'Asiatic Mode of Production'," *Karl Marx.* Edited by Tom Bottomore. Englewood Cliffs, N.J.: Prentice-Hall, 1973.

Lybyer, A. H. "The Ottoman Turks and the Routes of Oriental Trade." *English Historical Review* **XXX** (October 1915): 577–588.

Manivanna, Kéo. "Aspects socio-economiques du Laos médiéval." *La Pensée* 138 (1968): 56–70.

Moore, Barrington Jr. *Social Origins of Dictatorship and Democracy: Lord and Peasant in the Making of the Modern World.* Boston: Beacon, 1967.

Moore, Wilbert E. *Social Change.* Englewood Cliffs, N.J.: Prentice-Hall, 1963.

Myint, Hla. "The Peasant Economies of Today's Underdeveloped Areas," *Subsistence Agriculture and Economic Development.* Edited by Clifton R. Wharton. Chicago: Aldine, 1969.

Nash, Manning. "The Multiple Society in Economic Development: Mexico and Guatemala." *American Anthropologist* **LIX** (October 1957): 825–833.

Nicolson, Harold. *The Congress of Vienna: A Study in Allied Unity 1812–1822.* New York: Viking, Compass Books, 1961.

Nisbet, Robert A. *Social Change and History.* London: Oxford University Press, 1970.

Ostrogorsky, George. *History of the Byzantine State.* New Brunswick, N.J.: Rutgers University Press, 1957.

Pach, Sigismund P. "Sixteenth-century Hungary: Commercial Activity and Market Production by the Nobles," *Economy and Society in Early Modern Europe. Essays from Annales.* Edited by Peter Burke. New York: Harper Torchbooks, 1970.

Pach, Sigismund P. "La route de poivre vers la Hongrie médiévale," *Histoire économique du monde méditerranéen 1450–1650. Mélanges en l'honneur de Fernand Braudel.* Toulouse: Privat, 1973.

Parsons, Talcott. "Evolutionary Universals in Society." *American Sociological Review* **XXIX**, no. 3 (June 1964): 339–357.

Parsons, Talcott. *The System of Modern Societies.* Englewood Cliffs, N.J.: Prentice-Hall, 1971.

Pearson, Harry W. "The Economy Has No Surplus: Critique of a Theory of Development," *Trade and Market in the Early Empires.* Edited by Karl Polanyi, Conrad M. Arensberg, and Harry W. Pearson. New York: Free Press, 1957.

Polanyi, Karl. *Primitive, Archaic and Modern Economies.* Edited by George Dalton. New York: Anchor Books, 1968.

Polgar, Steven. "Population History and Population Policies from an Anthropological Perspective." *Current Anthropology* **XIII**, no. 2 (April 1972): 203–211.

Popper, Karl. *The Poverty of Historicism.* New York: Harper Torchbooks, 1964.

Pym, Christopher. *The Ancient Civilization of Angkor.* New York: Mentor, 1968.

Roe, Daphne A. *A Plague of Corn. The Social History of Pellagra.* Ithaca, N.Y.: Cornell University Press, 1973.

Rowe, John H. "Aspects of Inca Socio-Political Organization and Religion at the Spanish Conquest," *The Indian Background of Latin American History.* Edited by Robert Wauchope. New York: Knopf, 1970.

Runciman, Stephen. *A History of the First Bulgarian Empire.* London: G. Bell & Son, 1930.

de Santis, Sergio. "Les communautés de village chez les Incas, les Aztèques et les Mayas." *La Pensée* 122 (1965): 79–95.

Sédov, L. "La société angkorienne et le problème du mode de production asiatique." *La Pensée* 138 (1968): 71–84.

Seers, Dudley. "The Stages of Economic Growth of a Primary Producer in the Middle of the Twentieth Century," *Imperialism and Underdevelopment.* Edited by Robert I. Rhodes. New York: Monthly Review Press, 1970.

Seers, Dudley, and Joy, Leonard, eds. *Development in a Divided World.* Harmondsworth, England: Penguin Books, 1971.

Stinchcombe, Arthur. "Agricultural Enterprise and Rural Class Relations," *Class, Status and Power.* Edited by Reinhard Bendix and Seymour M. Lipset. New York: Free Press, 1966.

Stoianovich, Traian. "Le mais dans les Balkans." *Annales E.S.C.* **XXI**, no. 5 (September–October 1966): 1026–1040.

Wallerstein, Immanuel. *The Modern World-System: Capitalist Agriculture and the Origins of the European World-Economy in the Sixteenth Century.* New York: Academic Press, 1974.

Warriner, Doreen. "Some Controversial Issues in the History of Agrarian Europe." *The Slavonic and East European Review* **XXXII**, no. 78 (December 1953): 168–186.

Warriner, Doreen. *Land Reform in Principle and Practice.* London: Oxford University Press, 1969.

Wittfogel, Karl A. *Oriental Despotism: A Comparative Study of Total Power.* New Haven: Yale University Press, 1957.

Wolf, Eric. *Peasant Wars of the Twentieth Century.* New York: Harper and Row, 1969.

2. Works on Romania

The following references will use these abbreviations:

N.E.H.—*Nouvelles études d'histoire*, collections of articles published by the Academy of the Socialist Republic of Romania in Bucharest on the occasion of world history congresses. Volume I was published in 1955, II in 1960, III in 1965, and IV in 1970.

S.M.I.M.—*Studii și materiale de istorie medie*, a five-volume collection of articles on Romanian history in the Middle Ages (defined as extending to the start of the nineteenth century). All were published in Bucharest by the Academy of Romania. Volume I appeared in 1956, II in 1957, III in 1959, IV in 1960, and V in 1962.

E.R.—*Enciclopedia României*, a four volume encyclopedia about Romanian history, society, politics, economics, culture, and geography. The project was directed by Dimitrie Gusti, the editor of the series, and was published by the government of Romania. Volumes I and II appeared in 1938, III in 1939, and IV in 1943.

Alexandrescu-Dersca, Marie M. "Contribution à l'étude de l'approvisionnement en blé de Constantinople au XVIII-e siècle." *Studia et acta orientalia* I (1957): 13–37.

Bălcescu, Nicolae. *Question économique des principautés danubiennes.* Pamphlet. Paris, 1850.

Bănescu, N. *Un problème d'histoire médiévale. Création et caractère du second empire bulgare.* Bucharest: Institut roumain d'études byzantines, 1942.

Berindei, Dan. *Orașul București, reședință și capitală a Țării Romînești 1459–1862.* Bucharest: Societatea de științe istorice și filologie, 1963.

Berindei, Dan, and Adăniloaie, N. *Reforma agrară din 1864.* Bucharest: Editura academiei, 1967.

Berindei, Dan. *L'union des principautés roumaines.* Bucharest: Académie roumaine, 1966.

Berindei, Dan. "L'idéologie politique des révolutionnaires roumains de 1848," *N.E.H.* **IV**, 1970.

Berza, M. "Haraciul Moldovei și Țării Romînești in sec. XV–XIX," *S.M.I.M.* **II**, 1957.

Bodea, Cornelia. *Lupta românilor pentru unitatea națională 1834–1849.* Bucharest: Editura academiei, 1967.

Bogdan, Ioan. *Scrieri alese.* Edited by G. Mihăilă. Bucharest: Editura academiei, 1968.

Boicu, L. "Considérations sur la politique des Habsbourgs à l'égard des principautés roumaines (depuis le XVIIIe siècle jusqu'en 1848)," *N.E.H.* **IV**, 1970.

Brătianu, G. I. "Vicina I. Contributions à l'histoire de la domination byzantine et du commerce génois en Dobrodgea." *Bulletin de la séction historique* **X**, Académie roumaine (1923).

Bugă, Dragoș. "Repartiția geografică a așezărilor omenești dintre Carpați și Dunăre (Țara Românească) la jumătatea secolului al XIX-lea." *Comunicări de geografie* **VII** (1969): 183–196.

Câmpina, Barbu. "Le problème de l'apparition des états féodaux roumains," *N.E.H.* **I**, 1955.

Cantemir, Dimitrie. *Descriera Moldovei.* Bucharest: Cartea românească, 1923.

Căzănişteanu, C.; Berindei, Dan; Florescu, Marin; Niculae, Vasile. *Revoluţia Română din 1848.* Bucharest: Editura politică, 1969.

Chirot, Daniel, and Ragin, Charles. "The Market, Tradition and Peasant Rebellion: The Case of Romania in 1907." *American Sociological Review* 40 (August 1975): 428–444.

Chirot, Daniel. "The Romanian Communal Village: An Alternative to the Zadruga," *The Zadruga: The Extended Family of the Balkans. Essays by Philip E. Mosely and Essays in His Honor.* Edited by Robert F. Byrnes. South Bend, Ind.: Notre Dame University Press, 1975.

Ciobanu, Ştefan. "Populaţia în Ţările Româneşti la 1810." *Arhiva pentru ştiinţa şi reforma socială* **II** (1920): 85–97.

Ciurea, D. "Quelques considérations sur la noblesse féodale chez les Roumains," *N.E.H.* **IV**, 1970.

Claudian, Ioan. *Alimentaţia poporului român.* Bucharest: Fundaţia Regele Carol **II**, 1939.

Colescu, Leonida. *Statistiques des paysans devenus propriétaires par l'application de la loi de 1864.* Bucharest, 1900.

Constantinescu, Miron. *Cauzele sociala ale răscoalei lui Horia.* Doctoral dissertation. Bucharest, 1938.

Corbu, Constantin. *Ţărănimea din România între 1864 şi 1888.* Bucharest: Editura ştiinţifică, 1970.

Corfus, Ilie. *Agricultura Ţării Româneşti în prima jumătate a secolului al XIX-lea.* Bucharest: Editura academiei, 1969.

Creangă, G. D. *Contracte de învoeli agricole în vigoare pe anul 1906.* Bucharest: Carol Göbl, 1907.

Creangă, G. D. *Proprietatea rurală în România.* Bucharest, 1907.

Cronţ, Gheorghe. *Instituţii medievale Româneşti.* Bucharest: Editura academiei, 1969.

Despotopoulos, Alexandre J. "La révolution grecque, Alexandre Ypsilantis et la politique de la Russie." *Balkan Studies* **VII**, no. 2 (1966): 395–410.

Direcţia Centrală de Statistică. *Anuarul statistic al Republicii Socialiste România 1970.* Bucharest, 1970.

Dobrodgeanu-Gherea, Constantin. *Neoiobăgia.* 2nd ed. Bucharest: Viaţa românească, n.d. [probably 1921].

Dogan, Mattei. "L'origine sociale du personnel parlementaire d'un pays essentiellement agraire, la Roumanie." *Revue de l'Institut de Sociologie,* no. 2–3 (1953).

Donat, Ion. "Satele lui Mihai Viteazul," *S.M.I.M.* **IV**, 1960.

Dunăre, Nicolae. "Interdependenţa ocupaţiilor tradiţionale la Români." *Apulum* **VII** (1968): 529–550.

Dunăre, Nicolae. "Pastoritul de pendulare dublă pe teritoriul României," *Anuarul muzeului etnografic al Transilvaniei pe anii 1965–1967.* Cluj, 1969.

East, W. G. *The Union of Moldavia and Wallachia, 1859.* Cambridge: Cambridge University Press, 1929.

Eidelberg, Philip G. *The Great Rumanian Peasant Revolt of 1907. Origins of a Modern Jacquerie.* Leiden: E. J. Brill, 1974.

Eliade, Pompiliou. *De l'influence française sur l'esprit public en Roumanie.* Paris: Leroux, 1898.

Eliade, Pompiliou. *La Roumanie au XIXe siècle* **II**. Paris: Hachette, 1914.

Emerit, Marcel. "De la condition des esclaves dans l'ancienne Roumanie." *Revue d'histoire du sud-est européen* (October–December 1930).

Emerit, Marcel. *Les paysans roumains depuis le traité d'Andrinople jusqu'à la libération des terres (1829–1864).* Paris: Recueil Sirey, 1937.

Emerit, Marcel. "Reflexions sur le régime seigneural en Roumanie." *Revue historique du sud-est européen,* no. 4–6 (1938).

Filitti, Ioan C. *Proprietatea solului în Principatele Române până la 1864.* Bucharest: Fundaţiunea Regele Ferdinand II, n.d. [1930s].

Filitti, Ioan C. "Administraţia locală în România," *E.R.* I, 1938.

Floareş, C. I. "Amintiri cu privire la situaţia dinainte de împroprietări a unui sat de foşti clăcaşi." *Sociologie Românească* **II**, nos. 7–8 (July-August 1937): 362–364.

Florescu, Radu N. *The Struggle Against Russia in the Roumanian Principalities: A Problem in Anglo-Turkish Diplomacy 1821–1854.* Rome: Acata Historica II of the Societas Academica Dacoromana, 1962.

Florescu, Radu N. "The Fanariot Regime in the Danubian Principalities." *Balkan Studies* **IX**, no. 2 (1968): 301–318.

Garoflid, Constantin. "Regimul agrar în România," *E.R.* **I**, 1938.

Garoflid, Constantin. *Agriculture Veche*. Bucharest, 1943.

Georgescu, Valentin A. "Reflexions sur le statut juridique des paysans corvéeables et la politique agraire de la class dominante en Valachie dans la seconde moitié du XVIIIe siècle," *N.E.H.* **IV**, 1970.

Georgescu, Valentin A., and Popescu, Emanuela. *La Législation agraire de Valachie, (1775–82).* Bucharest: Editura academiei, 1970.

Georgescu-Roegen, N., Giurescu, C. C., and Romaşcanu, M. Gr. "Comerțul exterior," *E.R.* **IV**, 1943.

Giurescu, Constantin. *Studii de istorie socială*. Bucharest: Editura universul, 1943.

Giurescu, Constantin C. "Le commerce sur le territoire de la Moldavie pendant la domination tartare, 1241–1352," *N.E.H.* **III**, 1960.

Giurescu, Constantin C. *Istoria pescuitului și a pisciculturii în România,* **I**. Bucharest: Editura academiei, 1964.

Giurescu, Constantin C. *Viața și opera lui Cuza Vodă.* 2nd ed. Bucharest: Editura științifică, 1970.

Golopenția, Anton, and Georgescu, M. *60 Sate Românești,* vol. II. Bucharest: Institutul de științe sociale, 1941.

Gusti, Dimitrie. *D. Gusti: Opere,* vol. IV. Edited by Ovidiu Bădina and Octavian Neamțu. Bucharest: Editura academiei, 1970.

d'Hauterive, le Comte. *Mémoire sur l'état ancien et actuel de la Moldavie. Présenté à S.A.S. Le Prince Alexandre Ypsilanti, Hospodar regnant en 1787.* Bucharest: Carol Göbl, 1902.

Herseni, Traian. *Probleme de sociologie pastorală.* Bucharest: Institutul de științe sociale, 1941.

Holban, M. "Mărturii asupra rolului cnezilor de pe marile domenii din Banat în a doua jumătate a secolului al XIV-lea," *S.M.I.M.* **II**, 1957.

Ilies, A. "Stire în legătură cu exploitarea sării în Țara Românească pînă în veacul al XVIII-lea," *S.M.I.M.* **I**, 1956.

Iliescu, O. "Notes sur l'apport roumain au ravitaillement de Byzance d'après une source inédite du XIVe siècle," *N.E.H.* **III**, 1960.

Iliescu, O. "Despre natura juridică și importanța despăgubirilor oferite de Basarab Voievod regelui Carol Robert în 1330," *S.M.I.M.* **V**, 1962.

Ionescu-Șișești, G. "Agricultura României," *E.R.* **III**, 1939.

Iorga, Nicolae. *Geschichte des rumänischen volkes in rahmen seeiner staatsbildungen.* Gotha: F. A. Perthes, 1905.

Iorga, Nicolae. *Istoria comerțului românesc.* Bucharest: Tiparul românesc, 1925.

Iorga, Nicolae. *Histoire des Roumains et de la romanité orientale.* Bucharest: Académie roumaine, 1937–1945.

Iorga, Nicolae. *Istoria lui Mihai Viteazul.* New ed. Bucharest: Editura militară, 1968.

Jelavich, Barbara. *Russia and the Rumanian National Cause 1858–1859.* Slavic and East European Series, vol. XVII. Bloomington, Ind.: Indiana University Press, 1959.

Jormescu, C., and Popa-Burcă, I. *Harta agronomică a României.* Bucharest: Carol Göbl, 1907.

Kogălniceanu, Vasile M. *Chestiunea țărănească.* Bucharest: Joseph Göbl, 1906.

Lege rurala cu proclamațiunea Mariei Sale Domnitorului a Principatele Unite Române. Bucharest: Imprimeria Statului, 1864.

Lehr, Lia. "Comerțul Țării Romînești și Moldovei în a doua jumătate a secolului XVI și prima jumătate a secolului XVII, *S.M.I.M.* IV, 1960.

Lendvai, Paul. *Eagles in Cobwebs.* New York: Doubleday, 1969.

Liveanu, Vasile, *et al. Relații agrare și mișcări țărănești în România 1908–1921*. Bucharest: Editura politică, 1967.

Maciu, V. "Un centre révolutionnaire roumain dans les années 1845–1848: la société des étudiants roumains de Paris," *N.E.H.* **III**, 1965.

Manolescu, Radu. "Schimbul de marfuri dintre Țara Românească și Brașov în prima jumătate a secolului al XVI-lea," *S.M.I.M.* **II**, 1957.

Manolescu, Radu. *Comerțul Țării Romînești și Moldovei cu Brașovul (secolele XIV–XVI)*. Bucharest: Editura științifică, 1965.

de Martonne, Emmanuel. *La Valachie, essai de monographie géographique*. Paris: Armand Colin, 1902.

Mihăilescu, Vintilă. "Așezările omenești din Câmpia Română la mijlocul și la sfârșitul secolului al XIX-lea." *Memoriile*, Academia Română, secțiunii istorice series 3, vol. IV, no. 2. Bucharest, 1924.

Mihordea, V. *Relațiile agrare din secolul al XVIII-lea în Moldova*. Bucharest: Editura academiei, 1968.

Mihordea, V. "La crise du régime fiscal des principautés roumaines au XVIIIe siècle," *N.E.H.* **IV**, 1970.

Ministerul de agriculturei, industrie, comerțului, și domenilor. *Statistica mașinilor și instrumentelor agricole intrebuințate în 1905*. Bucharest, 1907.

Ministerul industrii și comerțului. *Anuarul Statistic al României, 1909*. Bucharest, 1909.

Ministerul industrii și comerțului. *Anuarul Statistic al României, 1912*. Bucharest, 1912.

Mioc, Damaschin. "Despre modul de impunere și percepere a birului în Țara Românească pînă la 1632," *S.M.I.M.* **II**, 1957.

Mioc, Damaschin, Chirca, H., and Ștefanescu, Șt. "L'évolution de la rente féodale en Valachie et en Moldavie, du XIVe au XVIIe siècles," *N.E.H.* **II**, 1960.

Mioc, Damaschin. "Cuantumul birului pe gospodăria țărănească în Țara Romînească în secolul al XVI-lea," *S.M.I.M.* **V**, 1962.

Mitrany, David. *The Land and the Peasant in Rumania: The War and Agrarian Reform 1917–1921*. London: Oxford University Press, 1930.

Montias, John M. *Economic Development in Communist Rumania*. Cambridge: M.I.T. Press, 1967.

Olteanu, Ștefan, and Șerban, Constantin. *Meșteșugurile din Țara Românească și Moldova în evul mediu*. Bucharest: Editura academiei, 1969.

Ornea, Z. *Țărănismul. Studiu sociologic*. Bucharest: Editura politică, 1969.

Oțetea, Andrei, *et al. Istoria Romîniei*, vols. II–IV. Bucharest: Editura academiei, 1962–1964.

Oțetea, Andrei. "Considerații asupra trecerii de la feudalism la capitalism în Moldova și Țara Romînească," *S.M.I.M.* **IV**, 1960.

Oțetea, Andrei. "La formation des états féodaux roumains," *N.E.H.* **III**, 1965.

Oțetea, Andrei. Les grandes puissances et le mouvement Hétairiste dans les Principautés Roumaines." *Balkan Studies* **VII**, no. 2 (1966): 379–394.

Oțetea, Andrei, *et al. Marea răscoala a țăranilor din 1907*. Bucharest: Editura academieie, 1967.

Panaitescu, P. P. "Les relations bulgaro-roumaines au moyen-âge." *Revista Aromânească* **I** (1929).

Panaitescu, P. P. *Interpretări Românești*. Bucharest: Editura universul, 1947.

Panaitescu, P. P. "Dreptul de strămutare al țăranilor în Țările Romîne pînă la mijlocul secolului al XVII-lea," *S.M.I.M.* **I**, 1956.

Panaitescu, P. P. "La grande assemblée du pays, institution du régime féodal en Moldavie et Valachie," *N.E.H.* **III**, 1965.

Papacostea, Șerban. "Contribuție la problema relațiilor agrare în Țara Românească în prima jumătate a veacului al XVIII-lea," *S.M.I.M.* **III**, 1959.

Pătrășcanu, Lucrețiu. *Un veac de frămîntări sociale 1821–1907*. 2nd ed. Bucharest: Editura politică, 1969.

Riker, T. W. *The Making of Roumania 1856–1866*. London: Oxford University Press, 1931.

Roberts, Henry L. *Rumania: The Political Problems of an Agrarian State*. New Haven: Yale University Press, 1951.

Rosetti, Radu [Verax]. *La Roumanie et les Juifs.* Bucharest: Socecu, 1903.

Rosetti, Radu. *Pământul, Sătenii și Stăpânii în Moldova.* Bucharest: Socec, 1907.

Rosetti, Radu. *Pentru ce s'au răsculat țăranii.* Bucharest: Socec, 1908.

Rusenescu, Constanța, and Bugă, Dragoș. "Territorial distribution and growth of the population between the Carpathians and the Danube, in the 19th and 20th centuries." *Revue roumaine de géologie, géophysique et géographie* série de géographie **X**, no. 1 (1966): 75–84.

Serafim, Gh. "Impărțirea pe moșii și pe trupuri de moșie a satului Negoești-Mehedinți." *Sociologie Românească* **III**, nos. 1–3 (1938): 32–35.

Seton-Watson, Hugh. *Eastern Europe Between the Wars.* 3rd ed. Hamden, Conn.: Archon, 1962.

Seton-Watson, R. W. *History of the Roumanians.* 2nd ed. Hamden, Conn.: Archon, 1963.

Stănică, Constantin. "Hotarul satului Orodel-Dolj." *Sociologie Românească* **II**, no. 1 (1937): 28–31.

Stahl, Henri H. "Organizarea socială a țărănimii," *E.R.* **I**, 1938.

Stahl, Henri H. *Nerej, un village d'une région archaïque.* Bucharest: Institut de sciences sociales, 1940.

Stahl, Henri H. *Contribuții la studiul satelor devălmașe.* românești. Bucharest: Editura academiei, 1958–1965.

Stahl, Henri H. "Paysages et peuplement rural en Roumanie," *N.E.H.* **III**, 1965.

Stahl, Henri H. *Les anciennes communautés villageoises roumaines.* Bucharest and Paris: Académie roumaine and C.N.R.S., 1969.

Stahl, Henri H. *Controverse de istorie socială românească.* Bucharest: Editura științifică, 1969.

Stahl, Henri H. *Studii de sociologie istorică.* Bucharest: Editura științifică, 1972.

Ștefănescu, Ștefan. "Considération au sujet des termes *Vlah* et *Rumîn* sur la base des documents internes de la Valachie des XIV–XVIIIe siècles," *S.M.I.M.* **V**, 1962.

Ștefănescu, Ștefan. "La situation démographique de la Valachie aux XIVe, XVe, et XVIe siècles d'après les conjonctures socio-politiques," *N.E.H.* **IV**, 1970.

Stoicescu, N. "Contributions à l'histoire de l'armée roumaine au moyen-âge." *Revue roumaine d'histoire* **VI**, no. 5 (1967): 731–763.

Sturdza, Dimitrie. "Suprafața și populațiunea Regatului României," *Buletin,* Societatea geografică Română, **XVI**, trim. 3–4. Bucharest, 1896.

Tappe, E. D. *Documents Concerning Rumanian History.* The Hague: Mouton, 1964.

Tucker, Jack. *The Rumanian Peasant Revolt of 1907: Three Regional Studies.* Ph. D. dissertation, University of Chicago, 1972.

Vâlsan, G. "O fază în popularea Țărilor Românești." *Buletin,* Societatea geografică Română, **XXXIII**. Bucharest, 1912.

Vlad, Matei D. "Mișcări demografice în cadrul colonizarii rurale din Țara Românească și Moldova (secolele XVII–XVIII)." *Studii și articole de istorie* **XIV** (1969): 73–90.

Voinea, Șerban. *Marxism oligarhic.* Bucharest: Editura Brănișteanu, 1926.

Warriner, Doreen. *Economics of Peasant Farming.* 2nd ed. New York: Barnes & Noble, 1965.

Warriner, Doreen, ed. *Contrasts in Emerging Societies.* Translations by E. D. Tappe. Bloomington, Ind.: Indiana University Press, 1965.

Weber, Eugen. "Romania," *The European Right.* Edited by Hans Rogger and Eugen Weber. Berkeley and Los Angeles: University of California Press, 1966.

Wolff, Robert L. *The Balkans in Our Times.* New York: Norton, 1967.

Xenopol, A. D. *A.D. Xenopol, Opere economice.* Edited by Ion Veverca. Bucharest: Editura academiei, 1967.

Zane, G. "Originea și desvoltarea economiei de schimb," *E.R.* **III**, 1939.

Zane, G. *Le mouvement révolutionnaire de 1840.* Bucharest: Académie roumaine, 1964.

Zane, G. *Industria din România în a doua jumătate a secolului al XIX-lea.* Bucharest: Editura academiei, 1970.

Zeletin, Ștefan. *Burghezia Română: origina și rolul ei istoric.* Bucharest: Cultura națională, 1925.

Index

A 6
B 7
C 8
D 9
E 0
F 1
G 2
H 3
I 4
J 5

www.ingramcontent.com/pod-product-compliance
Lightning Source LLC
LaVergne TN
LVHW090942080826
845145LV00003B/850

* 9 7 8 1 5 9 7 4 0 9 5 9 9 *